From reviews of *The Politics*

'In his soberly ordered, autl
sition and in his telling selecti
he has rendered sterling serv
demic, practitioner and sober citizen alike'

ANDREW CURRIE *TES*

'The argument of J. A. G. Griffith's book is short, clear and irrefutable'   *Tribune*

'Brilliant little book, which is all the more powerful for being closely and soberly argued and is no mere polemic'

ANTONY GREY *Freethinker*

'Informative, accurate, lucid, succinct, lively and provocative, without being extreme. John Griffith has satisfied all of these criteria. The work can be recommended with confidence to sixth formers and beginning law students as well as to a wider audience . . . a substantial contribution to public debate'

WILLIAM TWINING, *Public Law*

'The whole work is a magnificent survey of what is becoming a communal anxiety. All the relevant authorities are paraded and intelligently interpreted'   *Justice of the Peace*

'It is the achievement of Professor John Griffith's book to lift the debate to an altogether better level by advancing a new theory and by backing it with a wealth of concrete examples. The thesis of the book is simple and controversial . . . He has, in effect, thrown down the gauntlet to any believer in the neutrality of the judiciary, or in its independence from government'

MICHAEL ZANDER, *Guardian*

'Highly readable, and as much to be recommended to the general reader as to those having a special interest in the subject'

J. A. ANDREWS, *British Book News*

'An important book on an important issue'

Morning Star

'The first thinker to rip the mask off the sacred name of justice and reveal the political passions pulsing underneath was Thrasymachus. Justice, he asserted, was nothing but the interest of the stronger. In spite of the logical difficulties exposed by Socrates, Thrasymachus has not lacked for successors . . . *The Politics of the Judiciary* is a lively contribution to this traditon'

KENNETH MINOGUE, *TLS*

J. A. G. GRIFFITH was born in 1918 and educated at Taunton School and the London School of Economics and Political Science (LSE). He has been on the staff of the LSE since 1948, becoming Professor of English Law in 1959 and of Public Law from 1970 until his retirement in 1984. From 1956 to 1981 he edited *Public Law*. His books include *Principles of Administrative Law* (with H. Street), *Central Departments and Local Authorities, Government and Law* (with T. C. Hartley), *Parliamentary Scrutiny of Government Bills, Public Rights and Private Interests*, and *Parliament* (with Michael Ryle).

J. A. G. GRIFFITH

The Politics
of the Judiciary

Fourth edition

FontanaPress
An Imprint of HarperCollins*Publishers*

First published by Fontana in 1977
in the series 'Political Issues of Modern Britain',
edited by B. Crick and P. Seyd
Reprinted 1978 and 1979
Second edition published in 1981
Third edition published, in Fontana Press, in 1985

This Fourth Edition published in 1991 by Fontana Press,
an imprint of HarperCollins Publishers,
77–85 Fulham Palace Road, Hammersmith, London W6 8JB
Copyright © J. A. G. Griffith 1977, 1981, 1985, 1991

9 8 7 6 5 4 3 2 1

J. A. G. Griffith asserts his moral right to be identified
as the author of this work.

Phototypeset by Input Typesetting Ltd., London
Printed and bound in Great Britain by
HarperCollins Manufacturing, Glasgow

To BEN
who helped

Juger l'administration, c'est aussi administrer
J.-E.-M. PORTALIS, 1745–1807

The vanity of appearing as model employers of labour had not then, apparently, taken possession of the council, nor had the council become such ardent feminists as to bring about, at the expense of the ratepayers whose money they administered, sex equality in the labour market . . . The council would, in my view, fail in their duty if, in administering funds which did not belong to their members alone, they put aside all these aims to the ascertainment of what was just and reasonable remuneration to give for the services rendered to them, and allowed themselves to be guided in preference by some eccentric principles of socialistic philanthropy, or by a feminist ambition to secure the equality of the sexes in the matter of wages in the world of labour.

LORD ATKINSON in *Roberts v. Hopwood* [1925] AC 578

The Government recognizes that the judges are the great enemies of every government, because they're always supporting people who allege that they're being downtrodden by government.

LORD DONALDSON MR in an interview on Channel 4 on 10 February 1989 (as reported in the *Guardian*).

Contents

Preface to the fourth edition

Six years of much political change have passed since the last edition of this book was published. Even amongst the judiciary, attitudes have not remained the same. So the subject-matter of the politics of the judiciary has shifted somewhat. Judicial review of administrative action has developed, police powers have been statutorily redefined, *Spycatcher* has come but not gone, the labour injunction has been elaborated, there have been major miscarriages of justice, control over the press and freedom of speech has been tightened, new immigration and deportation problems have continued to puzzle the courts, the Lord Chancellor's reforms threaten further to politicize the judiciary.

Since the first edition was published in 1977, other authors have published books and articles dealing with judicial politics. Some have been good enough to tell me where I have gone wrong; some have gone as far as to do so with a degree of personal hostility which I have found particularly gratifying.

I have tried not to let this book develop a middle-aged spread and so have deleted much material. I have revised some opinions. But my simple thesis, once so controversial, remains that the judiciary cannot, under our constitution, act neutrally but must act politically. My hope is that the liberals will not succeed in persuading political leaders that, by enacting a Bill of Rights, judges should have even greater scope for their political adventures.

How Miss Colleen Etheridge still manages to cope with my manuscript and my temperament is a source of wonder to all. This book puts me even further in her debt. My thanks also to all others who have helped me, and especially to Cyril Glasser, SHAC, UKIAS, Bill Wedderburn, and

Eddie Yaansah. But none of these saw the final draft, so blame me for the mistakes.

MARLOW   JOHN GRIFFITH
October 1990

Part One

The Judiciary

*There is one matter which I ought to mention.
All the judges, without exception, are members
of the Athenaeum, and I presume you will wish
to be a member. If so, may I have the pleasure
of proposing you? There is a meeting of the
Committee early next week.*

Lord Cozens-Hardy, MR to Lord Buckmaster
– as he became – on the latter's appointment
to the Lord Chancellorship, in a letter dated
26 May 1915, quoted by R. F. V. Heuston,
The Lives of the Lord Chancellors 1885–1940,
p. 269.

*The most politically influential of the judges,
however, has been the Master of the Rolls, Lord
Denning . . . With his own modest roots he dis-
misses the attacks on a class-based judiciary:
'The youngsters believe that we come from a
narrow background – it's all nonsense – they
get it from that man Griffith.'*

Anthony Sampson, *The Changing Anatomy of
Britain* (1981), p. 159.

*I would think about 10 or 15 per cent [of judges
are Labour Party voters]. I would think it's a
diminishing number because I think that a large
number of judges who would have voted for Mr
Clement Attlee would look askance at voting for
some of his successors, with all respect to them.*

Lord Templeman, in an interview on Radio 4
with Hugo Young on 13 April 1988.

Since nearly all High Court judges are appointed when they are between about 45 and 57 it is likely that they will have shed such political enthusiasms as they may have had when young and have formed firm views about how the country should be run

Sir Frederick Lawton (former Lord Justice), *Solicitors Journal*, 2 November 1990.

1. Courts and judges

Introduction

This book is concerned with the relationship between the judiciary and politics. In the courts political questions may come before the judges because the matter is already in public controversy, like race or industrial relations; or because it is claimed that a public authority has exceeded its powers; or because the matter concerns the activities of the police; or because the matter impinges on the individual rights of citizens, affecting their freedom or their property.

The laws relating to civil and criminal wrongs are made either by Parliament in the form of Acts of Parliament (also called statutes) or by the judges themselves (called the common law). The common law is made as judges decide cases and state the principles on which they are basing their decisions, this accumulation of principles building into a body of law. Some parts of this common law have long fallen into disuse as having no contemporary relevance. Other parts have evolved to meet social changes. Statute law, however, predominates over common law wherever there is conflict, and much statute law is made to change and to replace parts of the common law.

Statute law itself cannot be a perfect instrument. A statute or one section of a statute may be made to deal with some particular subject – perhaps with immigration, or drugs, or housing or education – but a situation arises where doubt is cast on the meaning of the words of the statute. Does the situation fall within these words or not? For example, do the words 'national origins' include 'nationality' (see below, pp. 170–1)? The judges then must decide how to interpret the statute and by so doing they define its meaning. Not only therefore do the judges 'make law' through the development of the common law. They also do so by this process of statutory interpretation.

Judges are employed to decide disputes. Sometimes these disputes are between private individuals when neighbours disagree or one person is injured by another in an accident. Sometimes these disputes may be between large private organizations when companies argue about the terms of a commercial contract. But public bodies – Government departments, local authorities, and others – are also legal persons and also become involved in disputes which lead to judicial activity. The fact that one of the parties is a public body does not necessarily affect the nature of the dispute or the law applicable to it. If a Government department or Birmingham City Council enters into a contract with a building company for the construction of a block of offices, and a dispute arises, the law which governs the matter is essentially the same as it would be if the contract were between two private persons.

Such disputes are dealt with by the civil law and in the civil courts. The judgment given will say where the rights and wrongs lie and the court may award damages to one party or even order a party to take certain positive steps or to refrain from certain action.

In criminal law, the dispute is with the State. Over the years laws have been made and amended declaring certain kinds of action to be criminal and punishable with imprisonment or fines. This has been done because it is believed that the State has an interest in seeking to prevent those actions and to punish those who so act. So we have crimes called murder, manslaughter, rape, conspiracy, theft, fraud, assault, and hundreds of others, some of them quite trivial. They are dealt with in the criminal courts.

If the judicial function were wholly automatic, then not only would the making of decisions in the courts be of little interest but it would not be necessary to recruit highly trained and intellectually able men and women to serve as judges and to pay them handsome salaries.

It is the creative function of judges (see further, below, chapter 8) that makes their job important and makes worthwhile some assessment of the way they behave, especially in political cases. It must be remembered that in most cases for most of the time the function of the judge (with the help of the jury if there is one) is to ascertain the facts. But when questions of law do arise, their determination may be of the greatest importance because of the effect that will have on subsequent cases.

A note on the structure of the courts appears below (pages 38–41). From this it will be seen that the most senior judges are Lords of Appeal in Ordinary (or Law Lords) who are members of the House of Lords and sit, in their judicial function, in the Appellate Committee of that House. Each is referred to as Lord So-and-so. The next senior are Lords Justices of Appeal who sit in the Court of Appeal. Each is referred to as Lord Justice So-and-so. Next come judges of the High Court each of whom is referred to as Mr Justice So-and-so. The High Court, the Crown Court and the Court of Appeal are together called the Supreme Court. Next in seniority come the Circuit judges (often referred to as County Court judges when they are sitting in that court) each of whom is referred to as Judge So-and-so. Recorders and Assistant Recorders are senior barristers or solicitors who sit as judges a few weeks each year. Also there are District, Assistant District and Deputy District judges; stipendiary magistrates who act full time; and Justices of the Peace (JPs) who act part time and are unpaid.

The purpose of this book is to look at the ways in which judges of the High Court, the Court of Appeal, and the House of Lords have in recent years dealt with political cases which have come before them. By political I mean those cases which arise out of controversial legislation or controversial action initiated by public authorities, or which touch important moral or social issues.

When people like the members of the judiciary, broadly homogeneous in character, are faced with such political situations, they act in broadly similar ways. It will be part of my argument to suggest that behind these actions lies a unifying attitude of mind, a political position, which is primarily concerned to protect and conserve certain values and institutions. This does not mean that the judiciary inevitably and invariably supports what governments do, or even what Conservative governments do, though that is the natural inclination. Individually, judges may support the Conservative or the Labour or the Liberal parties. Collectively, in their function and by their nature, they are neither Tories nor Socialists nor Liberals. They are protectors and conservators of what has been, of the relationships and interests on which, *in their view*, our society is founded. They do not regard their role as radical or even reformist.

Appointment

The most remarkable fact about the appointment of judges is that it is wholly in the hands of politicians.[1] High Court and Circuit judges, Recorders, stipendiary and lay magistrates are appointed by the Lord Chancellor who is a member of the Government. Appointments to the Court of Appeal, to the Appellate Committee of the House of Lords,[2] and to the offices of Lord Chief Justice and President of the Family Division are made by the Prime Minister after consultation with the Lord Chancellor, who himself consults with senior members of the judiciary before making his choice or consulting with the Prime Minister. The Lord Chancellor has his own department headed, since the 1880s, by a permanent secretary. The department is the centre for the collection of information about the activity, the legal practice, and the reputation of members of the bar including those more senior, almost always Queen's Counsel (the conferment of which status is in the gift of the Lord Chancellor), from whom senior judicial appointments will be made. Inevitably the officials in the department exercise some influence

---

1. For general accounts see S. Shetreet, *Judges on Trial* (1976); R. E. Megarry, 'The Anatomy of Judicial Appointment' in *U.B.C. Law Review* (1985) 113; R. B. Stevens, 'The Independence of the Judiciary' in *Oxford Journal of Legal Studies* (1988) 222; R. Brazier, *Constitutional Practice* (1988), ch. 11. And see Courts and Legal Services Act 1990.

2. Referred to hereafter simply as the House of Lords.

but the extent of this varies and is difficult to assess.[3] By 1990, all but one of the Law Lords and all the Lords Justices of Appeal had been appointed by Mrs Thatcher.

When considering an appointment of a Circuit judge or a Recorder, the Lord Chancellor, through his officials,

> seeks the view of a wide range of High Court and Circuit judges, Leaders of Circuits and other sections of the Bar, and other senior members of the profession . . . Above all, the Presiding judges[4] are regularly consulted and play a key role in relation to appointments on their Circuits. The four heads of Division (the Lord Chief Justice, the Master of the Rolls, the President of the Family Division and the Vice Chancellor) are also involved.[5]

Those appointed to the senior status of High Court judge will have acted as Recorders and will often have sat as Deputy High Court judges, having been invited to do so from time to time. For the most part they will be senior practising members of the Bar but a few may be promoted from the Circuit bench (including, since 1 January 1990, those who were formerly solicitors). 'In every case', we are told, 'the Lord Chancellor personally reviews the field of choice in detail, in close consultation with the heads of Division, and other senior members of the Judiciary.'[6] But that is all we are told and the relative weight given to the many relevant considerations, both favourable and unfavourable, is not disclosed.

How far the Prime Minister uses his or her power of appointment or, to put this another way, merely accepts the Lord Chancellor's advice varies with different Prime Ministers and differing circumstances. It seems to be unusual for the Prime Minister or the Lord Chancellor to consult

3. According to *The Times* (19 April 1982) the Lord Chancellor's Department has agreed to include the Society of Black Lawyers in its consultations over judicial appointments.

4. Two High Court judges are appointed as such for each Circuit.

5. *Judicial Appointments* (1986), p. 6, published by the *Judicial Appointments Group of the Lord Chancellor's Department*.

6. Ibid., p. 17.

other ministers (except that the Lord Chancellor may discuss the matter with the Attorney-General and the Solicitor-General) unless any such minister happens to be also a distinguished member of the bar, as was Sir Stafford Cripps in Mr Attlee's administration from 1945. But it would be a mistake to assume that Prime Ministers are necessarily mouth-pieces of their Lord Chancellors when making the most senior appointments.

Lord Simon of Glaisdale has written: 'In 1951 Sir Winston [Churchill] particularly wanted [Sir Walter Monckton] in the unenviable post of Minister of Labour, and (presumably by way of compensation) undertook in writing that he should be appointed Lord Chief Justice on the next vacancy.'[7]

Such an undertaking must have been of very little value. Lord Goddard was then in only his sixth year as Lord Chief Justice, never looked like someone about to retire, and indeed continued in office for three years after Sir Winston gave way as Prime Minister in 1955. But the story shows that Sir Winston had no doubt that the office was solely in his gift.

Although Prime Ministers may from time to time use words which suggest that they are not unwilling to exercise their power of appointment, in recent times there is no direct evidence that they have done so. The likelihood is that a modern Prime Minister would depart from the recommendations of the Lord Chancellor only in the most exceptional case.

Solicitors and barristers may be appointed as Recorders or stipendiary magistrates. A Recorder who has served for five years may be appointed as a Circuit judge. Otherwise judges are appointed from the ranks of barristers of at least ten or fifteen years' standing and are likely to have had at least twenty years' practice at the bar. Judges in the Court of Appeal are usually appointed from amongst High Court judges and Law Lords from amongst Appeal Court judges.[8]

---

7. 81 *Law Quarterly Review* 295 (1965).

8. The Lord Chancellor need have no legal qualifications whatever, but in practice is appointed from the ranks of those senior barristers who are members of the political party of the government.

In 1990 Lords of Appeal in Ordinary (Law Lords) and the Master of the Rolls were paid £82,750; Lords Justices of Appeal (in the Court of Appeal) £79,500; judges of the High Court were paid £72,000; Circuit judges £48,100.

From these figures it will be seen that High Court judges gain little financially from promotion. And at present Circuit judges are not often promoted to the High Court. Judges of the High Court and above, with the exception of the Lord Chancellor, hold office during good behaviour subject to a power of removal by Her Majesty on an address presented by both Houses of Parliament, but no English judge has been removed under this provision which derives from the Act of Settlement 1701. Circuit judges and Recorders, however, may be removed from office by the Lord Chancellor on the ground of incapacity or misbehaviour.[9] Magistrates are removable by the Lord Chancellor for good cause. Senior judges must retire at seventy-five years of age, Circuit judges at seventy-two with possible extension to seventy-five, Justices of the Peace and stipendiaries at seventy.

In 1977 a full-time salaried judge in Scotland was removed from his office for misbehaviour because he was deemed to have engaged in public political activity. Sheriff Peter Thomson published a pamphlet advocating the holding of a plebiscite on Scottish home rule. In accordance with the Sheriff Courts (Scotland) Act 1971, the Secretary of State for Scotland asked two senior Scottish judges (the Lord President of the Court of Session and the Lord Justice Clerk) to investigate and they reported their finding of misbehaviour which, as for Circuit judges and Recorders in England and Wales, was a ground for dismissal. The Secretary of State, having taken into account that Sheriff Thomson had been previously warned, at the time of a similar offence in 1974, made an Order for his dismissal. Such an Order had to be laid before Parliament and was there debated on 6

9. Recorders are appointed for three-year terms which are renewable. Between 1981 and 1986, appointments of twenty-seven Recorders were not renewed, in some cases because the Lord Chancellor was not satisfied of their continued fitness or suitability: see 107 HC Deb. col. *429* (16 December 1986).

December 1977. The case caused much discussion especially as it could scarcely be said that his activity was directly connected with his duties as a judge.[10] Thomson asked for permission to make a statement at the bar of the House of Commons but this was denied.[11]

In December 1983, the Lord Chancellor dismissed for misbehaviour an Old Bailey Circuit judge who had been fined £2000 on two charges of smuggling whisky and cigarettes.

Judges of the superior courts may not be sued for anything done or said while acting in their judicial capacity even if they act from some malicious or corrupt motive. The law does permit judges to be prosecuted for crimes they may commit, while so acting, but proof of criminal intent would be extremely difficult to obtain, even if an appropriate charge could be devised.[12]

The danger of criticizing the appointment of particular judges was shown when in June 1980 a Belfast jury awarded £50,000 damages to a Northern Ireland county court judge for a libel contained in an article in the *Economist* suggesting that his appointment had been based, as *The Times* put it in a leading article, not so much on his ability but on the fact that he was a Roman Catholic. One of the principal witnesses for the judge was the Lord Chief Justice of Northern Ireland. The Lord Chancellor refused to disclose any of the correspondence concerning the judge's appointment on the ground that it was not in the public interest to reveal confidences about judicial appointments and this was accepted by the court. Yet the Lord Chief Justice, giving oral evidence, said that he and the Lord Chancellor were at one in their belief that religious affinity should not take precedence over ability in the appointment of judges and, said *The Times*, he gave the impression that his positive feelings towards the judge were shared by the Lord Chancel-

10. See 940 HC Deb. col. 1288–1332; also 939 HC Deb. col. 922–5.

11. A summary of the statement was contained in a letter from Mr Thomson to *The Times* on 16 December 1977.

12. See *Sirros v. Moore* [1975] QB 118, and Margaret Brazier, 'Judicial Immunity and the Independence of the Judiciary' in [1976] *Public Law* 397.

lor. So oral evidence was admitted on the kind of matter for which privilege from disclosure of documents was claimed by the Crown. The *Economist* appealed and the matter was settled on undisclosed terms, the damages being 'adjusted' and the editor expressing himself as being extremely satisfied.[13]

To what extent, if at all, do the Lord Chancellor and the Prime Minister take into account the political allegiance of those whom they appoint or promote to judicial office?

First, there is one special case. The Attorney-General and the Solicitor-General (the law officers of the Crown) are ministers, not in the cabinet, appointed by the Prime Minister from the ranks of Members of the House of Commons who are barristers. It is often said that by tradition they have a right to judicial appointment when vacancies occur and that this is particularly true of appointment to the office of Lord Chief Justice. In a famous essay, H. J. Laski recorded that between 1832 and 1906, out of 139 judges appointed, 80 were Members of the House of Commons at the time of their nomination and 11 others had been candidates for Parliament; that, of the 80, 63 were appointed by their own party while in office; and 33 of them had been either Attorney-General or Solicitor-General.[14] Laski suggested that it was 'probably undesirable' for law officers to be suddenly made judges and so required to act impartially. Laski treads very daintily here. 'It is not necessary to suggest that there will be conscious unfairness; but it is, I submit, possible that such judges will, particularly in cases where the liberty of the subject is concerned, find themselves unconsciously biased through over-appreciation of executive difficulty . . . Nothing is more disastrous than that any suspicion of the complete impartiality of the judges should be possible.'

From 1873 to 1945, 19 out of 23 Attorneys-General and over half the Solicitors-General later held high judicial office. But since 1945, the only Attorneys-General to do so became Lord Chancellors which, being an appointment to

13. *The Times*, 1 July and 9 December 1980.
14. H. J. Laski, *Studies in Law and Politics*, pp. 164–80.

political office, is distinguishable; and only two Solicitors-General became judges.[15] It is perhaps significant that none of the last four Lord Chief Justices – Lords Goddard, Parker, Widgery and Lane – had been law officers.

The wider question, also raised by Laski's figures, is the extent to which an active political life, and particularly Membership of the House of Commons, is regarded by the Lord Chancellor as a positive qualification for appointment to a judgeship. Practice has differed over the years.

Lord Halsbury was Lord Chancellor for far longer than any other during the last hundred years. He had three periods in that office which he held, in all, for over seventeen years between 1885 and 1905. His judicial appointments were much criticized on the ground in effect that 'Halsbury appointed to the High Court, and to a lesser extent to the county court, men of little or no legal learning whose previous career in public life had been largely in the service of the Conservative Party or else were relations of his own'.[16] Professor Heuston has examined such criticisms. Of the judges appointed by Halsbury to the High Court, eight were MPs at the date of their appointment and of these six were Conservatives. Five others had been unsuccessful Parliamentary candidates, three of them being Conservatives. One other had been a Conservative MP nearly twenty years before. So fourteen out of the thirty appointments were, in those senses, of politicians – and ten were Conservatives. Heuston concludes that of Halsbury's thirty appointments to the High Court, four or five were men of real distinction, eighteen or nineteen were men of competent professional attainments, leaving no more than seven 'whose appointments seem dubious'. Four of these seven were Conservative MPs at the date of the appointment, one had been a Conservative MP, and another had twice been an unsuccessful Conservative candidate. We may say, therefore (this is my conclusion not Heuston's), that of the ten Conservative politicians whom Halsbury appointed, six were bad appointments. Every Lord Chancellor, especially if he holds office as long as did Halsbury, will make some mistakes (and Heuston suggests that as many as three of the six were 'unlucky' appointments) but Halsbury's experience may suggest that the proportion of bad appointments is likely to be statistically higher amongst appointments made from the Lord Chancellor's political associates.

Certainly at that time it was accepted that a political career was likely to be an advantage for a barrister aspiring to a judgeship, though it was important that his seat should be safe, as no government would wish to run the possibility of diminishing its strength in the House. Heuston tells us how Lord Halsbury when he was a Parliamentary candidate was congratulated by Sir Edward Clarke on his election defeat by nine votes in 1874. Clarke explained that if Halsbury had won by such a majority he could not have expected elevation to a judgeship. But, as it was, he could expect to be made Solicitor-General and found a safe seat. This is indeed what happened although he held the office for over a year until the seat was found for him in 1877. (During the interval he was in fact offered a judgeship, which he declined, but it was made clear that the government could not long countenance a Solicitor-General without a seat in the House of Commons.)

In August 1895, arising out of argument about the fees payable to the law officers, Lord Salisbury, as Prime Minister, promised Sir Edward Clarke that he would be appointed Attorney-General if a vacancy occurred within two years. In 1897, a new Master of the Rolls had to be appointed. If the Attorney-General (Sir Richard Webster) took the post, Clarke would have to be appointed Attorney-General. Lord Salisbury, who had a poor opinion of Clarke's abilities (as had Halsbury), wrote in much perplexity to the Lord Chancellor but saying that the Rolls should be offered to Clarke 'on party grounds' because he would do less harm as a judge than as Attorney-General. Salisbury continued:

> There remains the third course, to throw Clarke over altogether and tell him that the highest point of his career has been reached. I confess that the more I con-

sider this alternative, the more I dislike it. It is at variance with the unwritten law of our party system; and there is no clearer statute in that unwritten law than the rule that party claims should always weigh very heavily in the disposal of the highest appointments . . . It would be a breach of the tacit convention on which politicians and lawyers have worked the British Constitution together for the last 200 years. Perhaps it is not an ideal system – some day no doubt the MR will be appointed by competitive examination in Law Reports, but it is our system for the present; and we should give our party arrangements a wrench if we throw it aside.

Lord Salisbury did offer the Rolls to Clarke, who declined it on the ground that it would put an end to his political career, though he added that he would accept being made a Law Lord. But that offer did not come.[17]

The change in the attitude to the appointment of barrister-politicians as judges is said to date from Lord Haldane's Chancellorship (1912–15) when legal and professional qualifications became the criteria, though at first the change was not extended to the most senior appointments. Lord Haldane himself expressed his 'strong conviction that, at all events for a judge who is to sit in the Supreme Tribunals of the Empire, a House of Commons training is a real advantage. One learns there the nuances of the Constitution, and phases of individual and social political life which are invaluable in checking the danger of abstractedness in mental outlook.'[18]

But a little later Lord Sankey, who was Lord Chancellor from 1929 to 1935, when resignations occurred, replaced five Law Lords who had had political backgrounds by others whose reputations rested on their professionalism as lawyers.[19]

In recent years Lord Chancellors have differed in their opinions about the value of judges having had experience as politicians. During the 1950s, being an MP came once again

17. On all this see Heuston, *op. cit.*, pp. 52–4, 323–4.
18. Quoted in Heuston, *op. cit.*, p. 39.
19. Abel-Smith and Stevens, *Lawyers and the Courts* (1967).

to be regarded as a qualification for appointment to a judge-ship. In 1964, Lord Gardiner, who shortly afterwards became Lord Chancellor himself, said that since 1951 'one or two' Lord Chancellors (there had been only three) 'felt that the standard of members of the bar going into the House of Commons has fallen noticeably since the war, and if you want the right men in the House of Commons then you must reward the man who votes the right way with a judgeship'.[20] Lord Gardiner himself thought that political views ought not to affect judicial appointments at all, and he pursued this policy during his period of office as Lord Chancellor (1964–70).

Today, being an active member of a political party seems to be neither a qualification nor a disqualification for appointment. But those barristers retained to represent the Government – called Treasury Counsel – are very likely to be offered High Court judgeships in due course.

It must be remembered that Lord Chancellors in making their appointments to the High Court have a relatively small group to select from. Effectively, the group consists of experienced barristers between the ages of forty-five and sixty and the number of genuine possibilities – the short list – may be as small as half a dozen.

Personal characteristics must be taken into account. A man or woman whose social or personal habits are uncon-ventional or uncertain is not likely to be risked. Homo-sexuality is likely to be a bar or, if discovered later, to result in resignation. On the other hand, it is obvious from the appointments made that the strength of a candidate's convic-tions, including his political opinions, is not considered a disadvantage. But those opinions should fall within the ordi-nary range represented in the House of Commons, excluding the more extreme.

Politically the most important judicial appointment is that of Master of the Rolls. As president of the Court of Appeal his view on the proper relationship between the Executive government and the individual, including powerful private organizations, is crucial. When Sir John Donaldson was

20. *Economist*, 28 March 1964, p. 210.

appointed to succeed Lord Denning in July 1982, this was seen as a strongly political appointment and one which the Prime Minister favoured. Sir John had been a Conservative councillor and had presided over the National Industrial Relations Court for the two and a half years of its existence during the Heath administration. On its demise he reverted to his position as a judge of the High Court and was not promoted during the years of the Labour Government 1974–9. From the beginning of 1984 when it seemed probable that Lord Hailsham would soon resign as Lord Chancellor, Sir John was widely discussed as his probable successor in the Thatcher cabinet. This highlighted his political characteristics and qualifications and may have led to his decision not to preside over the Court of Appeal when it considered the appeal by the Government against the decision of Glidewell J rejecting the decision to ban trade union membership at GCHQ.[21]

Social and political position

From time to time in recent years, analyses have been made, based on information in reference books, of the social background of the more senior judiciary.

The most comprehensive in terms of social class origins[22] covers the period from 1820 to 1968.

Over the whole period the dominance of the upper and upper middle classes is overwhelming. They account for 75.4 per cent to which may be added, proportionately, 10 per cent from those 'not known'. Moreover the total percentage of these first three groups in the most recent period is 76.8, which is higher than the overall percentage. Over the whole period covered by this analysis the dominance of the first three classes is unchanged.[23]

21. See below, p. 155.
22. Class assignment is according to father's occupation or rank. The judges in this table are those of the High Court, the Court of Appeal and the House of Lords or of their equivalents.
23. From an unpublished M. Phil. dissertation by Jenny Brock quoted in *The Judiciary*, the report of a Justice subcommittee (1972).

Period of Appointment	1820–1875	1876–1920	1921–1950	1951–1968	1820–1968	Number
Social class	%	%	%	%	%	
I Traditional landed upper class	17.9	16.4	15.4	10.5	15.3	59
II Professional, commercial and administrative upper class	8.5	14.6	14.3	14.0	12.7	49
III Upper middle class	40.6	50.5	47.3	52.3	47.4	183
IV Lower middle class	11.3	9.7	8.8	8.1	9.6	37
V Working class	2.8	1.0	1.1	1.2	1.3	6
Not known	18.9	7.8	13.2	14.0	13.5	52
	100	100	100	100	100	
Number	106	103	91	86	386	386

Another survey, published in 1975, covers the period 1876–1972 and, with a few omissions, analyses the 317 judges who sat in the High Court, the Court of Appeal and the House of Lords during that period. The author does not, however, break down these ninety-six years into shorter periods, so trends within the whole are not apparent. He considers school background and finds that 33 per cent attended one of the so-called Clarendon Schools (Charterhouse, Eton, Harrow, Merchant Taylors, Rugby, St Paul's, Shrewsbury, Westminster, Winchester), while 70 per cent attended Oxford or Cambridge Universities.[24]

School education is a good indicator of social and economic class background, particularly as the relative cost of attendance at one of the independent 'public' schools has changed little, until very recently. It must also be remem-

24. C. Neal Tate, 'Paths to the Bench in Britain', 28 *Western Political Quarterly* 108.

bered that university education at Oxford and Cambridge before 1945 (when those who are now judges attended) was also very largely a middle-class activity, within the first three groups of the table set out above.

In 1956 the *Economist*[25] published a short survey. This covered 69 judges of the Supreme Court, House of Lords and Judicial Committee of the Privy Council and showed that 76 per cent had attended 'major public schools' (not further defined) and the same percentage had been to Oxford or Cambridge. In May 1970 *New Society*[26] looked at 359 judges including those offices surveyed by the *Economist* but also, amongst others, county court judgeships and metropolitan magistrates. It found that 81 per cent had attended public schools and 76 per cent had attended Oxford or Cambridge. In 1969, Henry Cecil investigated the background of 117 out of 235 judges of the House of Lords, the Supreme Court, county courts and stipendiary magistrates. From a random group of 36 judges of the Court of Appeal and the High Court, he found that 31 had been to public schools (86 per cent) and 33 to Oxford or Cambridge (92 per cent). From a random group of 45 (out of 90) county court judges and 24 (out of 48) stipendiaries, he found that 52 had attended public schools (75 per cent) and 56 Oxford or Cambridge (81 per cent). In 1975 Hugo Young analysed the educational background of 31 appointees to the High Court during the previous five years. He found that 68 per cent went to public schools and 74 per cent to Oxford or Cambridge.[27]

These figures have changed very little over the last thirty or more years. In 1940 about 80 per cent of the judges of the Supreme Court had attended public schools. In 1969, this was true of 79 per cent of Henry Cecil's group of 117. A higher proportion of the earlier generation did not attend university at all – 8 out of 35 in 1940 but only 8 out of 135 in 1970. Of those who did attend, the bias in favour of Oxford and Cambridge has remained effectively

25. 12 December 1956, pp. 946–7.
26. 14 May 1970 (by Kevin Goldstein-Jackson).
27. *The Sunday Times*, 5 October 1975.

unchanged.[28] The *New Society* survey compared county court judges in three recent years. In 1947, in 1957 and in 1967, seven county court judges were appointed. Of these 21 judges, all but one in 1947, two in 1957 and one in 1967 had attended public schools; all but three in 1947, two in 1957 and three in 1967 had attended Oxford or Cambridge. In 1978, of 74 High Court judges listed, over 75 per cent had attended public schools and, of these, 41 per cent had attended one of the Clarendon Schools.[29] Of the 17 High Court judges appointed between 1 January 1980 and 1 May 1982, 76 per cent attended public schools and 88 per cent Oxford or Cambridge.[30] In 1986, 29 out of 34 Law Lords, and Lords Justices of Appeal had attended public schools and Oxford or Cambridge Universities.[31]

The decline in the number of 'political' judges is also shown. The *Economist*'s survey of 1956 recorded that 23 per cent of their 69 judges had been MPs or Parliamentary candidates. But fourteen years later, Henry Cecil could find only 10 MPs and 5 candidates out of his 117 judges (13 per cent). Since 1977, no judge sitting in the High Court, or the Court of Appeal or the House of Lords (as a Law Lord) had formerly been a Member of the House of Commons.

The age of the full-time judiciary has remained constant over many years: the average on appointment has been about fifty-two or -three and the average of all those in office has been about sixty. Inevitably, given the system of promotion, the average age is highest in the Court of Appeal and the House of Lords, at about sixty-five and sixty-eight years respectively. In 1988, of 509 judges (from the Circuit bench to the House of Lords), 91 had been born in or before 1920.

Between 1876 and 1972 there were 63 Lords of Appeal in Ordinary (Law Lords). An analysis of 49 of these showed

28. Henry Cecil, *The English Judge* (2nd edn, 1972). For a survey of judges sitting on 1 January 1970, see Fred L. Morrison, *Courts and the Political Process in England* (1974), ch. 3; the findings are very similar to those in the surveys quoted above.

29. 950 HC Deb. 16 May 1978, col. 108–10.

30. *LAG Bulletin*, August 1982 (Phil Cohen).

31. *Labour Research*, January 1987, p. 9.

that 18 had fathers who were lawyers, 16 had fathers of other professions (churchmen, doctors, teachers, architects, soldiers); 12 fathers were in business (of whom one was working-class), and 3 fathers were farmers or land-owners. Forty-six Law Lords had been to Oxford or Cambridge, seven to Scottish universities, four to Trinity College Dublin, two to London University (one of whom had also been to Cambridge) and one to Queen's Belfast. These facts and figures added relatively little to what was already known in outline. More interesting is the analysis of political background. The authors[32] divided their period into three groups. Group A included twenty Law Lords appointed in the period 1876–1914; group B had twenty-one appointed between 1918 and 1948; group C had twenty-two appointed in 1948–69. Of the twenty Law Lords in group A, eleven had been MPs and three Parliamentary candidates; of the twenty-one in group B, five had been MPs; of the twenty-two in group C, four had been MPs and two Parliamentary candidates. While these figures show the decline since the late nineteenth and early twentieth century of appointments of such politicians, they also show little change since 1918. It is, however, unwise to base generalizations on such figures. What matters more than prior political involvement is how far Law Lords consciously or otherwise are influenced in their judgments by their own political opinions, how far this is avoidable and how far it is undesirable. One highly 'political' Lord Chancellor – like Lord Hailsham of St Marylebone – can, if he chooses, make a considerable impact on judicial law-making at the highest level but, for this to be so, it is not necessary that he should have held political office or have been a Member of Parliament or a law officer.

All these figures show that, in broad terms, four out of five full-time professional judges are products of public schools, and of Oxford or Cambridge. Occasionally the brilliant lower-middle-class or working-class boy or girl has won their place in this distinguished gathering. With very few exceptions, judges are required to be selected from amongst practising barristers and it is difficult for anyone without a

32. L. Blom-Cooper and G. Drewry, *Final Appeal* (1972).

private income to survive the first years of practice. To become a successful barrister, therefore, it is necessary to have financial support and so the background has to be that of the reasonably well-to-do family which, as a matter of course, sends its sons or daughters to public schools and then to Oxford or Cambridge.

Nevertheless, some men and women have, since the middle 1960s, benefited from the expansion of university education, from the growth of law faculties in universities, and from the wider availability of this education and, with little private income, have been able (largely because of the increase in publicly financed legal aid) to make a living at the bar. In the 1990s some of these will move into the ranks of successful barristers from whom judicial appointments are made. Only then shall we be able to assess how far the dominance of the public schools and (what is of much less significance) of Oxford and Cambridge has begun to lessen. And not until the late 1990s shall we know whether (as seems most unlikely) judicial attitudes have changed as a result.

In March 1991, of the judges from the Law Lords to the Circuit bench (some 550 in all) only one was black. Two Lords Justice, two High Court judges and nineteen Circuit judges were women.[33]

Judicial independence means that judges are not dependent on governments in ways which might influence them in coming to decisions in individual cases, though their promotion, like their appointment, is effectively in the hands of the Lord Chancellor with, nowadays, a measure of Prime Ministerial intervention. As we have seen, in financial terms, such promotion is not of much significance. But life in the Court of Appeal and, even more, in the House of Lords is not so strenuous as in the High Court (or below), personal prestige and status are higher among the fewer, with a life peerage at the top. These are not inconsiderable rewards for promotion, and the question is whether there are pressures on, particularly, High Court judges to act and to speak in court in certain ways rather than others. Are there decisions

33. Lord Chancellor's Department 1991; Law Society 1989–90; quoted in *The Independent*, 8 March 1991

which could be classified as popular or unpopular in the eyes of the most important senior judges or the Lord Chancellor? Is a judge ever conscious that his reputation as a judge is likely to be adversely affected in their eyes if he decides one way, and favourably affected if he decides another way?

The answer is that such pressures do exist. For example, a judge who acquires a reputation among his seniors for being 'soft' in certain types of cases where the Lord Chancellor, the Lord Chief Justice, the Master of the Rolls and other senior judges favour a hard line is as likely to damage his promotion prospects as he would if his appointment were found to be unfortunate on other more obvious grounds. But this does not amount to dependence on the political wishes of governments or ministers as such. In no real sense does such direct dependence or influence exist. How far judges consciously or unconsciously subserve the wider interests of governments is another and more important question.

What is meant by saying that judges must be impartial and seen to be so? Judges themselves claim this as their great virtue and only occasionally is it seen to be departed from. Lord Haldane was a practising barrister in 1901 when he recorded:

> I fought my hardest for the Dutch prisoners before the Privy Council this morning, but the tribunal was hopelessly divided, and the anti-Boers prevailed over the pro-Boers. It is bad that so much bias should be shewn, but it is, I suppose, inevitable.[34]

D. N. Pritt in his autobiography told of his many political cases and of one which 'came before a judge of great experience and knowledge, so bitterly opposed to anything left-wing that he could scarcely have given a fair trial if he had tried'.[35]

Are such phrases applicable today? Every practising barrister knows before which judges he would prefer not to appear in a political case because he believes, and his col-

---

34. Quoted by Heuston, *op. cit.*, p. 195.
35. *From Right to Left* (1965), p. 142.

leagues at the bar believe, that certain judges are much more likely than others to be biased against certain groups, like demonstrators or students, or certain kinds of action, like occupations of property by trade unionists or the homeless. Sometimes counsel for one of the parties in a case will make objection to a particular judge hearing the case. And the judge may then decide not to sit. In 1978 Lord Denning MR acceded to such a request when told that the Church of Scientology of California felt that in his court there was an unconscious influence operating adversely to the church.[36] In January 1978, the Lord Chancellor announced that Judge Neil McKinnon had said that he wished not to preside in future over cases involving racial questions; and that this wish would be given effect to. Judge McKinnon had been widely criticized for comments made during his hearing of a case of inciting racial hatred.

Occasionally the Lord Chancellor will publicly reprimand a judge, as happened in 1978 when Mr Justice Melford-Stevenson was rebuked for describing an Act of Parliament as a 'buggers' charter'. In January 1982, Lord Hailsham repudiated the comment of a judge that a rape victim who hitch-hiked a lift was guilty of contributory negligence and that the rapist's penalty should accordingly be reduced. In January 1984, Lord Hailsham reprimanded a Recorder who attacked as an affront to British justice a decision by Wool-worths to prosecute a widow aged seventy-seven for shop-lifting.

More seriously, Judge Argyle was severely reprimanded by Lord Havers 'for a number of unfortunate remarks made by him in the course of a speech at Trent Polytechnic, Nottingham, on Friday, March 13, 1987'.[37] It was reported that he had said the Government 'had fallen flat on its face in dealing with the situation', adding that law and order did not exist in this country at the moment; that there could be up to five million illegal immigrants in Britain; and that judges should be able to impose the death sentence on

36. See *The Times*, 21 February 1978.
37. 488 HL Deb. col. 1376 (21 July 1987).

anyone convicted of an offence carrying more than a fifteen-year sentence.

In November 1988, Circuit Judge Cassel was reported as having said, when putting a husband on probation for indecent assaults on his 12-year-old daughter, during his wife's pregnancy, that the wife's lack of sexual appetite led to considerable problems 'for a healthy young husband'. The Lord Chancellor, Lord Mackay, said it was regrettable that the judge should have expressed himself in this way. It appeared that the judge had tendered his resignation on the grounds of ill health in a letter sent to the Lord Chancellor the day before his controversial comments.

It is generally agreed that making a bad decision (for which the remedy is an appeal) will not normally be treated as ground for dismissal of a Circuit judge as showing 'inability or misbehaviour'.

In May 1989, a registrar admitted a drink-driving charge and was severely reprimanded by the Lord Chancellor.

In February 1989, the Lord Chancellor was reported as having sought an explanation of remarks made at a dinner by Sir James Miskin, Recorder of London. Sir James was reported as having called for a return of capital punishment, launched an attack on the parole system, favoured the abolition of the right to silence for accused persons, referred to a black person as a 'nig-nog', and made a remark about 'murderous Sikhs' involved in a case he was hearing at the time. The Court of Appeal subsequently upheld convictions in the case, saying that although the remarks 'raised the appearance of bias', and were 'doubly deplorable' as involving a respected ethnic minority, they could not have affected the outcome of the trial.

A simplified note on the structure of courts

Civil cases are first heard either in county courts by Circuit judges (of whom there are some 430); or in the High Court by judges of the High Court[38] (of whom there are over eighty). Each case is heard by a single judge (very occasionally with a jury).[39] The High Court is divided into the Queen's Bench, Chancery and Family Divisions. The head of the Queen's Bench is the Lord Chief Justice, of the Chancery is the Vice-Chancellor, and of the Family Division is its President. For certain cases two or three judges of the Queen's Bench sit together and are then called the Divisional Court of the Queen's Bench Division.[40]

Appeal from county courts and the High Court lies to the Court of Appeal (civil division), which is presided over by the Master of the Rolls and where the other judges are Lords Justices of Appeal (of whom there are some thirty). Two or three judges sit on each case. From the Court of Appeal, appeal may lie to the House of Lords in important cases. The House of Lords for this purpose consists of the Lord Chancellor (who sits infrequently) and the Lords of Appeal in Ordinary (Law Lords, of whom there are not more than eleven). Other peers who hold or have held high judicial office may sit but rarely do so. Five usually sit on each case. For an appeal to the House of Lords, either the Court of Appeal or the House of Lords must give leave. It is possible, in certain circumstances, again if leave is obtained, to appeal direct from the High Court to the House of Lords, leap-frogging the Court of Appeal.

Less serious *criminal* cases are tried summarily (without a jury) by magistrates' courts where sit either two or more lay Justices of the Peace (of whom there are some 28,000) or a legally qualified stipendiary magistrate (of whom there are about sixty-five, most sitting in London). More serious criminal cases are first enquired into by magistrates' courts to see if there is sufficient evidence for the case to go further. If there is, the case goes to the Crown Court (sitting with a jury and in many different places), where it is heard by a

38. The numbers of judges etc are as they were at the beginning of 1990.
39. Also registrars (who are solicitors) frequently try small cases in county courts.
40. Very occasionally the other Divisions also adopt this device.

CIVIL JURISDICTION

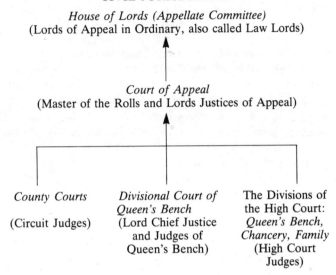

House of Lords (Appellate Committee)
(Lords of Appeal in Ordinary, also called Law Lords)

Court of Appeal
(Master of the Rolls and Lords Justices of Appeal)

County Courts (Circuit Judges)	*Divisional Court of Queen's Bench* (Lord Chief Justice and Judges of Queen's Bench)	The Divisions of the High Court: *Queen's Bench, Chancery, Family* (High Court Judges)

Queen's Bench or Circuit judge or by a Recorder (in certain circumstances joined by two to four Justices of the Peace). Recorders (of whom there are over seven hundred, plus some five hundred Assistant Recorders) are practising barristers or solicitors who are required to sit for a few weeks each year.

Appeals from decisions of magistrates' courts on less serious cases go either, if only a question of law is disputed, to the Divisional Court of the Queen's Bench Division or, where the appeal is on questions of fact and/or law, to the Crown Court. Appeals from decisions in more serious cases (heard originally by the Crown Court) go to the Court of Appeal (criminal division), which draws its members from the Lord Chief Justice, the Lords Justices of Appeal and the judges of the High Court. Normally, three sit on each case. From the Divisional Court and the Court of Appeal, further appeal lies to the House of Lords if leave is obtained.

Finally, the Judicial Committee of the Privy Council hears appeals from a very limited number of overseas territories. It is composed of Law Lords, and others who hold or have held judicial office in the United Kingdom or the Common-wealth.

CRIMINAL JURISDICTION

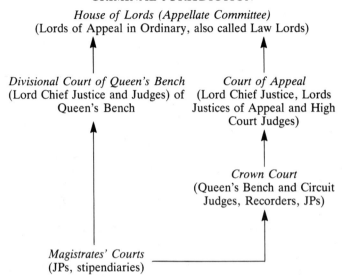

House of Lords (Appellate Committee)
(Lords of Appeal in Ordinary, also called Law Lords)

Divisional Court of Queen's Bench
(Lord Chief Justice and Judges) of Queen's Bench

Court of Appeal
(Lord Chief Justice, Lords Justices of Appeal and High Court Judges)

Crown Court
(Queen's Bench and Circuit Judges, Recorders, JPs)

Magistrates' Courts
(JPs, stipendiaries)

2. Extrajudicial activities

Commissions, inquiries, reports and the like

Judges are frequently called upon by the government of the day to preside over commissions, committees and administrative tribunals of different kinds. Some of these are concerned with matters deep in political controversy.

Royal Commissions are appointed by the Crown to enquire into selected matters of concern.[1] Committees are appointed by ministers for the same purpose. As the Crown acts on the advice of ministers in this matter, and as they deal with comparable matters, the distinction between the two is not substantial. Royal Commissions have more prestige but nothing of real consequence flows from this, and the matters which these bodies investigate vary greatly in importance.

Dr T. J. Cartwright has recorded that 640 such bodies were appointed between 1945 and 1969 and he examined 358. These included 24 Royal Commissions; and 334 'major' departmental committees which he defined as those dealing with matters of direct concern to the government of Britain and whose reports were published as command papers.

The mean size of the twenty-four Royal Commissions was thirteen members, but when comparable committees are added the mean size falls to eight members. Of the twenty-four Royal Commissions, judges chaired seven. Only academics equalled them in number of Royal Commission

---

1. See T. J. Cartwright, *Royal Commissions & Departmental Committees in Britain* (1975); see also G. Rhodes, *Committees of Inquiry* (1975).

chairs and no one group[2] of persons held half as many chairs of departmental committees. Altogether, judges chaired 118 out of Dr Cartwright's 358 bodies.

Judges chaired commissions or committees concerned with, among other things, Justices of the Peace (1946–8), medical partnerships (1948), police conditions of service (1948–9), the industrial health services (1949–50), State immunities (1949–51), taxation of profits and income (1951–5), marriage and divorce (1951), dock workers (1955–6), the interception of communications (1957), prison conditions (1957–8), the working of the monetary system (1957–9), legal education for African students (1960), security in the public service (1961), the security service and Mr Profumo (1963), children and young persons in Scotland (1961–4), jury service (1963–5), the port transport industry (1964–5), pay for dock workers (1966), tribunals of enquiry (1966), 'D' notices (1967), the age of majority (1965–7), trade unions and employers' associations (1965–8), Scottish inshore fisheries (1967–70), the constitution (1969–73), one-parent families (1969–74), the adoption of children (1969–72), contempt of court (1974), defamation (1975), and the Brixton disorders (1981). Many of these were highly political, some also highly controversial. Since 1969, important departmental committees chaired by judges have included those on the interrogation of terrorists (1971–2), crowd safety (1971–2), legal procedures to deal with terrorists (1972), the working of the Abortion Act (1971–4), the Red Lion Square disorders (1974–5), standards of conduct in public life (1974–6), and police pay (1977–8).

All those related to affairs within the United Kingdom. In addition, judges have frequently been employed on overseas matters. One of the most famous of these in post-war years was the Nyasaland Commission of Enquiry of 1959 led by Mr Justice Devlin who reported in terms of which the government of the day did not wholly approve. In 1972,

---

2. See Cartwright, *op. cit.*, p. 72. His other groups are civil service; retired central government; other government (active or retired); legal profession; business, finance, industry; medical profession; trade unions; other; no information.

Lord Pearce chaired a Commission on Rhodesian Opinion appointed to ascertain directly from all sections of the population of Rhodesia whether or not certain proposals for the government of that country were acceptable. The number of such judicial appointments for overseas territories is considerable.

In December 1973, Mr John Morris MP asked how many judges had carried out non-judicial duties in the form of inquiries, commissions and reports, or similar tasks, during the previous twenty years. He was told that, including Law Lords and Lords Justices but excluding standing bodies such as the Law Commission, the total was 79 judges. The Labour Government of 1964–70 appointed more, on average, than did the Conservative Governments during this period from 1953 to 1973.[3] On 12 July 1984, Mr Morris tried the same question again for the period since 1973. This time the Attorney General replied that the figures for the period before 1982 were 'not fully available or reasonably accessible', which can mean only that no one in his office was prepared to make the count. However he did say that in the years ending June 1983 and June 1984 the total number of High Court judges so involved was 28.[4] As no details were given, this figure is almost meaningless but if the categories counted were similar to those for the period of 1953–73 those two later years show almost a doubling, on average.

Most recently, in 1985–6, Mr Justice Popplewell reported on crowd safety and control at sports grounds, following the Bradford fire; in 1988, Lord Justice Butler-Sloss on suspected child abuse cases in Cleveland; in 1988 Mr Justice Barry Sheen on the sinking of the Herald of Free Enterprise; in 1988, Lord Cullen on the Piper Alpha oil rig explosion; in 1989, Lord Justice Taylor on the Hillsborough stadium disaster. In 1990, Lord Justice Woolf was appointed to inquire into the circumstances surrounding the riot at Strangeways prison and associated matters.

Judges are normally appointed as chairmen of those numerous committees which are concerned with reform of

---

3. For full details see 865 HC Deb. col. *478–82* (7 December 1973).
4. 63 HC Deb. col. *630* (12 July 1984).

substantive law or legal procedure. Specifically a judge is chairman of the Law Commission which is the permanent body concerned with law reform. Judges are therefore constantly involved in the process of making recommendations for improvement in the law and this includes not only technical legal subjects but also those on the boundaries of law and politics, like conspiracy. The Scottish Law Commission, also chaired by a judge, became deeply involved in the debate on devolution, submitting memoranda particularly dealing with the distribution of powers between the United Kingdom Parliament and the proposed Scottish Assembly.[5] These memoranda, although generally avoiding comment that might be regarded as politically partisan on the question of the desirability or otherwise of devolution, contain passages which were bluntly, even scathingly, critical of the statements of the means by which the government hoped to achieve their objectives.

One of the Scottish Law Commission's proposals was that if the area of devolution was sufficiently extensive, responsibility for the courts should also be transferred to the Scottish Assembly. A few months earlier Lord Wheatley spoke on behalf of all the High Court judges in Scotland. He accepted that a judge, as a member of a Royal Commission or a departmental Committee of Enquiry, might have to explain publicly the recommendations arrived at. However, he continued:

> When the subject enters the political arena and becomes politically controversial, we assume an elective silence on the political issues and confine ourselves, if we intervene at all, to constitutional or legal questions or views on practical matters affecting the law and its administration where our views may naturally be expected and sought.[6]

He went on to say that the unanimous view of the High Court judges in Scotland was that the Scottish courts should

5. See Scottish Law Commission: memorandum no. 32 incorporating also an earlier memorandum.
6. 367 HL Deb. col. 837 (27 January 1976).

remain the responsibility of the United Kingdom and not become the responsibility of the Scottish Assembly.

It is difficult to see how this disagreement between the Scottish Law Commission and the Scottish High Court judge could be thought of as other than political.

Judges are used to head permanent bodies concerned with national security. In April 1980, Lord Diplock was appointed to review the interception of communications (mostly phone-tapping) undertaken by the police, Customs and Excise, and the security services.[7] Mr Robin Cook MP, objected to Lord Diplock's suitability on the ground that he had been chairman of the Security Commission since 1971, and had not formerly indicated any understanding of the concern for civil liberties and privacy which had given rise to public and press anxiety about the procedures of the security services. Cook also referred to Diplock's 'evident distaste for trade unions' and said it was well known that 'taps' were frequently placed on trade unionists involved in trade disputes. The Home Secretary rejected the criticism.[8] Subsequently, the Speaker ruled in the House of Commons that it was offensive, even in relation to these extrajudicial activities, to refer to Lord Diplock as 'a Tory judge'.[9] Under the Interception of Communications Act 1985, the appointment was made statutory and Lord Justice Lloyd was the Commissioner in 1990.

The chairman of the Security Commission, which investigates breaches of security and advises generally on security matters, is presently Lord Griffiths. Under the Security Service Act 1989, Lord Justice Stuart-Smith was appointed Security Service Commissioner with a general supervisory role over the security services. Mr Justice Simon Brown was appointed as the president of the complaints Tribunal under the Act.

High Court judges are the deputy chairmen of the Parliamentary Boundary Commissions.

In February 1985, the Lord Chancellor (Lord Hailsham) set up a Review Body on Civil Justice consisting of a small

7. 982 HC Deb. col. 205–20.
8. 996 HC Deb. col. 824–6 (18 December 1980).
9. 987 HC Deb. col. *651* (3 July 1980) and *The Times*, 11 July 1980.

team of officials mostly from the Lord Chancellor's Department and an advisory committee. Lord Griffiths was a member of the committee. The Review Body reported in 1988.[10]

An important permanent body is the Judicial Studies Board. Its function is to provide training for judges, especially for those acting as Assistant Recorders or deputy Registrars, and for lay magistrates; but also for other judges through refresher seminars, also attended by civil servants. Originally limited to training in the criminal jurisdiction (with an emphasis on sentencing), the Board now is concerned also with the civil and family courts and tribunals. There is a Main Board, chaired by a Lord Justice of Appeal; the committees on the different jurisdictions are also chaired by judges.[11]

Judges also preside over enquiries set up under the Tribunals of Enquiry (Evidence) Act 1921. These enquiries are nowadays reserved for investigations into matters which may involve the reputation of ministers or public officials. Between 1945 and 1970 there were five: in 1948–9 into questions of possible bribery of ministers, chaired by Mr Justice Lynskey;[12] in 1957–8 into leakage of bank rate, chaired by Lord Justice Parker;[13] in 1959 into allegations of police assault on a boy, chaired by Lord Sorn;[14] in 1962–3 into a case of spying in which a minister's moral behaviour might have been involved, chaired by Lord Radcliffe;[15] and in 1966–7 into the responsibility for the Aberfan disaster, chaired by Lord Justice Edmund Davies.[16] Since 1970, this procedure has been used twice in Northern Ireland, as we shall see.[17] In 1972 a Tribunal of Enquiry presided over by Mr Justice James enquired into the collapse of the Vehicle and General Insurance Company and reported in terms

10. Cm 394.
11. See Report for 1983–87 (HMSO 1988).
12. Cmnd 7616.
13. Cmnd 350.
14. Cmnd 718.
15. Cmnd 2009.
16. HC 553 of 1966–7.
17. See below, pp. 52–5; see generally Cmnd 3121.

which were critical in particular of one civil servant.[18] In 1978 a Tribunal was appointed, under the chairmanship of Mr Justice Croom-Johnson, to investigate the activities of the Crown Agents.

Two outstanding examples of the use of the judiciary in politics have concerned industrial relations, and Northern Ireland.

Industrial relations

Under the Industrial Courts Act of 1919[19] the minister may set up a court of enquiry into a trade dispute. Since 1954, fourteen of such courts have been presided over by judges, normally with two experienced non-lawyers. Lord Pearson leads the field with five enquiries into disputes in the electricity supply, seamen's, civil air transport, steel, and port industries.[20] Lord Cameron follows with four: Ford's, port transport, printing, and building sites.[21] Lord Wilberforce presided over two enquiries into disputes in the electricity supply and coal industries;[22] Lord Morris into a shipbuilding and engineering dispute;[23] Lord Evershed into a London docks dispute;[24] and Lord Justice Scarman into the Grunwick dispute.[25]

These are far from being solely fact-finding enquiries. The terms of reference frequently require the court to have regard to the public interest or the national interest or the national economy or considerations like 'the need for an efficient and competitive' industry.[26] In one recent enquiry[27]

18. HC 133 of 1971–2.
19. I was helped by being able to read an unpublished thesis for MSc (Econ.) by David Cockburn (1972).
20. Cmnd 2361, 3025, 3211, 3551, 3754, 4429.
21. Cmnd 131, 510, 3184, 3396.
22. Cmnd 4954, 4903.
23. Cmnd 9084, 9085.
24. Cmnd 9302, 9310.
25. Cmnd 6922.
26. See Cmnd 3025 – the industry was shipping.
27. See Cmnd 4594.

into the electricity supply industry, Lord Wilberforce asked the Treasury to submit a memorandum on the significance of the dispute to the interests of the national economy and the Treasury responded with a document that argued for a progressive and substantial reduction in the levels of settlements.[28] This request from the court caused some difficulties as it was argued that the government was seeking to impose its views and even a favoured solution of the dispute upon the court. Lord Wilberforce sought to rebut this but the request clearly, in the minds of some, showed that the court was not independent or impartial.

The status and function of these courts came into question during one of the most critical of these enquiries, that presided over by Lord Wilberforce in 1972 into the dispute about miners' pay[29] which had led to a widespread stoppage of work. The extent to which the courts could become involved in the politics of such disputes had been shown a few years earlier when Lord Cameron presided over an enquiry into a dispute on London building sites.[30] The report then expressed the opinion that certain workmen should be eligible for re-employment if they sought it but not in any circumstances for election as shop stewards; and that other workmen should not be offered re-employment.

In the miners' dispute Lord Wilberforce became deeply enmeshed in job evaluation, the social and physical conditions in the pits and, above all, the need to produce a settlement under which the miners would go back to work. Lord Wilberforce discovered that there were two factors in any possible wage increase. One was the periodic factor – that wages did increase from time to time – and the other was what he called the adjustment factor which meant that a time might come in any industry when a distortion or trend had to be recognized as such for correction. 'The existence of these two quite separate factors', said the report, 'appears to have been overlooked until the present Enquiry brought

28. See Cmnd 4579.
29. See Cmnd 4903.
30. Cmnd 3396.

it to light.' If a large increase could not be paid for by the National Coal Board then the government should meet it.

The *Economist* referred to the device of 'calling in a High Court judge to write incredible economic nonsense',[31] but whatever view is taken of the justice or the wisdom of the report which recommended a considerable wage increase and which formed the basis of the settlement, the impression given was that the government had set up this enquiry to produce a report which would enable them to yield to the miners' claim without total loss of face.

Under other legislation, less formal committees may be set up to enquire into trade disputes, and in the 1960s Lord Devlin produced three reports on the port industry[32] and Lord Cameron reported on a dispute concerning bank employees.[33]

In 1962, the Royal Commission on the Press recommended that there should be set up a Press Amalgamations Court, like the Restrictive Practices Court, consisting of judges of the High Court and lay members appointed on the recommendation of the Lord Chancellor after consultation with the Trades Union Congress and the Press Council.[34] Lord Hailsham, then a minister, was doubtful about the value of the idea as he thought that the question of the public interest in a proposed amalgamation (which the court would have to consider) was 'not justiciable'. He went on to point out 'the danger of getting the judiciary into politics' especially as newspapers were often linked to political parties. The primary concern of the judiciary, said Lord Hailsham, must be 'to retain the respect of the public for their independence – which involves not merely their real independence of mind, but also the belief which the public can have that they are seen to be independent in every respect'.[35] Eight years later these considerations did not apparently deter Lord Hailsham

31. 26 February 1972.
32. Cmnd 2523, 2734, 3104.
33. Cmnd 2202.
34. Cmnd 1811 paras 337–49.
35. 250 HL Deb. col. 938–9.

(then Lord Chancellor) from supporting the setting up of the National Industrial Relations Court (NIRC).

When in 1970 the minister was introducing in the Commons legislation which created the NIRC, he said that the NIRC's existence showed 'in fact as well as in symbol' that the provisions of the Bill[36] would not be arbitrarily implemented by the Secretary of State of the day but would 'depend on the rule of the law'. The court, he said (inaccurately), would be 'something new in British justice' and would consist of judges and laymen sitting together.[37]

Many kinds of dispute arising out of industrial relations could find their way to the NIRC which, because of its status as a superior court of record and the powers given it by statute, was able to order the payment of fines and, if that or any other of its orders was disregarded, could imprison for contempt. The application of that sanction led to the involvement of the ordinary courts. Here I am concerned to emphasize that the NIRC was required by the legislation under which it operated to make decisions which were likely to lead, and did in fact lead, to considerable and widespread political protest.

Whether the NIRC always acted with the greatest wisdom may be debatable. But its failure was due not primarily to the way it performed its functions, but to the nature of those functions. Many people doubted whether the issues before the Restrictive Practices Court were justiciable. What the NIRC was required to do was to make binding decisions, and to see that they were enforced, in the context of dispute between trade unions, individual workmen, employers, and employers' federations. This, as many said at the time, was not a function which judges and courts could perform successfully.

Now under the Employment Protection Act of 1975 an Appeal Tribunal has been set up consisting of judges, and of others having special knowledge or experience of industrial relations, either as representatives of employers or as representatives of workers. So in structure, if not in other ways,

36. This became the Industrial Relations Act 1971.
37. 808 HC Deb. col. 982.

this tribunal is similar to the NIRC. It can hear appeals from tribunals under or by virtue of the Equal Pay Act 1970, the Sex Discrimination Act 1975 and others, as well as the Employment Protection Act itself. It is a somewhat curious body in that much of its jurisdiction is to hear appeals on questions of law, for which the lay members might appear unfitted. Perhaps we are seeing, as an evolution (the origins of which can be traced to the nineteenth century), the emergence of a genuine hybrid tribunal, in which case to suggest that this body is a further example of the use of judges for extrajudicial activities is only one way to describe it. It could also be said to be an example of the developed use of experienced laymen to assist in the determination of disputes.

Northern Ireland

The first involvement of judges, acting outside their courts, in Northern Ireland was in 1969 when the Governor appointed Lord Cameron to lead a commission of enquiry into disturbances.[38] Then in 1971 Sir Edmund Compton (not a judge but the former Parliamentary Commissioner for Administration) chaired an enquiry into allegations of physical brutality by the security forces. Sir Edmund found there had been cases of physical ill-treatment such as wall-standing, hooding, noise, deprivation of sleep, and diets of bread and water. The Home Secretary rejected any suggestion that the methods authorized for interrogation contained any element of cruelty but he appointed three Privy Councillors to consider those methods. One was Lord Parker (who had just retired as Lord Chief Justice) and another was Lord Gardiner (who had been Lord Chancellor from 1964 to 1970). Lord Parker and the third Privy Councillor (Mr J. A. Boyd-Carpenter) concluded that these methods, subject to proper safeguards, and limiting the occasions on which and the degree to which they could be applied, conformed to the authority given. Lord Gardiner said that they were secret, illegal, not morally justifiable and alien to the traditions of

38. Cmd (N.I.) 532.

what he believed still to be the greatest democracy in the world. The disagreement was wide.[39]

In April 1972, two reports were published. Lord Widgery (who had succeeded Lord Parker as Lord Chief Justice) had been appointed as a one-man tribunal of enquiry to enquire into the events of 'Bloody Sunday' which led to thirteen civilian deaths in Londonderry. This tribunal was set up under the Tribunals of Enquiry (Evidence) Act 1921 the procedure of which is designed to elicit facts. The line between matters of fact and opinions deduced from facts is not always easy to draw. Lord Widgery spoke about the justifiability of decisions taken by army commanders and soldiers, about actions which, he concluded, did 'not require censure', and in using such language caused dispute and argument about the nature of his findings.[40]

In the meantime Mr Justice Scarman had since 1969 been enquiring with two others into the violence and civil disturbances of that year. This tribunal also operated under the Act of 1921 and its report was substantial. It investigated a large number of incidents and drew conclusions about fault and responsibility. It assessed the social cost in terms of deaths, personal injuries, damage to property, damage to licensed premises, intimidation and displacement of persons.[41]

At the end of 1972 a commission under the chairmanship of Lord Diplock reported on the legal procedures to deal with terrorist activities in Northern Ireland. It concluded that the main obstacle to dealing efficiently with terrorist crime in the regular courts of justice was intimidation of would-be prosecution witnesses. It recommended that trials of scheduled terrorist offences should be conducted without a jury; that members of the armed services should be given power to arrest and to detain for up to four hours to establish identity; that bail should not normally be granted; that the onus of proof as to the possession of firearms and explosives should in certain circumstances be shifted to the accused;

and that the rules about the admissibility as evidence of confessions and signed statements should be relaxed.[42]

That commission led to the passing of the Northern Ireland (Emergency Provisions) Act 1973. In 1974 Lord Gardiner was appointed chairman of a committee to consider what provisions and powers, consistent to the maximum extent practicable in the circumstances with the preservation of civil liberties and human rights, were required to deal with terrorism and subversion in Northern Ireland, including provisions for the administration of justice; and to examine the working of the Act of 1973. The committee reported early in 1975,[43] and made a large number of recommendations, some endorsing the Diplock Commission and the Act, others being critical and proposing amendments to the law. In particular, it proposed the ending of detention without trial as soon as was politically possible, and it condemned as a serious mistake the establishment of a 'special category' for convicted prisoners claiming political motivation.

So from the beginning of 1972 there have been involved in five major enquiries relating to Northern Ireland a former Lord Chancellor (twice), a present and a former Lord Chief Justice, a Lord of Appeal, and a High Court judge. On one occasion, two of these were seen to be in open disagreement about the legitimacy and desirability of actions taken by the authorities; on another occasion, one of these was set up, in effect, to review recommendations made by another. It may be that a judge is well qualified to conduct enquiries to establish what took place on particular occasions. But it is impossible for him in his findings not to interpret events. He must draw deductions about what he thinks took place from the evidence that is presented to him. And so he will be involved in political controversy and, in circumstances like those prevailing in Northern Ireland, inevitably accused of bias, of whitewashing, of serving certain political masters. These accusations may be wholly untrue but they will be

42. Cmnd 5185.
43. Cmnd 5847.

made to an extent not paralleled by criticism of any judgment he may make from the bench of the regular courts.

Legislative process

The most senior judges sit in the House of Lords[44] and may take part in its legislative and other activities. Lords of Appeal in Ordinary – Law Lords – receive life baronies on appointment unless they are already ennobled. A survey has been made[45] of the twenty-six judges who were active Law Lords during the period 1952–68 together with two Lord Chief Justices, two Masters of the Rolls and one president of what was then the Probate, Divorce and Admiralty Division. The authors of the survey say that there was very little 'in the way of political activism' on the part of the Law Lords whose contribution to debates on bills was largely that of acting as 'resident technical consultants to the legislature on legal points' and it seems that those with records of overt political affiliation did not speak more than others.

While participating Law Lords agreed with one another more frequently than they disagreed, the authors of the survey list thirteen items between 1956 and 1967 where there was a substantial measure of disagreement and of these several were not matters of technical law. They included capital punishment, artificial insemination, adultery, the minimum age for the death penalty, corporal punishment of young offenders, and disputes concerning majority verdicts, suspended sentences and parole. In one recent debate, five Law Lords, in an unprecedented way, spoke against a legislative proposal which provided that in assessing damages payable to a widow on the death of her husband, her remarriage or prospects of remarriage should not be taken into account. Two other Law Lords participated and all the Law Lords with two exceptions attended the debate on 6 May 1971. 'In the face of almost certain defeat in the Lobby,' say Blom-Cooper and Drewry, 'the Law Lords, as decorously

---

44. I.e., the Upper House of Parliament.
45. L. Blom-Cooper and G. Drewry, *Final Appeal* (1972), ch. 10.

as they were able, withdrew their amendment and retired once more into their judicial shells.'[46]

Where technical law ends and political controversy begins is not always easy to determine. It is clear, however, that Law Lords while for the most part restricting themselves to the obviously technical are not averse to speaking on social questions like capital punishment, the treatment of offenders and adultery. They do occasionally assume the role of 'self-appointed guardians of the nation's conscience'.[47]

A well-known example from earlier in this century of a Law Lord speaking on a political matter in the House of Lords arose when Lord Carson in 1921 strongly attacked the proposal to establish an Irish Free State. His right to do so was challenged by Lord Chancellor Birkenhead and defended by former Lord Chancellor Finlay during a debate in 1922 on Law Lords and party politics.[48]

In 1963, Lord Hodson, already well known for his judicial views on matrimonial matters, strongly opposed provisions in Mr Leo Abse's Matrimonial Causes and Reconciliation Bill. He spoke once during the second reading debate, spoke or intervened thirteen times in committee, once on report, and once on third reading.[49] And Lord Hodson was concerned primarily with the substantive merits and demerits of the Bill, not with its legal technicalities.

But more dramatic and more political was Lord Salmon's contribution in 1975 to the debates on the government's controversial Trade Union and Labour Relations (Amendment) Bill. He said:

> We cannot shut our eyes to the fact that there are groups, very small numerically but extremely cohesive and tenacious, who have infiltrated the unions with the intention of seizing power if they can. Their objects and ideas are entirely different from those of the trade

46. Ibid., p. 215.
47. Ibid., p. 204.
48. 49 HL Deb. col. 931–73.
49. 250 HL Deb. col. 401–5, 1537, 1538–43; vol. 251 col. 1553–5, 1560, 1561, 1564, 1578–9, 1591–4, 1595, 1596, 1597, 1600; vol. 252 col. 419–20, 430.

unions, which we all know and respect. Their avowed purpose is to wreck the Social Contract and the democratic system under which we live. Their ethos derives from foreign lands where individual liberty is dead, and where the courts and trade unions are mere tools of the Executive, to do its will.[50]

The argument is familiar – Lord Gordon-Walker said he had heard it for forty years – but, even more, it is a political argument. Lord Salmon clearly felt strongly and spoke in the name of freedom and democracy. He posed the question whether the disadvantage of a judge speaking on matters which in one form or another – such as unfair dismissal from employment or from a trade union – might well come before him when he was on the bench was outweighed by the advantage of hearing his views or by the argument that he should not be prevented, by convention or otherwise, from speaking in Parliament on such a matter.[51]

In 1984, when the Police and Criminal Evidence Bill was being debated in the House of Lords, Lord Scarman, who had spoken at second Reading, moved two amendments during the Committee stage. The first concerned unlawfully obtained evidence and had the object of strengthening the deterrent effect of the Bill in dealing with problems of the misuse of police power. He returned to the same matter during the Report stage and his amendment was carried, against the Government, on a division. Subsequently, the Government inserted a clause of their own which went some way to meet Lord Scarman's amendment.[52] On third Reading, he moved a second amendment to make racially discriminatory behaviour by the police a specific disciplinary offence. This was also carried on a division; the Government accepted their defeat[53] and did not seek to reverse the decision. Both these matters were deep in political contro-

50. 358 HL Deb. col. 27.
51. For other, earlier, examples (mostly on more legal questions) see Shetreet, *op. cit.*, pp. 257–8, 345–7.
52. 452 HL Deb. col. 431–6 (4 January 1984); 454 col. 931–4, 946–8 (11 July 1984); 455 col. 653–74 (31 July 1984).
53. 455 HL Deb. col. 1219–27 (19 October 1984).

versy, the second in particular being strongly resisted by the police as well as by the Government.

Occasionally, a Law Lord may introduce a Bill, as did Lord Templeman in 1987–8 when he took the Land Registration Bill through the House of Lords on behalf of the Law Commission. The participation of judges in the debates on the Courts and Legal Services Bill 1989–90 is discussed below.[54]

Participation in public debate

In July 1955, the Director-General of the British Broadcasting Corporation (Sir Ian Jacob) wrote to the Lord Chancellor (Lord Kilmuir) about a project he had in mind for broadcasting a series of lectures about great judges of the past in which Sir Ian hoped members of the judiciary would participate. The Lord Chancellor consulted the Lord Chief Justice, the Master of the Rolls and the President of the Probate, Divorce and Admiralty Division of the High Court who all agreed with his reply. The Lord Chancellor began with the complacent and highly debatable observation that 'we are likely . . . to get a better assessment of the qualities of some eminent judge of the past through an existing member of the judiciary than from anyone else'. He continued in words which became known as the Kilmuir rules:

> But the overriding consideration, in the opinion of myself and my colleagues, is the importance of keeping the judiciary in this country insulated from the controversies of the day. So long as a judge keeps silent his reputation for wisdom and impartiality remains unassailable: but every utterance which he makes in public, except in the course of the actual performance of his judicial duties, must necessarily bring him within the focus of criticism. It would, moreover, be inappropriate for the judiciary to be associated with any series of talks or anything which could be fairly interpreted as

54. pp. 68–73.

entertainment . . . My colleagues and I, therefore, are agreed that as a general rule it is undesirable for members of the judiciary to broadcast on the wireless or to appear on television . . . We consider that if judges are approached by the broadcasting authorities with a request to take part in a broadcast on some special occasion, the judge concerned ought to consult the Lord Chancellor, who would always be ready to express his opinion on the particular request.

Lord Kilmuir added that he had no sort of disciplinary jurisdiction over Her Majesty's judges, each of whom, if asked to broadcast, would have to decide for himself whether he considered it compatible with his office to accept.[55]

In January 1986, the then Lord Chancellor (Lord Hailsham) said that the rules had been reviewed from time to time and the judiciary of the Supreme Court and the Circuit bench consulted. He himself had consulted the judges in 1971, 1979 and 1985. On each occasion the 'overwhelming consensus' was that there should be 'no change at all'. The course adopted, said Lord Hailsham, was to channel invitations for participation in journalism, appearances on the media, and other public engagements through the Lord Chancellor's office.

Certain kinds of publications seem not to have caused difficulties. Lord Scarman was a judge in the Court of Appeal when he gave and published the Hamlyn lectures in 1974, which were controversial, as was the Dimbleby lecture given by Lord Denning in 1980. There have been other examples.[56] There have also been conflicts. The 'controversies of the day' certainly included the dispute over clause 43 of the Administration of Justice Bill in 1985, by which the Government proposed to end the citizen's right to go to the Court of Appeal when a lower court refused to give leave to apply for judicial review of the decision of a Minister or other public authority. Among the many public critics were

55. For the full text of the letter see [1986] *Public Law* 383–6.
56. For the period between 1940 and the mid-1950s see R. B. Stevens op. cit. (above page 20, note 1).

two Lords Justices of Appeal. This, said Lord Hailsham, was 'utterly improper'. The judges were reported to have apologised. There were other reports that judges had been refused permission to appear on television in the early 1980s.

Extended to journalism, the rules were directly challenged by Circuit Judge Pickles. In March 1985, he came into conflict with the Lord Chancellor over an article he had written for the *Daily Telegraph* on Government pressure on the judiciary to shorten sentences and on the inadequacies of the prison system. The Lord Chancellor told him that, prima facie, the article constituted 'judicial misbehaviour' which is a ground for dismissal. In August 1985, Judge Pickles wrote a second article for the newspaper and was interviewed by the Lord Chief Justice.

In February 1986, he wrote an article in *The Guardian* attacking the Kilmuir rules as 'much too wide' and setting out the attempts to silence him, quoting letters from the Lord Chancellor (Hailsham). He also recorded programmes about law and society for the British Broadcasting Corporation. In other public statements he was openly critical of the Lord Chancellor and his department, accusing it of being secretive and antiquated. In April 1987, Judge Pickles published an outspoken autobiography. It was reported that in 1985 and 1986, objection was taken by the Lord Chancellor to Lord Justice Brown-Wilkinson's participation in public debates as a result of which he did not appear.

It seems to be accepted that peers are not expected to contact the Lord Chancellor's department before they speak extrajudicially in public. Lord McCluskey, in the Reith lectures of 1986, expressed many criticisms and warnings. Lord Templeman in the same year took part in radio and television programmes. In 1987, the Lord Chief Justice (Lord Lane) publicly backed police demands for the abolition of the suspect's 'right to silence';[57] and was reported as attacking politicians for delay in passing tougher laws on sentenc-

---

57. When this 'right' was abolished for proceedings in Northern Ireland in 1988, as part of anti-terrorist measures, three senior Ulster judges openly criticized the Secretary of State when he attended a social function in the province.

ing policy, a question on which the judiciary was divided. Whether these three informed the Lord Chancellor that they intended to speak on these lines is not known. It seems improbable. It is sometimes said that judges are entitled to make extrajudicial statements critical of the existing law and advocating reform. Perhaps Judge Pickles's utterances were disapproved of more for their style than for their content.

In November 1987, Lord Mackay, the newly appointed Lord Chancellor, ended the practice whereby judges were expected to seek the guidance of the Lord Chancellor's department before making public statements or taking part in radio or television programmes. They were now to be trusted to use their own discretion.

The consultative function

From mediaeval times, the sovereign and his or her principal ministers have consulted with the judges, those 'lions under the throne'. The advice they gave was not always to the sovereign's liking as the famous conflicts between James I and Chief Justice Coke showed. The peers also consulted the judges on occasion and when they did so in 1614 over the long-debated matter of the right of the King to tax through 'impositions' without Parliamentary approval, Coke took the view that the judges should not be required to give an opinion 'on the ground that they were expected in judicial course to speak and judge between the King's majesty and his people, and likewise between His Highness's subjects, and in no case to be disputants on any side'.[58] It is tempting to see this as the first occasion when the judges insisted on independence on this principle. We shall see that the conflicts between the different roles played by the judge in the political order persist today.

Government departments, especially the Home Office, frequently consult the judges on matters which require law reform, as do so many political changes. Departments have their own legal advisers but the view of the judges, who will

58. S. R. Gardiner, *History of England 1603–1642* (1883), vol. 2, p. 242.

be required to interpret and apply the legislation, may be thought valuable. The Judges' Council of the Supreme Court and the Council of Circuit Judges may be consulted. So may individual judges.

Thus on 7 June 1988, the House of Commons debated a proposal that juries should be empowered to recommend the use of the death penalty. The Home Secretary asked the Lord Chief Justice for his opinion and, said the Home Secretary, 'I can tell the House that he would be strongly opposed' to the proposal, on the ground that it was for Parliament, not the judges, to decide which types of murder should be met with death.

Sometimes the relationship goes beyond consultation. Lord Justice Butler-Sloss presided over the Cleveland inquiry into child abuse. Later, in June 1989, it was reported that she was proposing to the Lord Chancellor that the Children Bill should reverse a decision which she and other members of the Court of Appeal had felt obliged to make excluding hearsay evidence. In September 1989, following a private conference, the Lord Justice was reported as launching an education programme for judges on sentencing and treatment of child sex abusers.

It was also reported in August 1989 that Circuit Judge Bracewell was to play a vital role in the administration of the Children Act, advising on the system needed to match individual cases to the court best fitted to deal with them. In this connection, she was reported to have been co-opted to the Judicial Studies Board.

In September 1989, it was reported that the Home Secretary had begun a series of private discussions with public officials including the Lord Chancellor, the Lord Chief Justice (who had hitherto been reluctant to participate in such discussions lest they were seen as prejudicing judicial independence) and the senior Lord Justice of Appeal. The discussions were seen as preliminary to the Government policy paper on criminal justice.

Judges and the public service

The relationship between the judiciary and the Government has been changed by developments over the last twenty years and especially over the last five years or so.

The longer term has seen a greater willingness on the part of the judiciary to challenge the exercise by Ministers and civil servants of their discretionary powers. An early example is shown in *Padfield v. Minister of Agriculture* (1968).[59] The procedure by way of judicial review was simplified in 1977 and the number of applications rose considerably.[60] In some areas the judiciary seems more willing to limit the exercise of discretionary powers; in others, less willing, even reluctant. In 1987 a pamphlet, prepared by the Treasury Solicitor's Department in conjunction with the Management and Personnel Office of the Cabinet Office, was published under the title *The Judge Over Your Shoulder*. This was directed to civil servants as an introduction to the basic principles of judicial review. It attributed the growth of judicial review to, amongst other things, 'an increasing willingness on the part of the judiciary to intervene in the day-to-day business of government, coupled with a move towards an imaginative interpretation of statutes'. The pamphlet explained, in simple terms, how civil servants could protect themselves from the possibility of having their actions and decisions overturned by the courts.

A more direct conflict between the judiciary and the Government arose because of an alleged change in the attitude of the Lord Chancellor's Department. The conflict arose over the way in which the courts were administered and was a result of the application of managerial principles propagated by the Thatcher administrations of the 1980s. Before this, the judges themselves, and especially the Master of the Rolls, whose responsibility it was seen to be, considered and made the necessary recommendations to the Department on the staffing and other administrative arrangements of the courts. Because public expenditure was

59. [1968] AC 997; see below p. 116–17.
60. See below p. 125.

involved, the judges did not always get all the changes they wanted. But theirs was the initiative; and it was usually successful. Those arrangements can seriously affect the work of the courts, being concerned with assessing the needs of the courts and securing resources, organising the internal structures of the courts so that they can best deal with the caseloads arising, laying down pre-trial and trial procedures, managing the case-flow, measuring and monitoring court performance, managing court records, and planning necessary reforms to court structures and processes.[61]

In November 1987, the head of the Chancery Division of the High Court, Sir Nicolas Browne-Wilkinson, in a public lecture[62] spoke of a threat to the independence of the legal system arising 'by reason of the executive's control of finance and administration'. He was explicit: 'There appear to be those in the Lord Chancellor's Department who perceive its role as being far wider than is consistent with any concept of the independence of the judiciary.' He referred to the political reforms introduced by the Treasury in other Departments and to the Financial Management Initiative. This had affected staffing levels, prejudicing the proper administration of justice. It had resulted in the allocation of funds based not on the best interests of justice but on value for money.

Behind this lay the complaint that the judiciary had been effectively excluded from policy-making. A year later, the then Lord Chancellor (Lord Hailsham) replied by claiming that the essential function of the Lord Chancellor was to defend the independence and integrity of the judiciary. He denied that the Lord Chancellor was 'the lackey or dupe of the Chief Secretary of the Treasury' and scorned the idea that judges should be permitted 'to run a sort of legal Arcadia'.[63]

In 1988 the Lord Chief Justice (Lord Lane) re-instituted the Judges Council of the Supreme Court. The report of the

61. I. R. Scott, 'The Council of Judges in the Supreme Court of England and Wales' in [1989] *Public Law* 379.

62. 'The Independence of the Judiciary' in [1988] *Public Law* 44.

63. 8 *Civil Justice Quarterly* (1989) 308.

Review Body on Civil Justice[64] said the Council 'should enable the judiciary to plan for the allocation of High Court caseloads and judge power in the light of needs and resources of that court as a whole rather than of individual Divisions. It will also enable it to put a common view to the Lord Chancellor about needs for resources and about priorities for some needs.'

The Council consists of the Lord Chief Justice, the Master of the Rolls, the President of the Family Division, the Vice-Chancellor as head of the Chancery Division, the senior presiding judge and two judges of the High Court, one of whom is a presiding judge. Its staff is provided by the Lord Chancellor's Department. It is too early to assess its general impact. In the meantime, it is clear that many judges consider that the Lord Chancellor's Department has ceased to act as an intermediary or 'hinge' between themselves and the executive Government and has become as much a part of the governmental machinery as any other Department of State. Judges feel that in this process they have lost a privileged position which also helped to preserve their independence. This conflict between the judges and the Lord Chancellor's Department erupted when Lord Mackay put forward his proposals for the reform of the legal profession.[65]

So also, it must not be assumed that Ministers and civil servants regard judicial decisions as necessarily embodying the ultimate wisdom, especially where those decisions limit their powers. Indeed, their immediate reaction may be to seek ways which circumvent judicial pronouncements. A striking example of this occurred in 1989 when a decision of the Divisional Court interpreting immigration rules[66] was considered by the Treasury Solicitor's Department to be wrong and too advantageous to the prospective immigrant. As a result, a senior member of the Treasury Solicitor's staff sent an advisory letter to the President of the Immigration Appeal Tribunal saying that the decision undermined the

64. Cm. 394 para. 322.
65. See below pp. 68–73.
66. *R. v. Immigration Appeal Tribunal ex parte Khatab* [1989] Imm. AR 313.

rules and that the judge went 'much too far'. On the authority of the President, the letter was distributed to immigration adjudicators, with a copy of the decision and a briefing to counsel defending such applications for judicial review. The advice suggested: 'we must try, by adopting a uniformly more robust and aggressive approach, to recover some lost ground' and accused the Divisional Court 'almost invariably' of looking for errors or ambiguities so as to upset the determinations of adjudicators. As a result of the publicity given to these events,[67] it was decided that the Treasury Solicitor would no longer act as solicitor for the Tribunal.

A similar attitude was shown in 1986 when the Law Lords stated that the Trustee Savings Bank and its assets belonged not to depositors but to the state, shortly before the Bank was floated on the Stock Exchange. This view was contrary to that of the Government. It was ignored by the Treasury.

Sentencing policy is a source of disagreement between judges and the Home Office. Arguments have arisen over proposals to introduce automatic parole for short-term prisoners; also over the possibility of dividing every sentence of three years or under into three parts: imprisonment, supervised release, and remission (which Lords Justices on the criminal side of the Court of Appeal made clear they did not like). Ministers from time to time make statements seeming to indicate to judges generally what sentencing policy should be, within the range of punishments laid down by statutes for different crimes. Similarly, when life sentences are reviewed, the trial judge makes a recommendation to the parole board but complaints have been made that too frequently junior Ministers in the Home Office depart from the recommendation, usually by increasing the length of the period of imprisonment. This is seen by some judges as usurping their function.

A Government policy paper in 1990 on criminal justice would impose new duties on judges.[68] These include requiring a Court before giving a custodial sentence to consider a

67. In *The Independent*, 6 June 1989.
68. Crime, Justice and Protecting the Public (Cm 965); see new Criminal Justice Bill 1990–1.

report by the probation service and to give reasons for such a sentence, except for the most serious offences; also to satisfy itself that the offence was serious enough to justify the use of custody. The white paper proposed to give the courts power to give longer custodial sentences to persistent violent and sexual offenders.

The courts have always exercised considerable discretion, within the maximum penalties laid down by statute, depending on the particular facts of the cases before them. Inevitably they have been criticized, from time to time, for what was seen, usually, as undue leniency, sometimes as undue harshness. The Court of Appeal frequently gives sentencing guidance, for example on rape, incest and drug trafficking; where firearms are used; and on young offenders.

How far judicial discretion on sentencing should be directed by Government policy is problematic. The policy paper stated:

> No Government should try to influence the decisions of the courts in individual cases. The independence of the judiciary is rightly regarded as a cornerstone of our liberties. But sentencing principles and sentencing practice are matters of legitimate concern to Government, and Parliament provides the funds necessary to give effect to the court's decisions.[69]

This is unexceptionable, if not particularly helpful. The judges may be less happy with what follows:

> To help the courts in sentencing decisions, the Government also proposes that the legislation should place a new duty on the Secretary of State to inform the courts annually of the costs of implementing penalties . . . The courts, as well as other services, should know the costs of the decisions they take. Financial considerations can never be the deciding factor in sentencing. Even so the courts should take some account of the costs of implementing their decisions when they sentence,

69. Ibid., para. 2.1.

especially when they have a choice of suitable penalties.[70]

The general intention of the Government is to seek to reduce the prison population by encouraging judges to apply alternative penalties in many cases. Much will depend on the willingness of the courts to co-operate and, in particular, to give non-custodial sentences for repeated non-violent crimes, like burglary. Clearly the Government decided to tread carefully so as not to offend the judiciary by appearing to interfere directly with their discretionary powers to sentence as they think appropriate. In June 1990, it was reported that the Home Secretary was seeking a compromise with the judges on the proposals to limit custodial sentences.

Lord Mackay's proposals

In January 1989, the Lord Chancellor, Lord Mackay, published his proposals for reform of the legal profession in three policy papers.[71] Some of the proposals, including those which threatened the monopoly of barristers in superior courts, required all advocates to have certificates of competence, and permitted multi-disciplinary partnerships, aroused considerable opposition from within the profession. Most remarkable was the language used by some senior members of the judiciary. The Lord Chief Justice, Lord Lane, referred to the first paper on the profession as 'one of the most sinister documents ever to emanate from Government'. The Master of the Rolls, Lord Donaldson, said he had 'absolutely no disagreement' with Lord Lane over the main issues. Lord Scarman criticized the papers as being 'ill-considered', 'superficial' in their reasoning and 'flawed' in their logic. Lord Ackner spoke of the proposals as involving 'at the very least a substantial risk of the destruction of the Bar', of 'the myopic application of dogma' and

70. Ibid., paras 2.21, 2.22.
71. *The Work and Organisation of the Legal Profession* (Cm 570); *Contingency Fees* (Cm 571); *Conveyancing by Authorised Practitioners* (Cm 572). These are referred to also as the Green Papers.

much else besides. The former Lord Chancellor, Lord Hailsham, was reported as saying that the Government was 'thinking with its bottom and sitting on its head'.

It is, of course, common practice for Government departments to consult with affected interests before they publish proposals. By so doing they can often make modifications which buy off subsequent opposition. In the debate in the House of Lords on 7 April 1989, Lord Lane suggested that it would have been 'courteous or even helpful' if those responsible had seen fit to consult the judges upon the draft of the proposals.[72] But Lord Mackay drew attention to correspondence he had had with Lord Lane the previous autumn after the Government's announcement of their intention to publish proposals. The Lord Chief Justice had said then that it would be wrong for it to appear that the proposals had the backing of the judges or that they had had any hand in their preparation; and that it was essential that the judges remained at arm's length.[73]

This dispute emphasises the ambiguity of the judges' position. They want, at one and the same time, to be 'independent' of Government and to be involved in the processes of government. But, like everyone else, once they enter into discussions on policy with Ministers and civil servants they compromise their vaunted independence.

In the debate referred to, the senior judges renewed their attack. Lord Lane said:

> Oppression does not stand on the doorstep with a toothbrush moustache and a swastika armband. It creeps up insidiously; it creeps up step by step; and all of a sudden the unfortunate citizen realizes that [freedom] has gone . . . One asks whether we are now seeing tools being fashioned which by some future, perhaps less scrupulous, Government may be used to weaken the independent administration of justice and so undermine the rule of law.[74]

72. 505 HL Deb. col. 1329.
73. Ibid., col. 1475.
74. Ibid., col. 1331.

Lord Donaldson spoke of the further proposed fragmentation of the profession as 'an unmitigated disaster'; of 'an irreversible plunge into the unknown'; of 'an affront to the constitutional doctrine of the separation of power'; of freedom disappearing 'by gradual erosion'. And he reserved the right to say to the Government 'Get your tanks off my lawn'.[75] Lord Bridge spoke of a 'deep sense of unease' felt by the great majority of the judiciary and of 'hasty and ill-considered legislation'.[76] Lord Goff referred to multi-disciplinary partnerships as 'most objectionable',[77] and Lord Griffiths called them a 'profound mistake'.[78] Lord Ackner inveighed against 'political considerations, political dogma and doctrine which are about to do untold harm to the future quality of the administration of justice.'[79] Lord Oliver spoke of the Government taking 'a terrible and unjustifiable risk' and of the papers containing much that was 'quite unacceptable'.[80]

In May 1989, the Judges' Council set out the majority views of High Court and Court of Appeal judges. To a considerable extent these views supported those of the Bar Council in seeking to retain the monopoly of barristers in the superior courts, in rejecting multi-disciplinary partnerships, and in objecting to the Lord Chancellor having power to make final decisions on the training, conduct and rights of audience of advocates.

In July, Lord Mackay published a white paper which abandoned the proposal of a single accreditation for advocates, gave the judges a veto over the rules for accreditation of solicitors, and did not continue to propose multi-disciplinary partnerships. The effect may be to limit greatly the opportunity for solicitors to act as advocates in more serious criminal cases.

On 19 December 1989, the Courts and Legal Services Bill

75. Ibid., col. 1368–9.
76. Ibid., col. 1381–2.
77. Ibid., col. 1410.
78. Ibid., col. 1435.
79. Ibid., col. 1416.
80. Ibid., col. 1461.

was given a second reading in the House of Lords.[81] The general temperature of the debate was lower than that on 7 April. Much of the strongest criticism was voiced not by the judges in the House but by non-lawyers such as Lord Benson who had chaired the Royal Commission on Legal Services[82] which reported in 1979. Lord Ackner, however, remained unsubdued. He said:

> I am convinced that the probable long-term – and not all that long – collective effect of this Bill as it now stands will be to inflict serious damage on the quality of justice in this country . . . The ever-increasing megafirms, with their growing litigation departments, growing both in size and cost, with full rights of audience in all courts, will cause the Bar to wither away. The district attorney system will take over the criminal prosecutions, and the corrupt philosophy of the contingency fee will pervade the whole system. The strong and independent judiciary, acknowledged by the Government in the Green Paper to be one of the central supports upon which our liberties are based and upon which the rule of law depends, will be weakened by the diminishing quality of available recruits and the growing political influence in their appointments.

And he quoted Chief Justice Cardozo of the Supreme Court of the USA:

> We must always take care to safeguard the law against the assaults of opportunism, the expediency of the passing hour, the erosion of small encroachments, and the scorn and derision of those who have no patience with general principles.[83]

When the Bill was debated in committee and on report, language was again more restrained. To a remarkable extent, speeches and interventions by judicial peers were dominated by Lords Ackner and Donaldson. Lord Ackner

81. 514 HL Deb. col. 122–37, 146–248.
82. Cmnd. 7648.
83. 514 HL Deb. col. 204–5 (19 December 1989).

spoke on over 80 occasions and moved 17 amendments. Lord Donaldson spoke on 54 occasions. On third Reading, Lords Ackner and Donaldson spoke on 17 occasions, Lord Ackner moving two more amendments. During all these proceedings six other judicial peers spoke on a total of 16 occasions. On third Reading, Lord Ackner returned to the attack.[84]

With the particular merits and demerits of these proposals I am not here directly concerned. But the reaction of the most senior members of the judiciary – the Law Lords, the Lord Chief Justice and the Master of the Rolls – was felt by many of the general public, I believe, to conflict with the image which the judiciary have been at pains to promote. Judges, it was thought, did not enter into open controversy with politicians, certainly not in such outspoken language. Lord Benson referred to the debate of 7 April when he commented on 'the degrading spectacle of the Lord Chancellor and virtually the whole of the judiciary in open conflict'. This conflict was uncharacteristic both because judges usually avoided speaking against the Government on matters of party policy and because judges usually worked behind the scenes to advance their own causes or to influence legal reforms. Senior professional persons have traditionally not descended into the open political pit because they have not needed to, having more effective ways to achieve their ends. But, until recently, senior professional persons have not been directly challenged over what Bernard Shaw called their conspiracies against the laity. This conflict showed that judges, no less than physicians and surgeons, churchmen, academics, and practising lawyers would seek, for a variety of reasons (some being more elevated than others) to defend their professional status with much vigour and little subtlety.

Conclusion

If it is accepted, as I argue, that a judge, when sitting in his court, is frequently required to make decisions which involve

84. 516 HL Deb. col. 1758–9 (15 March 1990).

an assessment of where the public interest lies and so to make a political decision, then he cannot be said to act neutrally, although he may still be the person best suited to make that particular decision. Also he may be the best person to make certain extrajudicial decisions and his opinions on a range of public matters may be worth hearing. There is nothing inherently improper in consultations between a judge and public officials on general matters of policy concerning the administration of the judicial system. But judges should not be involved in the making of decisions for which they are unsuited.

The falseness arises when judges are presented, or present themselves, as neutral arbiters capable of providing unpolitical solutions to political problems or of expressing unpolitical opinions on political issues. It is when the claim to neutrality is seen, as it must be, as a sham that damage is done to the judicial system.

Part Two

Cases

The Court's position had not been made any easier by suggestions that it was possible for the Government to influence its decisions. The Court was surprised that those suggestions should have been made, and the Court owed it to its members and to all concerned to make it clear that no attempt had been made by anyone directly or indirectly, otherwise than in open court, to influence its decision.

Sir John Donaldson, President of the National Industrial Relations Court, in *Midland Cold Storage Ltd v. Turner and Others*, as reported in *The Times*, 28 July 1972.

It was a matter of real concern that the divisional court, exercising the power of judicial review, was increasingly . . . being used for political purposes superficially dressed up as points of law. The proper remedy was the ballot box and not the court. If a rating or precepting authority over-rated or over-precepted, the remedy was in the hands of the electorate . . . The impropriety of coming to the court when political capital was sought to be made could not be overstressed. It was perhaps even worse when public servants were or felt constrained to file affidavits which demonstrated a political purpose.

McNeill, J. in *R. v. Greater London Council*

ex parte Kensington and Chelsea LBC dismissing an application for judicial review of a precept issued by the GLC, as reported in *The Times*, 7 April 1982.

The intellectual isolation of appellate judges, who resolve 'hard cases' with reference to notions of social justice and public policy which they are singularly (and collectively) ill-equipped to understand . . . remains a deeply worrying feature of our judicial process.

Mr Gavin Drewry in 47 *Modern Law Review* (1984), p. 380.

Spycatcher is a very interesting case, in this respect. Some people say we're all establishment minded and other people say we're all something else minded. But in fact in Spycatcher we're not. No one can sack us, no one can take our pensions away, in Spycatcher three of us decided in favour of Mrs Thatcher and against the editor of The Sunday Times, *and those three of us didn't care a damn for the editor of* The Sunday Times. *Two of us decided in favour of* The Sunday Times *and against Mrs Thatcher, and those two didn't give a damn for Mrs Thatcher, we each of us decided it was a matter of principle, knowing that we were bound to be criticised, whatever we did, and we decided it, and there's an end of it.*

Lord Templeman, in an interview on Radio 4 with Hugo Young on 13 April 1988.

3. Industrial relations

The early cases

From the middle ages, Parliament has been concerned with the problems, central to the national economy, of productivity and the control of wages. And, for hundreds of years, workers who were thought to be failing in their duties were subjected to imprisonment and other penalties.

The use of the penal law against workers, especially when it involves imprisonment, or the possibility of imprisonment, is one of the most persistent sources of conflict between labour and management, and between labour and governments. Parliament legislated extensively against the combination of workers but the judges also, through their power of interpreting statutes and of making and extending the common law, were a powerful source of constraint on the emerging trade union movement in the industrial society of the nineteenth century. Two outstanding characteristics of labour law during the second half of that century were the intermittent recognition by politicians in government and Parliament that control of trade unionism by the imposition of penalties was of doubtful efficacy; and the recurrent attempts by the courts to preserve the penal method.[1]

Statutes of 1859, 1871 and 1875 were designed to relieve trade unions of criminal liability, especially for conspiracy. Specifically, the Conspiracy and Protection of Property Act 1875 provided that an agreement by two or more persons to do or procure to be done any act in contemplation or

---

1. I am much indebted to Lord Wedderburn on whose writings and advice I have freely drawn in preparing and revising this chapter. See *The Worker and the Law* (3rd edn. 1986) and 54 *Modern Law Review* (1991)1.

furtherance of a trade dispute should not be a criminal conspiracy unless the act itself was punishable as a crime. So to strike ceased to be a crime.

The last decade of the nineteenth century saw the development of a considerable antipathy to trade unionism among influential public opinion. This was in part due to the emergence of New Unionism which sought to organize unskilled workers. Professor Saville has written that the old unions 'were able to rely upon the skill of their members as a crucial bargaining weapon' but 'the new unionists were at all times, even in years of good trade, subject to the pressures of an over-stocked labour market'. So 'the employers, too, in the semi- and unskilled trades were more uncompromising than their fellows in industries where unionism had long been established'. The industrial offensive against the trade unions in the early years of the 1890s was 'most successful against the dockers, the seamen and the casual trades' but all the New Unions lost heavily in membership.[2]

It is against the background of this offensive that the judicial decisions[3] of 1896–1901 must seen. Although the right to strike had been established, some of the judges were not to be so easily defeated. In addition to the crime of conspiracy, there is the civil wrong (or tort) of conspiracy, consisting of an agreement which has been acted on and which is made in order to attain either an unlawful object or a lawful object by unlawful means. It was to this that some judges turned their attention.

In *Allen v. Flood*[4] a dispute arose between the ironworkers' union and woodworkers, the former objecting to certain work being done by the latter. Ironworkers told one of their officials that they would stop working if the woodworkers were continued in employment. The official informed the employers accordingly and the employers law-

2. John Saville, 'Trade Unions and Free Labour: the Background to the Taff Vale Decision' in *Essays in Labour History* (ed. Asa Briggs and John Saville, 1960) vol. 1, p. 317.

3. Including *Lyons v. Wilkins* (see below, p. 82).

4. [1898] AC 1.

fully dismissed the woodworkers, who then brought an action against the official.

The case was first argued in December 1895 before seven members of the House of Lords[5] including Lord Chancellor Halsbury, and a former Lord Chancellor, Herschell. 'From the very beginning,' says Professor Heuston, 'Lord Halsbury took a view strongly adverse to the position of the trade union and expressed his firm opinion that the plaintiffs . . . were entitled to damages for an interference with their right to work. It was also clear, however, that on this point he would be unable to carry with him a majority of his colleagues.' Apparently, Halsbury then 'conceived the idea that the case should be re-argued before an enlarged body of Law Lords and that, in addition, the House should adopt once more the practice of summoning the High Court judges to advise', a practice generally thought to be obsolete. Lord Herschell was angered by this idea and, says Professor Heuston, 'the High Court judges at that time, many of whom were Halsbury's own appointments, were not on the whole notable for progressive views on social or industrial matters.'[6]

Between 25 March and 2 April 1897 the case was re-argued before the original seven Law Lords and two others. Of the eight High Court judges who attended, and gave their 'opinions', six agreed with Lord Halsbury and two disagreed. But when the nine Law Lords delivered their judgments in December 1897, Lord Halsbury's views were supported by only two of his colleagues, with Lord Herschell and five others in the opposing majority. So the trade unions remained protected.

Then in 1901, in *Quinn v. Leathem*,[7] the effect of that decision was reversed. For many years, L supplied a butcher with meat. The trade union sought to persuade L not to employ non-union men. When this failed, the union

5. Here and elsewhere this means the House in its judicial capacity.

6. R. F. V. Heuston, *The Lives of the Lord Chancellors 1885–1940*, pp. 119–20; and see his article on 'Judicial Prosopography' in 102 *Law Quarterly Review* 90 (1986).

7. [1901] AC 495.

instructed their members working for the butcher that, if he continued to buy L's meat, they were to cease work. So the butcher took no more meat from L who brought an action against the union officials for conspiracy to injure him. The House of Lords decided unanimously in his favour.

From the trade unionists' viewpoint the effect of *Quinn v. Leathem* was seriously to curtail their power to operate in ways which would strengthen the working-class movement against employers. This was thought by trade unionists to be inconsistent with the leading decision of ten years before which had protected employers' associations from conspiracy on the ground that the acts had been done 'with the lawful object of protecting and extending their trade and increasing their profits' without employing unlawful means, although the consequence had been to injure their competitors.[8]

These judicial decisions caused great political upheaval and resulted in the passing of the Trade Disputes Act 1906 which followed the same pattern as the Act of 1875, protecting trade unions from actions for civil conspiracy if the acts were done in furtherance or contemplation of a trade dispute.

Another struggle centred on trade union funds. In law, property may be held either by a natural person, or by a number of such persons, or by an incorporated body such as a company. Trade unions fell into the second of these groups, but, because of their large and fluctuating membership and because of certain provisions in the Trade Union Act 1871, it was assumed that it was impracticable to bring actions against them so as to make their funds liable. In 1900 a dispute arose because it was said that the Taff Vale Railway Company had victimized a trade unionist who led a wage demand. The House of Lords held that trade unions could be sued, in effect, for losses sustained by employers as a consequence of strike action.[9] Lord Halsbury gave one of the five unanimous judgments. As Professor Heuston says, the decision left 'a legacy of suspicion and mistrust . . .

8. *Mogul Steamship Co. v. McGregor Gow & Co.* [1892] AC 25.
9. *Taff Vale Railway Co. v. Amalgamated Society of Railway Servants* [1901] AC 426.

to poison relations between the courts and the unions for many years'. He adds: 'One of Baldwin's favourite themes was the folly of this *Taff Vale* decision: "The Conservatives can't talk of class-war: they started it," he would remark to G. M. Young.'[10]

The *Taff Vale* decision was a serious blow to trade unionism. The law had seemed 'so clearly settled to the contrary', wrote Lord Asquith, that 'public opinion was unprepared for any such decision'. Liberal opinion strongly favoured its reversal. This was effectively carried through by the strong Liberal government elected in 1906 in the Trade Disputes Act of that year.

A few years later, the judiciary again intervened, this time by invoking the doctrine of *ultra vires*. This doctrine applies mainly to public authorities exercising statutory powers and to companies registered under the Companies Acts to pursue certain objects described in their constitutions. If powers or objects are exceeded, action can be brought to restrain those authorities or companies. Trade unions had for some time been supporting candidates for the House of Commons and spending union funds for this purpose. In 1909, a member of the Amalgamated Society of Railway Servants successfully challenged this practice.[11] This of course was also a severe blow to the emerging Labour Party and again the politicians had to try to restore what had been understood to be the position by passing the Trade Union Act 1913.[12]

For much of the interwar period and for some years after 1945, the judges seemed to withdraw from the conflict or, when asked to intervene, tended to adopt a neutral position. Indeed, such decisions as were made were markedly more generous in their recognition of the legitimacy of the purposes of trade unions. Moreover, during the 1930s, employers did not need to seek the help of the courts, the unions being in a weak condition. As we shall see, judicial

10. Heuston, *op. cit.*, p. 76; G. M. Young, *Stanley Baldwin* (1952), p. 31.

11. *Amalgamated Society of Railway Servants v. Osborne* [1910] AC 87.

12. See S. and B. Webb, *The History of Trade Unionism* (1920 edn), pp. 608–11.

intervention was not noticeably restrained at this time in other political cockpits.

But the 1960s gave rise to certain assumptions about the nature and the power of trade unions which, true or false, have coloured and affected the attitudes of the middle classes and, in consequence, the policies of the Conservative, Labour and Liberal parties. Once again, the judges have become central figures in these political issues.

Picketing

Picketing is a practice which stands uneasily across the boundary, as variously interpreted, of legal and illegal action. It can become conduct likely to cause a breach of the peace, or obstruction, or even assault. The Conspiracy and Protection of Property Act 1875 restated the criminal offence of 'watching or besetting' but excluded from that activity 'attending at or near the house or place where a person resides, or works, or carries on business, or happens to be . . . in order merely to obtain or communicate information'. But in *Lyons v. Wilkins*[13] the Court of Appeal had decided against the officers of a trade union who, having ordered a strike against the plaintiffs and against S (who made goods for the plaintiffs only), organized pickets to seek to persuade work-people not to work for the plaintiffs. That, said Lindley LJ, was not merely obtaining or communicating information. It was putting pressure on the plaintiffs by persuading people not to enter their employment. And that was illegal. It was further decided that such watching and besetting might be a nuisance at common law and illegal on that ground also. Once again the legislature reversed the courts and by the Trade Disputes Act 1906 made picketing lawful if in contemplation or furtherance of a trade dispute and if the purpose was peacefully obtaining or communicating information or 'peacefully persuading any person to work or abstain from working'.

The interpretation of the law remained contentious.

13. [1896] 1 Ch. 811; [1899] 1 Ch. 255.

During a trade dispute in 1960, a police officer found two pickets standing at the front entrance of a factory, four standing at the back entrance and ten or twelve outside the back entrance. The officer told the defendant three times that he considered two pickets at each entrance were sufficient but the defendant, persisting in his intention to join the pickets, 'pushed gently past' the police officer, 'was gently arrested', and was charged with obstructing the police in execution of their duty. The Divisional Court held that he was properly convicted on the ground that the police officer had reasonable grounds for anticipating that a breach of the peace was a real possibility.[14] In *Tynan v. Balmer*[15] (1966) forty pickets in a continuous circle around a factory (which had the effect of sealing off the highway) were held not to be legalized by the Act of 1906 because their action was a nuisance at common law and an unreasonable use of the highway. In 1972, a strike picket held a placard in front of a vehicle on a highway, urging the driver not to work at a site nearby and preventing him from proceeding along the highway. The picket was charged with obstruction of the highway although the whole incident lasted for not more than nine minutes. The House of Lords upheld the prosecution.[16] Lord Reid said it would not be difficult to infer, as a matter of fact, that pickets who assemble in unreasonably large numbers do have the purpose of obstructing free passage. The following year, a police cordon prevented pickets from approaching a coach carrying workers out of a site. The defendant was involved in a scuffle with a constable and was successfully charged with obstructing him in the execution of his duty.[17] The result of these cases was greatly to limit the right to picket. They enlarged the scope within which the police could prevent picketing and they greatly narrowed the scope within which picketing could lawfully be undertaken.[18]

14. *Piddington v. Bates* [1960] 3 All ER 660.
15. [1967] 1 QB 91.
16. *Hunt v. Broome* [1974] AC 587.
17. *Kavanagh v. Hiscock* [1974] 2 WLR 421; see also *Hubbard v. Pitt* [1975] 3 WLR 201 (see below, pp. 246–8).
18. For the *Shrewsbury* case, see below, p. 236.

Moreover, the use by the courts of these common law devices of obstruction, breach of the peace and nuisance is difficult to legislate against as the essential purpose (which before the 1960s had been more or less achieved with police co-operation) is to permit 'reasonable' picketing, including the right to accost for a short period within which arguments can be advanced, without putting persons in fear or to immoderate inconvenience.

'The attendance', said counsel for the defendant in *Hunt v. Broome*, 'is for the purpose of peacefully persuading a man not to work so the attendance must be in a position where the persuasion can be carried out; otherwise its purpose is frustrated . . . Attendance for the purpose of peaceful persuasion is what is protected by the Act . . . not mere attendance, standing with banners; the attendance is for oral communication.'[19]

As the courts presently interpret the law this purpose is often difficult and sometimes impossible to achieve. It is also true that the right to picket may be abused.

The right to strike

In 1964 the House of Lords in *Rookes v. Barnard*[20] delivered a judgment which seemed like a return to the early heady days of the century. R worked for BOAC with whom his union had an agreement that all workers should be union members. In 1955 R left the union after a disagreement with union members. Two local union members, and a district union official employed by the union, threatened BOAC that labour would be withdrawn if R were not removed within three days as required by a resolution passed at a members' meeting. Such a strike would have been a breach of contract by each member. BOAC gave R long notice and lawfully discharged him. R sued the two members and the official for conspiracy.

Under the Trade Disputes Act 1906 no action for con-

19. Mr John Mortimer, QC.
20. [1964] AC 1129.

spiracy would lie unless the act would be unlawful if done
by a person alone. So the Law Lords considered whether a
threat to strike could be 'unlawful' in this sense. And they
held it could be.

This decision was seen by trade unionists as a direct attack
on the right to strike. The Law Lords certainly seemed to
stretch themselves to arrive at their conclusion. Lord Devlin,
for example, could find 'nothing to differentiate a threat of
a breach of contract from a threat of physical violence'. It
was a time when strikes were being blamed for most of the
country's ills, and Lord Hodson said: 'The injury and suffer-
ing caused by strike action is very often widespread as well
as devastating and a threat to strike would be expected to
be certainly no less serious than a threat of violence.' Once
again the politicians had to seek to reverse their Lordships'
decision and passed the Trade Disputes Act 1965.

Inducing breach of contract

In 1952, certain drivers and loaders told Bowaters Ltd, the
paper suppliers, that they might not be prepared to deliver
paper to the plaintiffs who were printers and publishers.
Bowaters told the plaintiffs and they brought an action
against officers of the unions to which the drivers and loaders
belonged. The Court of Appeal held that the evidence did
not establish that there had been any direct procurement by
the defendants of any wrongful acts by the drivers or loaders
or that the latter had committed any wrongful acts; also
that there was no evidence of any actual knowledge by the
defendants of any contract between Bowaters and the plaintiffs. So the plaintiffs lost their action.[21]

In 1964, the House of Lords considered a case in which a
union were met by a refusal of a company to negotiate
with them on terms and conditions of service although they
organized the majority of the men concerned, being water-
men in the Port of London. Another union organized the
minority. So the first union issued instructions that none of

21. *Thomson & Co. v. Deakin* [1952] 1 Ch. 646.

their men would man, service or tow empty barges belonging to the company. The company owned and hired out barges but did not employ any of the union men, but their action meant that barges were not returned and so the company's business came to a standstill. The company brought an action against the union officials. The House of Lords found for the company on the ground that the union had knowingly induced breaches of the hiring contract and their members' contracts of employment. Most importantly, their Lordships decided that there was, on the facts, no trade dispute within the meaning of the Trade Disputes Act 1906 because the basis of the embargo was trade union rivalry.[22]

This attitude of the courts was strengthened by the decision of the Court of Appeal in *Torquay Hotel v. Cousins*.[23] Union members picketed the Torbay Hotel, cutting off fuel oil supplies, and later, when the manager of the plaintiff hotel was reported as having called for a stand against the union, picketed that hotel with the same result. The union also told an alternative oil supplier not to supply the plaintiff hotel. The Court of Appeal held that as the plaintiffs employed no union members the union's actions were not in furtherance of a trade dispute and injunctions were issued against the union. As Professor Wedderburn has observed, the result of this decision could be that where an association of employers is fighting off a trade union, it may be able to 'keep its smaller members in the front line and avoid any of its bigger members being parties to the dispute'.[24] The trade unions' 'golden formula' of action 'in furtherance of a trade dispute' looks weaker as a protection than it did.

No wonder that, in 1968, a member of the Royal Commission on Trade Unions and Employers' Associations wrote:[25]

A thing that worried me all through the deliberations . . . was this: supposing we made all the right recommendations and supposing the Government gave

22. *Stratford v. Lindley* [1965] AC 269.
23. [1969] 2 Ch. 106.
24. Wedderburn, *op. cit.*, (2nd edn) p. 336.
25. Quoted by Wedderburn, *op. cit.*, (2nd edn) p. 8.

effect to them in legislation, how long would it be before the judges turned everything upside down?

Industrial Relations Act 1971

But the most dramatic judicial intervention was yet to come. In 1971 was passed the Industrial Relations Act. This measure of a Conservative government was strongly opposed, in and out of Parliament, by the trade union movement and the Labour Party. It established the National Industrial Relations Court (NIRC), presided over by Sir John Donaldson, formerly a judge of the High Court. The NIRC had wide jurisdiction to consider complaints arising under the Act, to impose penalties, and to punish those who disregarded its orders.

In recent years, the amount of work available for dockworkers has drastically declined because of the growing practice of loading and unloading goods in containers at depots outside the port areas. From mid-1971, the Transport and General Workers' Union authorized the practice of selective 'blacking' of the goods carried by certain road haulier firms to ports. When the Act of 1971 came into force in February 1972, the union became liable to complaints and penalties for this blacking. The first complaint was made on 23 March 1972 and the NIRC ordered the union, its officers, servants and agents to refrain from certain specific blacking. The union's officers advised their shop stewards to obey this order but the advice was rejected. On 29 March the NIRC found the union in wilful contempt of the order and, following subsequent complaints, imposed fines totalling £55,000.[26]

On 13 June the Court of Appeal decided that the union was not accountable for its shop stewards and set aside the fines.[27] But the next day the NIRC ordered three London dockers who had defied an order against blacking made on 12 June to be committed to prison for contempt of court. The warrants for their arrest were to be issued on 16 June,

26. *Heaton's Transport (St Helens) Ltd v TGWU* [1972] 1 ICR 285.
27. Ibid. 308; [1973] AC 15.

and widespread strikes became imminent. However, as the result of a curious intervention by the Official Solicitor (an officer of the court), the Court of Appeal was able to review the decision to imprison, although the three dockers did not ask for it to be reviewed; and the decision was set aside. So the dockers did not go to prison and the strikes were avoided.[28]

For a fortnight there was a breathing space. Then on 3 July another complaint was lodged with the NIRC against seven dockers including two of the original three. On 7 July, the NIRC ordered them to refrain from their actions and, after further proceedings, on 21 July committed five of the seven to prison for contempt. Unofficial dock strikes began at once and the threat of widespread stoppages of work became very real.

On 24 July the General Secretary of the Trades Union Congress went to see the Prime Minister who said, according to *The Times*, that he would not intervene. On 25 July, the Official Solicitor visited the dockers in prison, but they made clear that they did not intend to give any undertakings of obedience to the NIRC or to apologize – which is normally essential before those in contempt are released. Nevertheless the Official Solicitor on that day tried to persuade the NIRC to convene immediately so that he could apply for the committal orders to be discharged. But he was told to come back not later than the afternoon of the next day.

On 25 July the situation seemed to have reached an impasse. Sir John Donaldson, president of the NIRC, had said in June: 'By their conduct these men are saying they are above the rule of law. No court should ignore such a challenge. To do so would imperil all law and order.' On 21 July he said: 'These breaches are serious and were deliberately committed, quite literally in contempt of this court . . . The issue is whether these men are to be allowed to opt out of the rule of law . . . It is a very simple issue but vastly important for our whole way of life is based upon acceptance of the rule of law.' The NIRC had committed the men to prison. The men showed no intention of modifying their

28. *The Times*, 12 and 14 June 1972.

position. Dock strikes were occurring and a general strike was clearly impending. How could industrial action on a wide scale be avoided and the face of the NIRC be saved?

We have seen that on 13 June the Court of Appeal had decided in *Heaton*'s case that the Transport and General Workers' Union was not accountable for the action of its shop stewards. From that decision, leave was given to appeal to the House of Lords. That appeal was heard between the 10th and 19th of July. Their Lordships reserved judgment and then, with almost unprecedented speed (at least eight weeks normally elapse), Lord Wilberforce delivered their joint opinion, on the morning of 26 July – that 'next day' intimated to the Official Solicitor. And the House of Lords reversed the Court of Appeal and decided that the union was responsible for its shop stewards.[29] Immediately the NIRC convened and, avowedly because of that decision, released the dockers from prison.[30]

The difficulty is finding any necessary connection between two cases. The House of Lords' decision determined an important question of law concerning the liability of trade unions for the actions of their shop stewards. But the five dockers' case was about the 'very simple issue' of punishment for men who had defied the order of the NIRC and had expressed their intention to continue in that defiance. In releasing the dockers, the president of the NIRC said that, because of the House of Lords' decision, the situation was 'entirely changed'. The unions were accountable and the burden of their task would be 'immeasurably increased' if the dockers remained in prison. 'The cause of the rule of law will not be advanced by placing an avoidable burden upon the unions.' Nevertheless five men, who had been imprisoned because they deliberately and flagrantly disobeyed the orders of the NIRC, and so imperilled the rule of law and 'our whole way of life', were released although

29. [1972] 1 ICR 308; [1973] AC 15. Subsequently, however, it appeared that this was not a proposition of general application: see *General Aviation Services v. TGWU* [1976] IRLR 224, a decision which seemed to indicate a desire by the House of Lords (Lord Salmon dissenting) to put the decision in *Heaton*'s case behind them.

30. *The Times*, 27 July 1972.

they had not asked to be released and had made clear that they had no intention of apologizing to the court for their behaviour or of desisting from that behaviour.

A political and economic crisis of possibly considerable dimensions was avoided by two actions. First, the speeding-up of the delivery of the House of Lords' decision; and secondly, the discovery by the NIRC that, because of that decision, they could release the dockers. It appeared very much as if the judicial system had bent itself to the needs of the politicians and that, in particular, the principles of the rule of law to which the NIRC earlier paid such respect had been sacrificed to the expediency of the political and economic situation.

This last example of judicial activism in political affairs differs from the others. The latter have shown a conservative judiciary interpreting legislation and developing the common law in ways which government and Parliament sought to reverse. The establishment of the NIRC was a political act aimed at trying to contain trade union power within particular rules prescribed by the Industrial Relations Act 1971. The experiment failed and the NIRC was abolished in 1974. But the apparent willingness of the House of Lords to expedite the delivery of their judgment coupled with the highly eccentric use made of that judgment by the NIRC to release the five dockers was so convenient for the government of the day that it aroused the strong suspicion of judicial compliance with political expediency.

A later industrial dispute was a pretty example of the intermingling of the exercise of powers in the high places of government in the United Kingdom. In October 1973, the NIRC fined the Amalgamated Union of Engineering Workers £100,000 for contempt of court when they refused to obey the court's order to call off a strike.[31]

To obtain payment of the fine the court sequestrated against assets held in the political fund of the union. Labour MPs put down a motion in the House of Commons calling for the removal from office of the president of the NIRC for 'political prejudice and partiality'. Sir John Donaldson

31. *Con-Mech (Engineers) Ltd v. AUEW* [1973] ICR 620.

defended himself in a public speech saying that the court had not known that the assets had been earmarked for a political or any other purpose. At this point Lord Hailsham, then Lord Chancellor, in a public speech and as head of the judiciary, attacked those who had signed the motion and said that the public should note the identity and party of the Members concerned. Whereupon Labour Members tabled another motion condemning the Lord Chancellor and alleging 'a gross contempt of the House of Commons'.[32]

In the event neither of the motions was debated and the matter lapsed.

The conflict between the courts and trade unions showed itself in the second half of the nineteenth century and the first decade of the twentieth as an expression of class conflict. The trade unions were growing in militancy, especially during the years after 1890, and were displaying powers which dismayed a large part of middle-class society. The dismay was in part because of the anticipated economic consequences of this militancy, but also because it threatened the existing social order of late Victorian England.

Many politicians, from Disraeli onwards, had realized that trade union power was an economic factor which had to be taken seriously into account and certainly was not capable of being overcome by crude shows of force. Her Majesty's judges, however, were less prescient and less capable of adjusting legal principles and traditions to the new pressures. So, under men like Halsbury, they reacted to the legislation of the later nineteenth century with all the inflexibility of those who are determined that what was good enough for their fathers' social and economic structures was good enough for them. And in the more general upheaval of political beliefs which accompanied 'the strange death of liberal England', influential judges were more often to be found towards the right of the spectrum of opinion.

The most recent developments may prove to be of the utmost importance and to have the most lasting consequences. What litigation might have been promoted by the

32. See 865 HC Deb. col. 1089–91, 1291–7.

Labour government's aborted proposals in the late 1960s[33] we shall never know. But the much more rigorous policy embodied in the Conservatives' Industrial Relations Act of 1971 was a revolution in the long story. For this Act deliberately sought to use the courts and the judges to achieve political ends. The institution of the NIRC reflected the new techniques and reintroduced the old arguments. The identification of 'law' and 'policy' made almost impossible the continuance of the interplay between the judges and politicians which had provided a valuable tolerance. Had the Act succeeded, the damage to the reputation of judicial institutions would have been considerable; but it was always highly probable that this attempt to use the judges for these political purposes would fail. The failure was forecast by almost all those with the greatest knowledge of the working of industrial relations in this country and, more particularly, abroad. But the circumstances of its failure, and the manoeuvrings of politicians and judges which accompanied that failure, combined to produce a calamity which went far beyond the collapse of a doomed policy, for the failure directly resulted in a deep distrust of the judicial system. Trade unionists, as we have seen, had little cause to look to the judiciary for the protection of their statutory rights. Now the suspected subservience of the judiciary to the politicians seemed to be made manifest. There is no evidence that the judges at any time protested to Her Majesty's government in or out of Parliament against the proposals to involve them directly and indirectly in the administration of the act of 1971. Their failure to do so rests with the Lord Chancellor (Lord Hailsham), the Master of the Rolls (Lord Denning), and, to a lesser extent, the Lord Chief Justice (Lord Widgery).

The events of 1972 finally persuaded the leaders of organized labour (and the great mass of trade union members) that the judges were not to be trusted. Today the relations between the trade unions and the judiciary are worse than they were in the period immediately following the *Taff Vale* decision in 1901. Mr Heath deliberately employed the judges

33. See *In Place of Strife* (Cmnd 3888).

as instruments of his policy, enmeshed trade unionists in new legal rules, and then, in chorus with the judges, condemned them, in the name of the rule of law, for seeking to extricate themselves.

Less easy to understand is the apparent willingness of the judiciary to lend themselves to this manoeuvring. It is difficult to believe in the political naïveté of judges, but Sir John Donaldson, president of the NIRC, looking back on the short history of that court, has expressed views which are bewildering in their ingenuousness. He emphasized the need for guidelines in all aspects of industrial relations and continued:

> With such guidelines, the courts could be given their traditional role of investigating the merits of disputes and helping the party who is right . . . The public suffers from every industrial dispute. Ought they not to know who is right? Adopting this new approach they *would* know, for the court which investigated the dispute would tell them. Those who suffered injustice would then be supported by the courts.[34]

On this evidence it seems possible that a large part of the conflict that arose in the administration of the NIRC was the result of a belief of its president that, in industrial conflicts, one side can be discovered, after proper examination by judges, to be 'right' and the other side 'wrong'. But industrial conflicts are not of this kind. They can be solved only by compromise and by the exercise of economic and political strength, not by the application of legal principles or guidelines. This may be unfortunate but it is the reason why the NIRC was bound to fail.

The Law Lords restrain Denning

In a group of cases in 1978 and 1979 the Court of Appeal sought considerably to limit the immunities of trade unionists from criminal and civil liabilities for acts done 'in contem-

34. *Lessons from the Industrial Court* (1975) 91 LQR at 191–2.

plation or furtherance of a trade dispute'.[35] Then, in three
cases decided between July 1979 and February 1980, the
House of Lords reversed this development. Both the substance and the manner in which this was done throw further
light on the politics of the judiciary in dealing with industrial
relations.

The first of these cases was *NWL Ltd v. Woods*.[36] The
International Transport Workers' Federation blacked a ship
in an attempt to force its owners to pay wages in accordance
with the Federation's scales. Since the crew of the ship were
not directly involved, the owners argued that there was no
trade dispute. Two years before, in *BBC v. Hearn* (1977),[37]
trade union officials had threatened that their workers would
refuse to allow the BBC to televise the cup final so that
it could be seen in South Africa, because of the union's
disapproval of the racial policies of the government of that
country. The Court of Appeal had held that there was no
trade dispute and so no protection for the trade union
officials. In *NWL* the House of Lords did not question that
decision. But in 1978, the Court of Appeal had decided, in
'*The Camilla M*',[38] where the facts were similar to those in
NWL, that the presence of an 'extraneous motive' for trade
union action was sufficient to prevent that action being a
'trade dispute'.[39]

In *NWL* the House of Lords rejected this test. Lord
Diplock said that even if the predominant motives were 'to
bring down the fabric of the present economic system by
raising wages to unrealistic levels', that would not make the
dispute any less one connected with the terms and conditions
of employment and therefore a trade dispute. Similarly Lord
Scarman said that if the dispute were connected with one of

35. *Beaverbrook v. Keys* [1978] ICR 582; *Star Sea Transport of Monrovia
v. Slater 'The Camilla M'* [1978] IRLR 507; *Associated Newspapers Group
Ltd v. Wade* [1979] ICR 664.

36. [1979] 1 WLR 1294.

37. [1977] 1 WLR 1004.

38. See note 35.

39. The Court of Appeal in *NWL* discharged the injunction given in the
lower court on the ground that the union had not made 'impossible
demands' and so distinguished '*The Camilla M*'.

the matters referred to in the statute (for example, terms and conditions of employment) then 'it is a trade dispute, and it is immaterial whether the dispute also relates to other matters or has an extraneous, e.g. political or personal, motive. The connection is all that has to be shown.' The legislative purpose of the Trade Union and Labour Relations Act 1974, said Lord Scarman, was 'to sweep away not only the structure of industrial relations created by the Industrial Relations Act 1971, which it was passed to repeal, but also the restraints of judicial review which the courts have been fashioning one way or another since the enactment of the Trade Disputes Act 1906 . . . Briefly put, the law is now back to what Parliament had intended when it enacted the Act of 1906 – but stronger and clearer than it was then.'

In *Express Newspapers v. McShane*,[40] there was a dispute over pay between the proprietors of provincial newspapers and members of the National Union of Journalists. The national executive of the union called out on strike all its members on provincial newspapers. These newspapers used news copy supplied by the Press Association and the union called on PA journalists to strike also. This strike affected national newspapers. The union instructed its members on the *Daily Express* and other nationals to refuse to use copy sent out by the PA.

The plaintiffs sought an injunction against the members of the national executive of the union to restrain them from inducing or procuring their members not to use PA copy. The defendants claimed that what they were doing was in furtherance of their dispute with the provincial newspapers. The judge at first instance granted the injunction and the Court of Appeal upheld his decision, Lord Denning MR saying that there was no evidence that the blacking at the *Daily Express* had had any effect on the provincial dispute. So the Court of Appeal held that the acts were not done in furtherance of a trade dispute. 'Furtherance' was to be tested objectively by the courts as well as subjectively by reference to the defendants' intentions.

40. [1979] 2 All ER 360.

The House of Lords overruled the Court of Appeal,[41] giving its reasons on 13 December 1979. Four of their Lordships held that 'in furtherance' referred only to the subjective state of mind of the defendant and that he so acted if his purpose was to help the parties in the dispute to achieve their objectives and if he honestly and reasonably believed his actions would do so. Lord Wilberforce, while agreeing in the result, said that the test was whether the act done, pursuant to the general intention, was reasonably capable of achieving its objective. Lord Denning, said Lord Wilberforce, 'finally settled, I think, upon practical effect. This, I think, with respect goes too far.'

Six weeks later, on 26 January 1980, the Court of Appeal decided *Duport Steels v. Sirs.*[42] Steelworkers in the public sector had for some time been in dispute with their employers, the British Steel Corporation, and had come out on strike. Their union, the Iron and Steel Trades Confederation, in order to bring pressure on the government (who, the union hoped, would then put pressure on the BSC to settle the strike), decided to extend the strike to the private sector of the steel industry. Certain private steel companies sought injunctions to prevent this.

The Court of Appeal granted the injunctions on the ground that the extension had generated a second dispute, between the ISTC and the government, which was separate from the union's dispute with the BSC, and not a trade dispute because the government was not the employer. Lord Denning MR added the further reason that the acts done were too remote to be regarded as furtherance. As a leading article in *The Times* put it: 'Undaunted by the superior timidity of the House of Lords the Court of Appeal persevered in its determination to set limits to the scope of the immunities granted to trade unions by statute.'[43]

This 'second dispute' argument was not advanced by counsel for the steelworkers but emanated from the bench. Counsel thought so little of it that he did not seek to sustain

41. [1980] 2 WLR 89.
42. [1980] 1 All ER 529.
43. *The Times*, 28 January 1980.

it before the House of Lords. On the legal substance of the case, the House of Lords had little to add to the principles on which they had decided *Express Newspapers v. McShane*. The 'connection' between the strike in the private sector and the strike in the public sector was obvious, as was the honest and reasonable belief of the union that that extension would further their dispute with the BSC. So their Lordships again overruled the Court of Appeal.[44]

In another group of cases the courts grappled somewhat variously with a new institution.

The Advisory, Conciliation and Arbitration Service (ACAS) was established by the Employment Protection Act 1975. It is charged with the general duty of promoting the improvement of industrial relations, and in particular of encouraging the extension of collective bargaining and the development and, where necessary, reform of collective bargaining. One of its powers is to make recommendations requiring an employer to recognize a particular trade union as a negotiating body. Its functions were not at first regarded by the courts with much enthusiasm.

> It is therefore clear that as a result of the statutory machinery an individual can have a substantial measure of control over his own working life compulsorily delegated to an agent, a trade union, which he has not selected and may even have his own contract of service varied without his consent. These are very large powers, every bit as large as powers of compulsory acquisition of property; and, in my judgment, the court should seek to ensure that, just as in the case of compulsory purchase powers, the conditions for the exercise of the powers conferred by the 1975 Act are strictly observed.[45]

In the case from which that quotation is drawn the court set aside a questionnaire issued by ACAS on the ground that it was an unlawful exercise of discretion. Much more seriously, the House of Lords in *Grunwick Processing Lab-*

---

44. [1980] 1 All ER 529.
45. Browne-Wilkinson J in *G. C. Powley v. ACAS* [1977] IRLR 190.

oratories Ltd v. ACAS (1978)[46] effectively made the resolution of recognition disputes dependent on the co-operation
of employers. This could be seen as an example, from the
other side, of the dangers of seeking to impose legal and
compulsory arbitration over industrial relations. The union
request for recognition was referred to ACAS which sent
questionnaires to union members at Grunwick's but not to
the rest of the workers because the employers would not
supply ACAS with their names and addresses. The duty of
ACAS under the statute was to 'ascertain the opinion of the
workers to whom the issue relates'. The failure of ACAS
to ascertain the opinion of the non-union members (who
numbered two-thirds of all those employed) rendered void
ACAS's recommendation of recognition for the union.

The next two cases, however, show a broader understanding of what ACAS was supposed to be doing. In *United
Kingdom Association of Professional Engineers v. ACAS*
(1980)[47] the Association sought recognition from a company
already well supplied with trade unions. ACAS refused to
recommend recognition partly because to do so would
arouse strong opposition from the other unions with a risk
of industrial action which would be damaging to the industry.
In the Court of Appeal, Lord Denning MR saw this as
'another story of David and Goliath . . . a small union pitted
against a great one'. He set aside ACAS's report, saying
that the threats of industrial strife should have been ignored.
But the House of Lords (Lord Scarman delivering the main
opinion) reversed the Court of Appeal and upheld the
report. Similarly, in *Engineers' and Managers' Association
v. ACAS* (1980)[48] the House of Lords by a majority held
that ACAS had not acted unreasonably in postponing its
statutory enquiries for the time being because another union
was also seeking recognition and the plaintiff Association
was also suing the Trades Union Congress. Lord Scarman
said: 'ACAS has to form its view as to what is best for
the promotion of industrial relations and the extension of

46. [1978] AC 655.
47. [1979] 2 All ER 480 (CA); [1980] 1 All ER 612 (HL).
48. [1980] 1 All ER 896.

collective bargaining. The Court of Appeal erred in substituting its judgment for that of ACAS.'

ACAS has had a troubled life and its powers have been limited and subjected to greater ministerial control by the Employment Act 1980.

The Conservative attack

Legislation since 1979 has greatly affected industrial relations, often in line with the expressed views of the Court of Appeal and the House of Lords.

Section 17 of the Employment Act 1980 is designed to limit 'secondary action', that is action taken by workers in support of a trade dispute between other workers and their employers. The section defined secondary action in relation to a trade dispute as arising when a person induces another to break a contract of employment if the employer under the contract of employment is not a party to the trade dispute.

Marina Shipping Ltd v. Laughton (1982)[49] was one in a long line of cases[50] arising out of attempts by the International Transport Workers Federation (ITF) to force ship owners employing cheap labour recruited abroad to pay European standard rates of wages. In this case, ITF officials blacked a ship with the result that lock keepers, in breach of their contract with port authorities at Hull, refused to operate gates and so prevented the ship from sailing. Section 17(3) of the Act permits secondary action if (a) the purpose or principal purpose of the secondary action was directly to prevent or disrupt the supply during the dispute of goods or services between an employer who is a party to the dispute (here the ship owners) and the employer under the contract of employment to which the secondary action relates (here the port authorities); and (b) the secondary action was likely to achieve that purpose. This would seem to cover the action of the lock keepers in this case. But section 17(6) provides

49. [1982] 2 WLR 569.
50. See, for example, *NWL v. Woods* (above, p. 94).

that references to the supply of goods and services between two persons are references to the supply by one to the other in pursuance of a contract between them. The Court of Appeal held that there was no contract between the owners and the port authority and so the secondary action was illegal.

Very similar facts were considered by the House of Lords in *Merkur Island Shipping Corporation v. Laughton* (1983).[51] Here the ITF persuaded tugmen, in breach of their contract with their employers, to refuse to operate tugs to enable the ship to leave port. The House of Lords held that since the ship owners were not party to any contract with the tug owners (the arrangements had been made by the charterers of the ship) the secondary action was, again, illegal.

The effect of these decisions is to prevent the ITF from pursuing its aim of requiring owners of ships flying 'flags of convenience' to pay wages at levels compatible with collective agreements made by 'bona fide organizations of shipowners and seafarers' in accordance with the recommendations of the International Labour Organisation. It has been strongly argued that the interpretation is mistaken. As the law stands, everything turns on the fortuitous circumstance of the existence or non-existence of a formal contract between two parties even though the reality of the supply of goods and services from one of the principals to another within the meaning of section 17(3) is not in question. If the *purpose* is to interrupt an apparent contract and the secondary action would be likely to achieve that purpose, then the secondary action should be legitimate even if no such contract exists in fact.[52]

In *Cheall v. Association of Professional, Executive, Clerical and Computer Staff*,[53] the House of Lords overruled a majority of the Court of Appeal. Cheall resigned from one trade union (ACTSS) and joined another (APEX). In

51. [1983] 3 All ER 914. See also *Union Traffic v. TGWU* [1989] ICR 98 and *Shipping Company Uniform v. ITF* [1985] IRLR 71.
52. See Wedderburn, 45 *Modern Law Review* (1982) 317, and 46 *Modern Law Review* (1983) 632. See also Employment Act 1990 section 4.
53. [1983] 2 WLR 679.

accepting Cheall, without first enquiring of ACTSS whether it objected, APEX breached the Bridlington principles designed to prevent unions poaching members from one another. As a result the Trades Union Congress Disputes Committee required APEX to dismiss Cheall and advise him to rejoin his former union. This APEX did, in accordance with its own rules, whereupon Cheall sought a declaration that his dismissal was invalid. In the Court of Appeal,[54] Lord Denning MR decided in favour of Cheall, invoking the European Convention on Human Rights, which declared that everyone had a right to join a trade union, which proposition Lord Denning identified with the common law. He also referred to the case of the three railwaymen, dismissed for refusing to join a trade union, who had succeeded before the Court of Human Rights[55] and he reached the conclusion that the relevant article of the Convention was 'part of the law of England or at any rate the same as the law of England'. Had this view been upheld, it would have destroyed the Bridlington principles. Slade LJ also decided in favour of Cheall but on more modest grounds. Donaldson LJ disagreed. He quoted Lord Atkin that the doctrine of public policy 'should only be invoked in clear cases in which the harm to the public is substantially incontestable, and does not depend upon the idiosyncratic inferences of a few judicial minds'.[56] Donaldson LJ continued:

> Above all I think that judges must beware of confusing political policy with public policy . . . Whether judges are better or less able than others to assess the merits and demerits of political policies is beside the point, because that is not their function.
> . . . We are being invited to apply considerations of political rather than public policy. This I absolutely decline to do.

The Law Lords unanimously rejected Cheall's application on the ground that there was no principle of law which

---

54. [1982] 3 WLR 685.
55. *Young v. United Kingdom* [1981] IRLR 408.
56. *Fender v. St John-Mildmay* [1938] AC 1.

prevented the union from relying on its own rules which also bound Cheall. 'My human sympathies', said Lord Diplock, 'are with Mr Cheall, but I am not in a position to indulge them; for I am left in no doubt that upon all the points that have been so ingeniously argued, the law is against him.' But Lord Diplock suggested that different considerations might apply if the effect of Cheall's expulsion from APEX were to have put his job in jeopardy because of the existence of a closed shop or for some other reason.

In *Carrington v. Therm-A-Stor Ltd*,[57] a group of employees decided to try to introduce a trade union into the factory where they worked. By late April 1980 between sixty and sixty-five of the seventy employees had joined or applied to join. The district secretary of the union wrote to the managing director setting out the union's case for recognition. Two days later the employers' managing committee decided to dismiss twenty of the employees and instructed the chargehands to decide who should be chosen. Four of those chosen brought this action for unfair dismissal. The industrial tribunal found that the reason for the dismissals was that the managing director was strongly anti-union but that none of the four could show that the reason for his dismissal was his own union membership or activities. The Court of Appeal, with regret, rejected their claim on the ground that, although the relevant statutory provision declared a dismissal to be unfair if the reason for it was that the employee proposed to join a trade union or take part in union activities, the provision was 'not concerned with an employer's reactions to a trade union's activities, but with his reactions to an individual employee's activities in a trade union context' (Sir John Donaldson MR). The narrowness of this interpretation is self-evident.

The British Telecommunications Act 1981 established BT as a public corporation and transferred telecommunication functions to it from the Post Office. By a government licence under the Act, Mercury Communications, a private company, was authorized to establish a communications system. An agreement between BT and Mercury provided for inter-

57. [1983] 1 WLR 138.

connections between the two systems. The Post Office Engineering Union waged a campaign against the licensing of competitors of BT and against proposals, in a Bill before Parliament, on privatization of BT. The union instructed its members not to make the interconnection, there was a day of action and a series of selective strikes. The union also instructed its members to 'black' BT services at Mercury's premises. There was a threat of industrial action against Mercury's shareholders. Mercury applied to the court for interlocutory injunctions to restrain the union and its members from inducing breach of contract between Mercury and BT.

We have seen that a persistent principle since 1906 had been that an act done by a person in contemplation or furtherance of trade dispute could not be actionable in tort on the ground of inducing another person to break a contract. By the Employment Act 1982 the definition of a trade dispute is narrowed. Disputes between workers and workers – demarcation disputes – are excluded; so are disputes between workers and an employer unless he is their own. Also it is no longer sufficient that the dispute should be 'connected with', in the instant case, termination of employment; now it had to relate 'wholly or mainly' to that. The Court of Appeal readily allowed new evidence to be admitted and held that since the risk to jobs did not appear to be a major factor in the dispute, it seemed unlikely that the union would be able to bring itself within the definition of a trade dispute and so the injunction should be granted.

Sir John Donaldson MR said it was important in such disputes, which gave rise to strong, indeed passionate, feelings, that 'everyone should know where the courts stand. They are on neither side. They have an independent role, akin to that of a referee . . . Parliament makes the law and is solely responsible for what the law is. The duty of the court is neither to make nor to alter nor to pass judgment on the law. Their duty is simply to apply it as they understand it.'[58] The effect of the decision was to make clear that the courts, under the new legislation, will decide in what

58. *Mercury Communications v. Scott-Garner* [1983] 3 WLR 914.

circumstances industrial action is, in their view, 'political' and when not. And this, far more than in the past, will determine the legality or illegality of the action.

The House of Lords shows every sign of adopting a hard line against trade unions when interpreting the new legislation, as this next case demonstrates.

The Dimbleby newspapers had been printed by an associated company, Dimbleby Printers Ltd, which became engaged in a closed shop dispute with the National Graphical Association. As a result of that dispute, the NGA members were on strike and the Dimbleby newspapers were not being printed. So the Dimbleby company turned to TBF (Printers) Ltd, which was itself a company closely associated with (same shareholdings, same management) T. Bailey Forman Ltd, with whom the NUJ was engaged in a trade dispute and had been since 1979. The NUJ instructed its members employed by Dimbleby newspapers not to supply copy to Dimbleby newspapers and argued that, because of their effective identity, TBF (Printers) Ltd, as well as T. Bailey Forman Ltd, was an 'employer who is party to the dispute' between the NUJ and T. Bailey Forman Ltd, within the meaning of that phrase in section 17(3) of the Act of 1980. But the House of Lords rejected this argument.[59]

Lord Wedderburn has summarized several of these recent developments thus:

> So, workers may picket, but only at their own place of work. Sympathy or solidarity action must be made tortious *because* it is 'secondary', i.e. it transgresses the rule about staying within employment unit boundaries. Access to tribunals for unfair dismissal of strikers is narrowed to victimization in the complainant's own 'establishment'; workers taking part in it elsewhere no longer count as his fellows. And the 'trade dispute' itself – the central concept of the system of immunities – is now confined to disputes with a worker's *own* employer only and to disputes which relate wholly or mainly to

59. *Dimbleby and Sons Ltd v. National Union of Journalists* [1984] 1 WLR 427.

the industrial conditions of the workers in that employment unit only. As it faces the power of capital organized in interlocking but legally separate corporate entities, labour is now cut up into atomized units of which the boundaries are by law coterminous with the employers' definitions of employment units in both private and public sectors. Trans-enterprise solidarity is no longer acceptable to the law. Any doubtful points are increasingly swept aside by Law Lords who found that the old immunities stuck in their 'judicial gorges'. And if need be, there are always new common law liabilities ready to hand not necessarily protected by immunities.[60]

The last sentence refers particularly to the development of the notion of 'economic duress' as creating liabilities for trade unions.[61]

The uses of the labour injunction

An injunction may be issued whenever the court 'finds it just and convenient to do so'. This very wide discretion the judge may exercise in different ways in different cases or in different types of cases. Labour injunctions are sought by employers or dissident trade unionists or others to prevent or to stop industrial action, including strikes, by trade unions or their officials which the plaintiff claims is illegal. If the action continued, he argues, damage would result to his business or personal interests which would be irreparable and for which the subsequent payment of compensation would be an inadequate remedy. The plaintiff seeks an interim or interlocutory injunction, being an order of the

60. 'Labour Law Now: a Hold and a Nudge' in 13 *Industrial Law Journal* (1984) 73.
61. See *Universe Tankships of Monrovia Inc. v. International Transport Workers Federation* [1982] 2 WLR 803; but note *Hadmor Productions v. Hamilton* [1982] 2 WLR 322; see also the new tort liability invented by the Court of Appeal in *Associated British Ports v. TGWU* [1989] 1 WLR 939 not commented on by the House of Lords when reversing on other grounds; and see *Dimskal Shipping Co v. ITWF* [1990] IRLR 102.

court requiring the defendant to desist from his action in order to maintain the status quo until its legality or illegality can be determined at a subsequent trial. Where the case is urgent, the application to the court is made *ex parte*, that is, without the other side being present. If not urgent, two clear days' notice is required but is often waived.

The question for the court used to be whether the applicant had shown prima facie evidence, or a probability, that his legal rights were being infringed. He also had to show that he would suffer more harm if the interim remedy were not granted than the defendant would suffer if it was (the 'balance of convenience'). But in 1975, the Law Lords said this test caused confusion. Lord Diplock said the court need be satisfied only that the applicant's claim was not 'frivolous or vexatious' and that there was 'a serious question to be tried'.[62]

This made the granting of an interim injunction much easier to obtain. The balance of convenience still had to be shown by the plaintiff to be in his favour but, as Wedderburn says, the threat of irreparable harm to the employer's 'property' in his business interests could not be out-weighed by the defendant union. Failure to abide by the terms of an injunction leads to proceedings for contempt of court, followed by fines and by possible sequestration (seizure) of the assets of the union.[63]

For the union, an interim injunction prevents the calling of a strike or other action at a time which the union has decided is the most effective. As the full trial is not likely to take place until weeks or months later, the bargaining position of the union is greatly weakened. Very frequently the full trial never takes place because the dispute is ended one way or another. Throughout the 1980s Government legislation progressively reduced the number of situations in which unions or individuals could legally take industrial action.

62. *American Cyanamid Ltd. v. Ethicon* [1975] AC 396.
63. See Wedderburn 'The Injunction and the Sovereignty of Parliament' in 23 *The Law Teacher* (1989) 4.

In *Messenger Newspapers Group v. NGA* (1984)[64] the union called a strike to support the policy of 100 per cent union membership which had been departed from in some subsidiary companies belonging to the Group. Picketing led to violence and one company dismissed the union workers on strike. The Group company obtained injunctions to stop secondary picketing and attempts to prevent advertisers taking space in the newspapers. The union disregarded the injunctions and was fined £50,000 for contempt of court. When mass picketing continued a further £100,000 fine was levied and the union's assets were sequestrated. Further violent demonstrations by mass pickets led to £525,000 additional fines being imposed. Also the union had to pay aggravated and exemplary damages amounting to over £125,000. It was this case that first showed the considerable legal sanctions available against unions under the new legislation.

During the miners' strike in 1984, members of the South Wales area of the National Union of Mineworkers supported the strike call but, months later, a few of them returned to work under extensive protection from the police. Demonstrations and pickets collected at pit gates and shouted abuse at them, as they passed through in coaches. Injunctions were sought to prevent this, but the judge had some difficulty in finding that the demonstrators were acting illegally. However he decided that the protest was 'a species of private nuisance, namely unreasonable interference with the victim's right to use the highway'.[65] This was an example of judicial creativity at its most blatant.

In another case,[66] the National Union of Mineworkers was fined £200,000 for refusal to obey an interim injunction and the judge ordered sequestration of its assets, some of which had been transferred abroad. It was claimed that trustees of the NUM (the President, the Vice-President and the Secretary) were in breach of their duties and the High Court ordered them to recover these assets and hand them over to

---

64. [1984] IRLR 397 (the 'Eddie Shah' case).
65. *Thomas v. NUM (South Wales area)* [1985] 2 WLR 1081.
66. *Clarke v. Heathfield* [1985] ICR 203, and (No. 2) at 606.

the sequestrators. When this was not done the judge ordered a receiver to be appointed as an officer of the court in place of the trustees.

The powers of the courts in such cases spread very wide. A strike was called by a joint negotiating committee of several unions, one of which (TASS) had two representatives on the committee of thirty-six members. Contrary to statutory requirements, no ballot had been held and interim injunctions were granted requiring the unions to withdraw and cancel their instructions and take all practical steps to inform their members to desist. Contempt proceedings were brought for failure to comply. TASS argued that they had nothing to withdraw, not having taken the original decision to strike. Nevertheless they were held to be in contempt but, the strike having collapsed, no penalty was imposed.[67]

The statutory liability of unions for the actions of their members has given rise to many difficulties. In *Express and Star v. National Graphical Association*,[68] the plaintiff newspapers obtained an interim injunction requiring the union to withdraw a direction to their members to take industrial action. The union circulated all its branches accordingly. But the court subsequently found two specific breaches involving officers of the union and held the union guilty of contempt. The Court of Appeal upheld this decision and ruled inapplicable to contempt proceedings statutory protection provided to unions under the Employment Act 1982.

The *Spycatcher* litigation[69] may have serious implications for trade union liability. Injunctions were issued against *The Observer* and *The Guardian* newspapers to prevent them from publishing extracts from Peter Wright's book and the Court of Appeal, overruling the judge at first instance, held that although publication by *The Independent* newspaper and others could not be a breach of those injunctions neverthe- less, since they knew of their issue, they could be guilty of

67. *Austin Rover Co. v. AUEW (TASS)* [1985] IRLR 162. But a penalty of £250,000 was imposed on the TGWU after the strike was settled.
68. [1986] ICR 589.
69. See below pp. 207–15.

contempt of court if their publication interfered with the course of justice. Presumably this principle would apply to trade unions taking action in the same dispute where their fellow members had been injuncted.

In no recent case has the Court of Appeal gone further in its attempt to control trade union activity than in the dispute over the Government's suddenly announced decision in April 1989 to abolish the National Dock Labour Scheme. In May, Associated British Ports sought interim injunctions to prevent the Transport and General Workers Union from calling a national docks strike after a favourable ballot of 9,400 dockers employed under the Scheme. The Court of Appeal, overruling the High Court judge, granted the injunction on the ground that in 'the balance of convenience' the wish to strike at this time was more than counterbalanced by the financial loss to the employers and the inconvenience to the public. The Court of Appeal said the strike was not in the public interest. This was a novel formulation. The 1967 Scheme provided that workers should 'work for such periods as are reasonable' and the employers argued that this made the strike illegal. The Court of Appeal said that difficult questions of law were raised, that there was a 'serious issue' to be decided and that, pending the full trial, the injunction should be granted. Not surprisingly and not for the first time, trade union leaders wondered whether it had become impossible to mount a legal strike. Over 2,000 dock workers immediately walked out despite the judgment and despite the advice given by their leaders not to do so.

The union appealed to the House of Lords and the unofficial action was abandoned. The Law Lords allowed the appeal on the ground that the clause in the Scheme relied on by the employers could not have the meaning attributed to it.[70] The Bill to abolish the Scheme was meanwhile being rushed through Parliament, and a fresh ballot was needed for the strike. A few days later a second action brought by the newly created Commissioner for the Rights of Trade Union Members seeking an injunction was rejected by the High Court. When the Act was passed, the strike collapsed.

70. *Associated British Ports v. TGWU* [1989] 1 WLR 939.

During the dispute in 1984, striking miners travelling in convoy on the motorway in Nottinghamshire were stopped within a few miles of four collieries. They were told by the police that there was reason to fear a breach of the peace if they proceeded and, when they attempted to push through, they were arrested for obstructing the police.[71] In another case, the judge suggested that mass picketing was of itself capable of amounting to intimidating conduct, echoing Lord Reid in *Hunt v. Broome* (above page 83) and so contrary to section 7 of the Conspiracy and Protection of Property Act 1875.[72] In *Read (Transport) Ltd v. NUM (South Wales)*,[73] road hauliers with contracts to take coke from British Steel Corporation works were subjected to mass picketing, abuse and threats. They obtained an interim injunction directed against the union, which then agreed to comply. But breaches of the injunction continued and the union officials were held to be in contempt, the union being fined £50,000 with sequestration of assets to follow, if needed.

In 1984, it became common for bail conditions, following arrests during the strike, to require those charged not to visit any premises or place for the purpose of picketing or demonstrating in connection with the current trade dispute between the NUM and the National Coal Board other than peacefully to picket or demonstrate at their usual place of employment. In *R. v. Mansfield Justices ex parte Sharkey*[74] the court added: 'It does a bench of justices no credit if their clerk is affixing standard conditions to bail forms while applications for unconditional bail are being made.' But that was the limit of their comment, except to admit that the large numbers involved did sometimes make it difficult to avoid an appearance of 'group justice'.

The dispute between, on the one side, the News International newspapers (*Sun* and *News of the World*), the Times Group (*The Times* and *The Sunday Times*) and others, and,

71. *Moss v. McLachlan* [1985] IRLR 76. This was not a case on injunctions.
72. *Thomas v. NUM (South Wales Area)* [1985] IRLR 136 (see above p. 107).
73. [1985] IRLR 67.
74. [1985] QB 613. This was not a case on injunctions.

on the other side, the unions (SOGAT 82, the NGA and others) which centred on the new site at Wapping, followed the breakdown of negotiations and the dismissal of all those on strike. There were daily (and nightly) demonstrations involving thousands of protestors and large numbers of police. Actions were begun by the employing newspapers alleging nuisance, intimidation, harassment, and interference with commercial contracts.[75] Injunctions were issued and some of the unions instructed their members to stop the forbidden activities. Several unions were held to be in contempt, were fined and had their assets sequestrated.

The requirements of a ballot before strike action have been variously interpreted by the courts. The requirements in Area union rules were held not to have been fulfilled by the NUM in Derbyshire and an order followed restraining the union from using funds in this connection.[76] But British Rail failed to obtain an interim injunction against the NUR, the court holding that the union was likely in the highest degree to be able to show that their ballot was valid.[77] London Underground, however, were granted an injunction to prevent a ballot being held on the ground that the issues did not constitute trade disputes.[78] And when the Employment Act 1988 tightened the ballot requirements, the Union of Communication Workers had their ballot declared invalid.[79]

In 1988, disputes arose between British shipowners, who proposed to introduce changes to existing terms and conditions of work for their employees, and the National Union of Seamen. The union decided to ballot its members on industrial action but P & O and Sealink successfully applied

75. *News Group Newspapers and others v. SOGAT 82 and others* [1986] IRLR 337; and [1987] ICR 716 where the assets of a union branch were held not subject to sequestration.

76. *Taylor v. NUM (Derbyshire)* [1984] IRLR 440; [1985] IRLR 65, 99.

77. *British Rail v. NUR* [1989] IRLR 345, 349.

78. *London Underground v. NUR* [1989] IRLR 341, 343. But see Millet J. in *Associated British Ports v. TGWU* [1989] IRLR at 301.

79. *Post Office v. Union of Communication Workers* [1990] 1 WLR 981.

for injunctions to prevent the holding of ballots.[80] The basis of these decisions was that strikes would result in unlawful 'secondary' action involving employers who were not parties to the dispute. Unofficial strike action followed and the union's own bankers were granted an injunction prohibiting the NUS from transferring any of their property abroad, on the principle that third parties must ensure that they gave no aid to any action which might occur if the union's property were sequestrated as a result of some future contempt of court. Such a sequestration was ordered on the application of Sealink. The NUS persuaded its members to end their unlawful industrial action but the courts 'transferred' the sequestration to apply to a separate complaint by P & O that NUS workers were unlawfully picketing its premises. Fines were also imposed and crippling fines were threatened.

At the same time as the dispute over the Dock Labour Scheme was moving rapidly through the courts,[81] the British Railways Board was being denied an injunction against the National Union of Railwaymen. The Board claimed that a ballot on industrial action had not been validly conducted but the High Court judge said the evidence for this 'did not come anywhere near justifying injunctive relief'. The judge seemed unimpressed by the argument that a rail strike would cause 'enormous public inconvenience'. The Court of Appeal dismissed the appeal, Lord Donaldson MR taking the high ground that the function of the independent judiciary under the rule of law was simply to decide whether there had been compliance with the statute requiring the holding of a ballot, however unpopular the strike might be with the travelling public.[82]

The extent to which trade unions are disadvantaged by the rules developed by the judiciary is shown in a case involving the National Union of Teachers. It is well known that teachers undertake a number of tasks which appear to be

---

80. *P & O European Ferries (Portsmouth) Ltd. v. NUS*, *The Independent*, 28 March 1988.

81. See above p. 109.

82. *British Railways Board v. National Union of Railwaymen* [1989] IRLR 345, 349.

additional to their contractual duties and so voluntary. The union called on teachers in certain schools to take action by refusing to supervise in lunch periods, or to attend meetings outside school hours. No ballot was held, as was legally required if the action was in breach of contract. An interim injunction was granted to the local authority employers by the judge on the ground that it was 'improbable' that there was 'no serious issue to be tried'.[83] As Wedderburn says, a further advantage accrues to the plaintiff when the test is turned into this negative form. And he continues: 'The judge may as easily say "This is all too difficult for interlocutory motion. It must go to trial, so I will *not* grant an injunction", as he may conclude, "so I *will* grant an injunction".'[84] But the judge usually takes the second course in cases concerning industrial relations.

83. *Solihull MB v. NUT* [1985] IRLR 211.
84. Op. cit., p. 700.

4. The control of discretionary powers

The earlier cases

During the inter-war period, the courts showed little reluctance in overruling the decisions of Ministers and local authorities especially where, as in slum clearance and compulsory purchase cases, property rights were interfered with. The exercise of statutory powers was closely scrutinized and any procedural or substantive defect was generally found to be sufficient to nullify a decision. Typical of this attitude was that of Swift J in *Re Bowman*:

> When an owner of property against whom an order has been made under the Act comes into this court and complains that there has been some irregularity in the proceedings, and that he is not liable to have his property taken away, it is right, I think, that his case should be entertained sympathetically and that a statute under which he is being deprived of his rights to property should be construed strictly against the local authority and favourably towards the interest of the applicant, in as much as he for the benefit of the community is undoubtedly suffering a substantial loss, which in my view must not be inflicted upon him unless it is quite clear that Parliament has intended that it shall.[1]

1. [1932] 2 KB 261; and see *Carltona v. Commissioners of Works* [1943] 2 All ER 560, *Point of Ayr Collieries v. Lloyd George* [1943] 2 All ER 546, *Robinson v. Minister of Town and Country Planning* [1947] KB 702, *Franklin v. Minister of Town and Country Planning* [1948] AC 87.

Similarly in *Errington v. Minister of Health*,[2] Maugham LJ said:

> It seems to me a matter of the highest possible import-ance that where a quasi-judicial function is being exer-cised, under such circumstances as it had to be exercised here, with the result of depriving people of their prop-erty, especially if it is done without compensation, the persons concerned should be satisfied that nothing unfair has been done in the matter, and that *ex parte* statements have not been heard before the decision has been given without any chance for the person concerned to refute those statements.

Decisions such as these show that the courts inclined to the view that in a conflict between the common law property right of an individual and the statutory powers of a local authority to interfere with those rights, the benefit of any doubt in statute was to be given to the individual – and that this was particularly so if the statute gave less than full compensation to the individual. This is, indeed, often said to be a presumption to which judges should have regard in interpreting statutes. The idea that Parliament, in this field, was 'interfering' with the common law died hard.

The changes in attitudes and the growth of interventionism

But during 1939–45 and for some years after the war, there was a marked change in judicial attitudes. The classic judg-ment was that in *Associated Provincial Picture Houses Ltd v. Wednesbury Corporation*.[3] On the one hand, Lord Greene MR indicated the strict limits on the powers of the courts to set aside an administrative decision where the public author-ity acted within its jurisdiction. On the other hand, such an authority must act in good faith, use the powers for the purpose for which they were given, take into account rel-evant matters and disregard the irrelevant, and must not act

2. [1935] 1 KB 249.
3. [1948] 1 KB 223.

in a way so unreasonable that no reasonable authority could have so acted. But it was no part of the courts' function to replace the discretionary decision of the public authority with one of its own.

The highest point in this reluctance to intervene with governmental activities was reached in the mid-1950s when the House of Lords interpreted a statutory provision, which limited the courts' jurisdiction to review a compulsory purchase order on land, so broadly that even fraud by public servants was held not to entitle the owner to bring an action.[4]

From the early 1960s, the courts reverted to their former attitude and became increasingly willing to review governmental activities on a variety of grounds; the reluctance of the 1940s and 1950s disappeared.

In *Ridge v. Baldwin*[5] the House of Lords held that a chief constable, who had been acquitted on a criminal charge but criticized for lack of leadership by the judge, was entitled, under the common law rules of natural justice, to a hearing before he could be dismissed by the local authority who employed him. This decision led the way to a general concept of the need for 'fairness' in the administrative process.

The earlier distinction between those matters which fell within ministerial or local authority discretion and those which were within the competence of the courts to adjudicate became increasingly blurred. Thus in *Padfield v. Minister of Agriculture, Fisheries and Food*[6] milk producers from the south east asked the minister to appoint a committee of investigation, alleging that the price they were paid by the Milk Marketing Board was too low having regard to transport costs. The relevant statute empowered the minister to set up such a committee but in this case he refused to do so on the ground that the complaint was unsuitable for investigation because it raised wide issues; that if the committee upheld the complaint he would be expected to make an

4. *Smith v. East Elloe RDC* [1956] AC 736; and see *Jones v. Department of Employment* [1988] 2 WLR 493.

5. [1964] AC 40.

6. [1968] AC 997. Contrast *British Oxygen v. Minister of Technology* [1971] AC 610 where the House of Lords refused to interfere with a ministerial discretion about investment grants.

order to give effect to the committee's recommendations; and that the complaint should be dealt with by the Board rather than by the committee of investigation. A majority of the House of Lords found these reasons insufficient and ordered the minister to set up the committee. They agreed that he had a discretion under the statute whether or not to do so but said that he was not justified in refusing if the result was to frustrate the policy of the Act of Parliament. Lord Morris of Borth-y-Gest disagreed. In his view, the court could intervene only if the minister (a) failed or refused to apply his mind to or to consider the question whether to refer a complaint to the committee or (b) misinterpreted the law or proceeded on an erroneous view of the law or (c) based his decision on some wholly extraneous consideration or (d) failed to have regard to matters which he should have taken into account. And he held that none of these was the case. The view taken by the majority was surprising as the decision of the minister not to intervene was clearly one of policy with which the courts are usually reluctant to interfere.[7]

The decision of the House of Lords in *Anisminic Ltd v. Foreign Compensation Commission*[8] shows how, on occasion, the courts will resist the strongest efforts of the government to exclude them from reviewing executive discretion. The Foreign Compensation Commission was empowered by statute to deal with claims to compensation under agreements with foreign governments. The plaintiffs owned property in Egypt which they lost at the time of the Suez crisis in 1956. The Commission made a provisional determination that the plaintiffs had failed to establish a claim according to the rules laid down under the statute. The statute provided that: 'The determination by the Commission of any application made to them under this Act shall not be called in question in any court of law.'

Despite these last words the plaintiffs applied to the courts for an order declaring that the Commission had miscon-

---

7. See, for example, *Bushell v. Secretary of State for the Environment* [1980] 3 WLR 22.
8. [1969] 2 AC 147.

strued the rules. The House of Lords, not for the first or for the last time, held that 'determination' should not be construed as including everything which purported to be a determination but was not, and so the court was not precluded from deciding that the order of the Commission was a nullity. Looking at the way the Commission had construed the rules, the House decided that the determination was a nullity.

Lord Morris of Borth-y-Gest again dissented. He agreed that the courts could intervene if the question was whether or not the Commission had acted within its powers or its jurisdiction. But 'what is forbidden is to question the correctness of a decision or determination which it was within the area of their jurisdiction to make.'

This distinction has a long and respectable history. If an Act of Parliament says that A (who may be a minister or a commission or a local authority or an individual) shall be the person to settle certain specified questions and that there shall be neither appeal to nor review by any other body or person (including the courts), then A's decisions are unchallengeable so long as (a) it is A, not another, who decides, (b) A decides those specified questions and not others and (c) A does not act in bad faith or with similar impropriety. The *Anisminic* decision goes much further than this and says in effect that A's decision can be set aside by the courts if they disagree with his interpretation of the rules which he is required to apply. In a later case Lord Denning MR said,

> So fine is the distinction that in truth the High Court has a choice before it whether to interfere with an inferior court on a point of law. If it chooses to interfere, it can formulate its decision in the words: 'The court below had no jurisdiction to decide this point wrongly as it did.' If it does not choose to interfere, it can say: 'The court had jurisdiction to decide it wrongly, and did so.' Softly be it stated, but that is the reason for the

difference between the decision of the Court of Appeal in *Anisminic* . . . and the House of Lords.[9]

As Lord Diplock said in *Re Racal Communications Ltd*, 'The breakthrough made by *Anisminic* was that, as respected administrative tribunals and authorities, the old distinction between errors of law which went to jurisdiction and those which did not, was for practical purposes abolished.' In *Racal* the House of Lords held that where a statute provided that the decision of a High Court judge should 'not be appealable', it could not be reviewed or appealed from.

This extreme case of judicial interference with the powers of public authorities may be contrasted with the attitude of the Court of Appeal in *Secretary of State for Employment v. ASLEF*[10] *and Others (No. 2)*.[11] The Secretary of State exercised his powers to apply to the NIRC under the Industrial Relations Act 1971 for an order requiring a ballot of trade union members to be held. This power existed where, as the statute provided, it appeared to him that there were reasons for doubting whether the trade union members, in taking part in industrial action, were acting in accordance with their own wishes. The trade union appealed against the order given by the NIRC. Lord Denning first considered how far the words 'if it appears to the Secretary of State' put his decision beyond judicial challenge. He said:

> In this case I would think that, if the minister does not act in good faith, or if he acts on extraneous considerations which ought not to influence him, or if he plainly misdirects himself in fact or in law, it may well be that a court would interfere; but when he honestly takes a view of the facts or the law which could reasonably be entertained, then his decision is not to be set aside simply because thereafter someone thinks that his view was wrong . . . Of course it is to be remembered here

9. *Pearlman v. Harrow School* [1978] 3 WLR 736, a decision of the Court of Appeal criticized by Lord Diplock in *Re Racal Communications Ltd* [1981] AC 374.

10. Associated Society of Locomotive Engineers and Firemen.

11. [1972] 2 QB 455. The 'others' included the other railway unions.

that we are concerned with a grave threat to the national economy. The steps that are proposed do not imperil the liberty, livelihood or property of any man. The issue is simply: should a ballot be held of the railwaymen to ascertain their views?

Lord Denning then turned to the claim that the minister had acted improperly.

It is said that it must 'appear' to the minister that there are 'reasons' for doubting whether the workers are behind their leaders: and that the minister has given no reasons. We have been referred to several recent cases, of which *Padfield v. Minister of Agriculture, Fisheries and Food* is the best example, in which the courts have stressed that in the ordinary way a minister should give reasons, and if he gives none the court may infer that he had no good reasons. Whilst I would apply that proposition completely in most cases, and particularly in cases which affect life, liberty or property, I do not think that it applies in all cases.

Lord Denning concluded that the proposition did not apply in this case and that there were reasons which a reasonable minister could entertain and so there was no ground on which the court could interfere with the minister's decision to ask for a ballot order. He was supported by the other members of the Court of Appeal. In the event the union leaders were wholly justified, as the result of the ballot showed, in their claim that there were no reasons for doubting that the industrial action was in accordance with the wishes of the workers.

Two cases exemplify greater willingness of the courts to control ministerial discretion. In *Secretary of State for Education and Science v. Tameside Metropolitan Borough Council*[12] the minister acted under section 68 of the Education Act 1944 which provided:

If the Secretary of State is satisfied . . . that any local education authority . . . have acted or are proposing to

12. [1976] 3 WLR 641.

act unreasonably . . . he may . . . give such directions
. . . as appear to him to be expedient.

In March 1975 the Labour-controlled Tameside Council
put forward proposals to the Secretary of State for the reor-
ganization of secondary education along comprehensive lines
to come into effect in September 1976. The proposals were
approved in November 1975. The council made many of the
necessary arrangements for the changeover and told pupils
which schools they would be going to.

At the local elections in May 1976, the Conservatives won
control of the council and on 7 June told the Secretary of
State that they proposed not to implement the plans for the
conversion of the five grammar schools into comprehensives
and sixth-form colleges. On 11 June the Secretary of State
gave the council a direction under section 68, requiring them
to implement their predecessors' plans, and on 18 June the
Divisional Court ordered the council to comply. On 26 July
the Court of Appeal overruled the Divisional Court and on
2 August, moving with impressive speed, Lords Wilberforce,
Diplock, Salmon, Russell and Dilhorne upheld the Court of
Appeal.

The basis of their Lordships' decisions was that the minister could give a valid direction only if he was satisfied that
no reasonable local authority could have decided as the
Conservative majority did; and that he could not have been
so satisfied.

The second case was that of Laker Airways. Under the
Civil Aviation Act 1971, the Civil Aviation Authority was
empowered to grant licences to those wishing to operate air
transport lines. The Authority granted a licence to Mr
Freddy Laker for the period from 1973 to 1982 to operate
a cheap passenger service known as 'Skytrain' between the
United Kingdom and the USA. The Conservative government supported the project but in February 1976 the Labour
government (which had previously supported Mr Laker)
through its Secretary of State for Trade in a White Paper
announced a change of civil aviation policy.

The Act of 1971, empowered the Secretary of State to
'give guidance' to the Authority with respect to their statu-

tory functions. The White Paper purported to contain such guidance which, in accordance with the Act, was approved by a resolution of each House of Parliament. The crucial phrase in the White Paper guidance was that the Authority should not license more than one British airline to serve the same route, with British Airways as the preferred airline to the USA. That prevented Skytrain from coming into operation.

The Court of Appeal held that the power of the Secretary of State to give guidance to the Authority did not extend to such a discretion. Said Lord Denning MR:

> 'Guidance' could only be used to explain, amplify or supplement the general objectives or provisions of the Act. If the Secretary of State went beyond the bounds of 'guidance' he exceeded his powers; and the Civil Aviation Authority was under no obligation to obey him.

So Mr Laker succeeded in his action.[13]

These two cases while comparable are also dissimilar. In both cases two public authorities were in conflict. In *Laker's* case the minister was seeking to require the Civil Aviation Authority to follow his policy but he chose a way of doing this which the Court of Appeal considered not to be within his powers. In *Tameside* the central department and the local authority were in direct conflict over a matter of administrative feasibility. The minister did not believe that Tameside Council could properly implement the change within the limited time available.

The decision in *Tameside* may be contrasted with *ASLEF (No. 2)*[14] where the trade union's complaint that the minister had no reason to believe that the members were not behind their leaders was not supported by the court. In *Tameside* the minister had sound administrative reasons for believing that the local authority was acting unreasonably but it was held that merely to have such reasons was insufficient. A remarkable feature of this decision of the House of Lords

13. *Laker Airways Ltd v. Department of Trade* [1977] 2 WLR 234.
14. See above, p. 119.

was that it was based on almost no judicial authority at all. One of their Lordships referred to *ASLEF (No. 2)*, and to one other decision. The other three referred to none. Yet this is hardly an area where judicial pronouncements have been lacking. It concerns the whole matter of judicial control over ministerial discretion.

Professor de Smith[15] wrote that Parliament might purport to restrict judicial review by conferring powers in subjective terms, the public authority being entitled to act when it 'is satisfied' or when 'it appears' to it that, or when 'in its opinion', a prescribed state of affairs exists. Then the courts interpret such phrases so as to give themselves more or less control as they wish. This depends on the judges' views of the merits of the case before them or (I would add) the direction their political inclinations lead them – what I call below their 'view of the public interest'.[16] If trade unions are being restricted by ministerial action (as in *ASLEF [No. 2]*) then statutory limitations on ministers' powers will be interpreted loosely. If ministers appear to the courts to be acting in a way which is arbitrary or unfair (as in *Padfield* and *Tameside* and *Laker*) then the limitations will be insisted on. Little attempt is made to treat like situations in a like manner or to act consistently within a framework of judicial analysis. And one is often left with a feeling that in this area of the law judges rely almost entirely on their own sense of justice or on their own personal conception of what is best.

Another case in which the courts appeared to be in conflict with ministers was *Gouriet v. Union of Post Office Workers*,[17] in which the plaintiff sought an order from the court to restrain the defendant trade union from breaking the law by refusing to handle mail to South Africa. Usually a person, like the plaintiff, who suffers no special damage from a breach of the law must ask the Attorney-General either to institute proceedings or to give his consent (in a relator action) to the plaintiff's proceeding. In this case the Attorney-General refused to do either. One question that

15. *Judicial Review of Administrative Action* (3rd edn, pp. 318–20).
16. See chapter 9.
17. [1977] 2 WLR 310 (CA); [1978] AC 435 (HL).

arose in the Court of Appeal was whether this decision was subject to judicial review. Lord Denning said:

> The Attorney-General tells us that when he refuses his consent, his refusal is final. It cannot be overridden by the courts. He is answerable to Parliament, and to Parliament alone. He declines even to give his reasons for his refusal. This is, to my mind, a direct challenge to the rule of law . . . Suppose that he refused his consent for corrupt motives, or in bad faith . . . or for party-political reasons, and not in the interests of the public at large . . . or because he considered that the information was laid by a pressure group, of which he disapproved . . . These instances are, of course, entirely hypothetical. I would not suggest for one moment that they existed here. But the possibility of them convinces me that his discretion to refuse is not absolute or unfettered. It can be reviewed by the courts. If he takes into account matters which he ought not to take into account, or fails to take into account the matters which he ought to take into account, then his decision can be overridden by the courts. Not directly, but indirectly. If he misdirects himself in coming to his decision, the court can say: 'Very well then. If you do not give your consent, or your reasons, we will hear the complaint of this citizen without it.'

But in this Lord Denning was in a minority, both the other Lord Justices (Lawton and Ormrod) holding that the Attorney-General's exercise of his discretion to refuse his consent to the bringing of relator proceedings in his name could not be reviewed or questioned by the courts.

In the House of Lords Lord Wilberforce said:

> The distinction between public rights, which the Attorney can and the individual (absent special interest) cannot, seek to enforce, and private rights is fundamental in our law. To break it, as Mr Gouriet's counsel invited their Lordships to do, was not a development of the law, but a destruction of one of its pillars.

So Mr Gouriet could not bring his action, the Attorney-

General being the only person entitled to represent the public in a court of justice.

Judicial review

The growth of interventionism during the 1960s and 1970s was consolidated by a procedural change introduced in 1977 when the Supreme Court Rule Committee created a specific new remedy of judicial review. This brought together in a simplified form a number of remedies obtainable from a Divisional Court of the Queen's Bench Division consisting of two or three judges.[18] The grounds on which this remedy could be sought were summarized by Lord Diplock in the GCHQ case[19] under the three headings of illegality, irrationality and procedural impropriety. These cover the situations where a public authority is alleged to be acting outside its statutory powers, to be acting in a grossly unreasonable way, or to be abusing the rules of natural justice governing procedure. So review is not an appeal on the merits of a decision but limited to those grounds. Sometimes the distinction between a fair procedure and a fair decision is very narrow. Since 1977 a case law has been built up to define the limits of the availability of this remedy, which proved very popular.[20] In early days the judiciary greatly encouraged litigants to use it and the number of civil applications rose from 356 in 1981 to 1580 in 1989, the House of Lords having ruled in 1983 that those seeking redress for an infringement of public law rights must proceed by way of this remedy only.[21]

As a consequence of government policy, many of the challenges to the exercise of ministerial discretion in recent

18. There is a preliminary step as 'leave' to apply for judicial review must be first obtained from the High Court.

19. *In re the Council of Civil Service Unions* [1984] 3 All ER 935; see p. 155.

20. See M. Sunkin 'What is Happening to Applications for Judicial Review?' in 50 *Modern Law Review* 432 (1987).

21. *O'Reilly v. Mackman* [1983] 2 AC 237; but see *Wandsworth London Borough Council v. Winder* [1985] AC 461.

years have been instituted by Labour local authorities. These have been largely unsuccessful. In *ex parte Norwich City Council*,[22] the local authority were not proceeding with the sale of council houses as expeditiously as the minister wished. Under the Housing Act 1980 he was empowered to 'do all such things as appear to him necessary or expedient' to enable tenants 'to exercise the right to buy'. The minister decided to use his powers of intervention. He was upheld by the Court of Appeal. Given the statutory provisions, it is difficult to see how the court could have decided otherwise.

The introduction of the new block grant system for local authorities under the Local Government, Planning and Land Act 1980 resulted in one hiccough for the minister when the Divisional Court held that he had not listened to further representations when he should have done.[23] This decision is in line with those, like *Padfield*,[24] where the courts have been willing to limit ministerial discretion on various grounds, some of them relatively new, at least in their present application. Attempts in the Court of Appeal to set aside ministerial decisions on other aspects of the new block grant on more technical and precise grounds failed.[25] The lesson seems to be that a plaintiff has a better chance of attacking the exercise of ministerial power if he can show that in some general way, especially procedural and not substantive, the minister has not played the game according to the newly enlarged rules of natural justice.

Hackney LBC tried another line of attack which was repulsed when the Divisional Court held that there was no requirement for the Secretary of State, issuing guidance to a local authority as to the level of its expenditure, to have regard to whether or not the authority would by restricting

22. *R. v. Secretary of State for the Environment ex parte Norwich City Council* [1982] 2 WLR 580.
23. *R. v. Secretary of State for the Environment ex parte Brent LBC* [1982] 2 WLR 693.
24. See above, pp. 116–17.
25. *R. v. Secretary of State for the Environment ex parte Hackney LBC and Camden LBC* [1984] 1 All ER 956.

its expenditure in such a way render itself unable reasonably to discharge any of its statutory duties.[26]

The decision in *Lambeth LBC v. Secretary of State for Social Services*[27] where Woolf J struck down the minister's decision to use his statutory powers to suspend the members of an area health authority and to appoint commissioners in their place was strongly interventionist. The power of the minister arises under the National Health Service Act 1977 if he considers that by reason of an emergency it is necessary for a specified period to transfer functions from one body to another. The disagreement between the minister and the area health authority was caused by the overspending by the authority and its unwillingness to make economies. The court held that such a power could not be used, where there was no particular crisis and no specified power, so as to control the authority's financial affairs. The minister had a separate power, which he did not use, to issue directions to the authority. Woolf J referred to the *Tameside* decision[28] and to *ASLEF (No. 2)*.[29] 'There can be no question', he said, 'of my substituting my view of the facts for that of the Secretary of State.' He seems nevertheless to have come very close to substituting his view of the statutory power and the discretions within it for that of the minister.

Mr Louis Blom-Cooper QC appeared for the applicants in that case. He has told us that the minister relied on the legal advice from within the Department when he issued his directive to the area health authority and put in the commissioners. 'Long, and refreshingly frank, affidavits were addressed in evidence which revealed the faulty advice given to the minister. The drafters of the affidavits had forgotten the lesson that the mother whale gave to her off-

---

26. *R. v. Secretary of State for the Environment ex parte Hackney LBC*, *The Times*, 26 March 1984.

27. (1981) 79 LGR 61.

28. See pp. 120–1.

29. See pp. 119–20.

spring: "It is only when you begin to spout that you get harpooned!" '[30]

The Fares Fair litigation

The decision of the House of Lords in *R v. Greater London Council ex parte Bromley London Borough Council* (1981),[31] confirming that of the Court of Appeal, has been widely regarded as a political decision, no doubt because it gave a ruling in an acutely political controversy. Both the ruling itself and the judicial reasoning adopted by the Court of Appeal and the House of Lords exemplify what is meant by the politics of the judiciary. The case is of great importance and interest because it illuminates the weaknesses inherent in the role of the judiciary when required to adjudicate in such matters.

In July 1981, the GLC passed a resolution implementing a commitment in the election manifesto of the Labour Party to reduce fares charged by the London Transport Executive (LTE) by 25 per cent and to meet this cost (some £69m) issued a supplementary precept for rates of 6.1p in the £ to all London boroughs. In addition this policy resulted in the GLC losing some £50m of rate support grant from the government. Bromley London Borough Council applied to the High Court to quash the supplementary rate as *ultra vires*.

Under the Transport (London) Act 1969, the GLC was placed (by section 1) under the general duty to develop policies, and to encourage, organize and, where appropriate, to carry out measures, which would promote the provision of integrated, efficient and economic transport facilities and services for Greater London. The LTE consisted of persons appointed by the GLC with the function of implementing

---

30. 'Lawyers and Public Administration' in [1984] *Public Law*, pp. 225–6. The decision in this case was given on 25 February 1980. On 20 March 1980 the National Health Service (Invalid Direction) Act 1980 was enacted to reverse the decision.

31. [1983] 1 AC 768; also known as *Bromley v. GLC*.

the policies of the GLC (section 4). The GLC was empowered by the Act to make grants to the LTE for any purpose (section 3) and the GLC intended in this way to reimburse the LTE for the revenue lost by the fares reduction and so enable the LTE to balance its books, this being an obligation placed on the LTE 'so far as practicable'. Subject to that obligation, the LTE was under a duty to exercise and perform its functions, in accordance with principles laid down or approved by the GLC, in such manner as, and with due regard to efficiency, economy and safety of operation, to provide or secure the provision of such public passenger transport services as best met the needs for the time being of Greater London (section 5). If the LTE accounts showed a deficit, the GLC was required to take such action as appeared necessary and appropriate to enable the LTE to balance its books (section 7(6)). Additionally the GLC was empowered to give the LTE general directions, and the approval of the GLC was required for the general level and structure of fares to be charged by the LTE (section 11).

The Divisional Court of the Queen's Bench Division which first heard the action refused Bromley's application but the Court of Appeal and the House of Lords upheld it and quashed the precept and so the scheme.

The five Law Lords were Wilberforce, Diplock, Keith, Scarman, and Brandon. All agreed that the GLC's power to make grants to the LTE included a large degree of discretion to supplement revenue received by the LTE from fares, including anticipated or prospective revenue deficits. But they put limitations on this discretion. All except Lord Diplock founded their decision on the ground that the LTE was under a general duty to run its operations on ordinary business principles and that this had been breached by the reduction of fares without regard to those principles. All except Lord Diplock (and in this he positively disagreed) held that the GLC had to have regard, when making a grant, to the LTE's obligation to run its operations so far as practicable, on a break-even basis; so the GLC could make grants to the LTE only to make good unavoidable losses and not to further a particular social policy. All except Lord

Keith also held that the GLC was under a fiduciary duty to its ratepayers which they had breached by the scheme, Lord Diplock particularly emphasizing the loss of rate support grant, and that they had acted thriftlessly.

Much argument centred on the proper meanings to be attached to particular words such as 'economic' and on the recent history of transport legislation. But the concept of the fiduciary duty said to be owed by the GLC to its rate-payers was most widely emphasized by their Lordships. It is a judge-made concept and wholly imprecise. Lord Scarman, for example, rejected the GLC's interpretation of the 1969 Act on the ground that it 'would make mincemeat of the fiduciary duty owed to the ratepayers'. If Parliament had intended to depart from the break-even basis, he argued, this would have been enacted expressly in Part 1 of the Act where the general duties of the policy-maker, the GLC, were set; and added: 'But section 1(1) says nothing to suggest the exclusion of the fiduciary duty to the ratepayers.' The answer is, of course, that 'Parliament' never thought about the fidu-ciary duty at all. And this for the very good reason that the only relevant decision on the fiduciary duty – *Prescott v. Birmingham*[32] – had been immediately negatived by Parlia-ment[33] in its application to the power of local transport authorities to fix the level of fares.

The doctrine of the fiduciary duty, being judge-made, is capable of extended application as the courts please. In this case, the Law Lords chose to say that the GLC had not adequately taken into account the interests of the ratepayers and that the interests of the users of public transport had been unduly preferred.[34] Such an argument can logically be applied whenever public authorities spend the ratepayers' (or the taxpayers') money to further some statutory purpose. Particular public expenditure can always be criticized on the ground that it is excessive or wrongly directed, whether on

32. [1955] Ch. 210.
33. By Public Service Vehicles (Travel Concessions) Act 1955.
34. Cf. *Pickwell v. Camden LBC* [1983] 1 All ER 602 (see below, p. 315); *R. v. Greenwich BC ex parte Cedar Transport, The Times*, 3 August 1983.

defence or education or the building of motorways or any other public service. The constitutional reply is that public authorities, being directly or indirectly elected, are the representatives of the public interest and that their function is precisely that of making such decisions. The criticism is then seen as being political and if the electors of Greater London disapprove of what is done in their name by their representatives, the remedy lies in their hands at the next election. Nor is this merely constitutional or political theory, divorced from reality, for without doubt the election in 1985 for the GLC would have turned very largely on this issue and on the view taken of the controversial Labour administration at County Hall during its four years in office. It is surely no more the function of the judiciary to tell the GLC where the public interest lay in its spending of public money than it is the function of the judiciary to make similar judgments about spending by the Departments of the central government. The application of the doctrine of the fiduciary duty in this case was gross interference by the judiciary in the exercise of political responsibility of an elected local authority.

There remains, however, the much more substantial argument that the GLC had exceeded its statutory powers as laid down in the Transport (London) Act 1969.

We may take Lord Wilberforce's argument as typical of the Lords' approach. He emphasized sections 5 and 7 as 'critical'. Section 5 provided that, subject always to section 7(3), it was the general duty of the LTE to exercise and perform their functions with due regard to efficiency, economy and safety of operation. He said that those last three sets of words 'point rather more clearly than does section 1 in the direction of running on business-like or commercial lines'. And, he said, the word 'economy' prevented the LTE from conducting its undertakings on other than economic considerations. He called the initial words of section 5 important as drawing attention to the 'paramount' financing provisions of section 7(3).

This section 7(3) required the LTE so to perform their functions as to ensure so far as practicable that at the end of each accounting period the aggregate of the net balance of the consolidated revenue account of the LTE and of their general reserve was such as might be approved by the GLC; and that if, at the end of any accounting period, the aggregate showed a deficit, the amount properly available to meet changes to revenue account in the next following accounting period should exceed those charges by at least the amount of that deficit. In order words the LTE was to balance its books taking one year with the next. Further, under section 7(6), the GLC was required to have regard to section 7(3) and, where there was a deficit, the GLC was to take such action as appeared to the GLC necessary and appropriate to enable the LTE to comply with the requirements of section 7(3). As Lord Wilberforce said, the GLC might direct fares to be raised or services to be adjusted; or might make a grant to the LTE. Lord Wilberforce read this as meaning that the GLC could not exercise its powers 'unless and until' the LTE had carried out its duty. 'It appears to me clear', he said, 'that neither the LTE in making its proposals, nor the GLC in accepting them, could have power totally to disregard any responsibility for ensuring, so far as practicable, that outgoings are met by revenue, and that the LTE runs its business on economic lines.'

The alternative view is that 'revenue account' did not mean internally generated revenue only but included GLC grants. This is reinforced if the intention of Parliament in passing the Act was that deficits on internally generated revenue would most likely be incurred, not merely casually, but deliberately as a consequence of treating transport as a social service. This view argued that section 7 was meant as an accounting section only and contained only a prohibition against annual accumulation deficits. The GLC was meant to be the dominant authority (see section 1), with the LTE as its instrument, and the power of the GLC to make grants to the LTE 'for any purpose' was strong evidence of this.

Lord Wilberforce answered this alternative view in these words:

There is indeed, and has been for some years, discussion on the political level as to whether, and to what extent, public transport, particularly in capital cities, should be regarded, and financed, as a social service, out of taxation whether national or local. We cannot take any position in this argument; we must recognize that it exists. But I am unable to see, however carefully I re-read the 1969 Act, that Parliament had in that year taken any clear stance on it.

The other Law Lords (Lord Diplock excepted) also placed great reliance on section 7(3) and correspondingly less on sections 1 and 3.

Before we discuss this decision further, there is an aftermath to consider. The Law Lords' speeches in *Bromley* were delivered on 17 December 1981. Almost immediately commercial ratepayers on Merseyside sought to quash a similar scheme. Following the May 1981 elections, the new Labour majority on Merseyside County Council set about implementing its own manifesto which had promised no reduction in transport services but a reduction in fares. The precept required an additional supplementary rate of 6p in the £. The Merseyside authorities operated under the Transport Act 1968 which, though similar, was not the same in its provisions as the Transport (London) Act 1969. Thus the County Council as Transport Authority and its subordinate, the Transport Executive, had to have regard to the promotion of 'a properly integrated and efficient system of public transport to meet the needs of that area with due regard to the town planning and traffic and parking policies' of the other councils. Also the Transport Authority was expressly empowered to require the Executive to provide a service at a cost the Executive considered to be too high, so long as the Transport Authority provided the necessary additional cost. Woolf J also found that the Authority had properly considered the interest of the ratepayers and that the financial duties were not overriding. Further, there was no automatic loss of rate support grant as a result of introducing the scheme. On these and other grounds the judge distinguished *Bromley v. GLC.*

As a result of the decision in *Bromley v. GLC* the fares were doubled and Camden London Borough Council contemplated taking legal proceedings to challenge their validity. Legal advice from learned leading counsel on both sides was contradictory, and at one stage the Attorney-General advised the Minister of Transport that if the GLC should adopt a certain budgetary policy he thought the courts would accept it. He then made this advice public, thus instituting a free legal aid service of a novel kind.

The reality was that the decision in *Bromley v. GLC* was one which no one wished to be bound by. It seemed to suggest that the GLC and the LTE must try to break even, a course which was certainly feasible if fares were sufficiently increased and services sufficiently reduced, but which was politically as unacceptable to the government as it was anathema to the GLC.[35]

The GLC, bloody but unbowed, next produced a new scheme. This directed the LTE to reduce fares by 25 per cent and involved a grant to be made to the LTE to meet the resulting deficit on revenue account. The LTE objected to the direction on the ground that it failed to have regard to the LTE's financial duty under section 7(3) to break even so far as is practicable.[36]

Kerr LJ said that some of the public comments on *Bromley v. GLC* gave the misleading impression that the judgments in the Court of Appeal and the House of Lords were designed to thwart the wishes of the majority on the GLC for political motives. 'Such reactions,' he said, 'whether based on ignorance or whatever, can only be described as utter rubbish . . . It is to be hoped that nothing like that will happen again.'

All three judges in the Divisional Court (the others were Glidewell J and Nolan J) found the speeches of the Law Lords in *Bromley v. GLC* not easy to understand and impossible to reduce to agreed principles. As Mr George Cunningham MP said in the House of Commons on 22 December 1981, referring to those speeches:

> Each of the five judgments rambles over the territory in what can only be called a head-scratching way, making it

---

35. In order to enable the GLC to finance concessionary fares out of transport funds, the Travel Concessions (London) Act 1982 had to be passed very rapidly.

36. *R. v. LTE ex parte GLC* [1983] 1 QB 484.

impossible for the consumer of the judgment to know at the end just what the law is held to be, except negatively, and then only negatively on a few points. When one puts the five judgments together, the effect is chaos.[37]

The Divisional Court upheld the scheme adopted by the GLC but the ground on which they did so seemed to be no more than that 'since the LTE could exercise its function to balance its revenue account by a grant from the GLC, a policy that reduced fares by means of such a grant was not unlawful'. Those words are taken from the headnote in the Law Reports and seem a fair if wholly circular summary. To this was added the proviso that the GLC had not acted arbitrarily and had considered both its duties to the ratepayers and the statutory duties imposed by the 1969 Act on it and on the LTE.[38] This reinforces the view that what upset the Court of Appeal and the House of Lords in *Bromley v. GLC* was, above all, the way in which the Labour majority went about implementing their election promises rather than their statutory powers to do so. Local authorities would be well advised in future to preface all their decisions with the words: 'Having had regard to all relevant matters and having disregarded all irrelevant matters, and having considered the interests of all those likely to be affected, *resolved that*' etc.

When all this has been said, it is still very difficult to see how the Divisional Court in *R. v. LTE ex parte GLC* managed to come down in favour of the GLC in the face of the unanimous decision of the Law Lords. That decision was based primarily not on procedural defects but on interpretations of the words of the statute and on the notion of the fiduciary duty. The new scheme, upheld by the Divisional Court in the later case, was made under the same statute and did not appreciably hold a different balance between ratepayers and transport users. The decision of the Divisional Court bears the marks of a rescue operation, seeking to save some sanity for transport policy in London and for

37. 15 HC Deb. col. 905.
38. See now Transport Act 1983.

the right of statutory authorities to exercise statutory powers within the statutory terms given to them.

The later cases

An important limitation on the availability of judicial review arose when a senior nursing officer employed by a Health Authority was dismissed for misconduct. At the first hearing the judge held that the public was concerned to see that a great public service acted lawfully and fairly towards its officers and so judicial review was available. But the Court of Appeal, no doubt alarmed by the prospect of large numbers of public sector employees seeking similar review, held that such cases should be treated as ordinary master-and-servant situations governed by private law.[39] This principle was extended to civil servants who had the alternative remedy of taking their complaints to an industrial tribunal.[40] A similar reason was given for refusing the remedy to a convicted prisoner who brought an action against the Home Secretary and the prison governor requiring them to provide him with the necessary medical treatment in accordance with the Prison Rules.[41] But the remedy was made available by the House of Lords to a prisoner who alleged breaches of procedural rules by a deputy governor inquiring into disciplinary offences.[42]

Judicial policy-making was apparent in the decision of the House of Lords in *R. v. Secretary of State for the Environment ex parte Nottinghamshire County Council* in 1986.[43] This was an attempt by a local authority to object to the level of grant it was deemed to be entitled to from the central

39. *R. v. East Berkshire Health Authority ex parte Walsh* [1985] QB 152.

40. *R. v. Civil Service Appeal Board ex parte Bruce* [1988] ICR 649; but the Board may be required to give reasons, *R. v. Civil Service Appeal Board ex parte Cunningham*, *The Independent*, 30 May 1990.

41. *R. v. Secretary of State for the Home Office ex parte Dew* [1987] 1 WLR 881.

42. *Leech v. Deputy Governor of Parkhurst Prison* [1988] 2 WLR 290.

43. [1986] 2 WLR 1; and see *R. v. Inland Revenue Commissioners ex parte Preston* [1985] AC 835.

government. Their Lordships expressed the opinion that in the absence of some exceptional circumstance such as bad faith or improper motive on the part of the Minister it was inappropriate for courts to intervene on the ground of unreasonableness in a matter of public financial administration of this kind. Lord Templeman said that such matters were not for judges 'who are not qualified to listen' but for the Minister, for Members of Parliament, and ultimately for the electorate. The courts could intervene only if unfairness was such as to amount to an abuse of power. Such an 'abuse' was exemplified by the courts in *Wheeler v. Leicester City Council*[44] where the City Council (which had adopted an anti-apartheid policy) banned the Leicester Rugby club from using a Council recreation ground because three members of the club had joined an English touring side to South Africa. The majority of the Court of Appeal held that the council was entitled to have regard to the need to promote good race relations under the Race Relations Act 1976. But the House of Lords held that in the absence of any infringement of the law or any improper conduct by the club the banning was unreasonable and a breach of the council's duty to act fairly, hence a procedural impropriety and a misuse of statutory powers.

The Monopolies and Mergers Commission may, under the Fair Trading Act 1973, have referred to it by the Director of Fair Trading or a Minister for investigation and report whether a monopoly, as defined, is or is not against the public interest. On several occasions judicial review has been sought of the Commission's recommendations. In 1986, the Argyll group of companies and Guinness were rival bidders in attempts to take over Distillers Ltd. After bids and counter bids the Secretary of State referred the Guinness proposal to the Commission for inquiry and report. Then Guinness decided to divest itself of certain whisky brands to reduce its market share and the chairman of the Commission ruled that this meant its bid had been abandoned and that

---

44. [1985] 3 WLR 335; and see *R. v. Lewisham LBC ex parte Shell UK Ltd* [1988] 1 All ER 938; *R. v. Barnet LBC ex parte Johnson, The Independent*, 17 August 1990.

the reference should be set aside. Argyll applied unsuccessfully for judicial review based on a restrictive view of the Commission's substantive and procedural powers.[45] In another case, the objection was that the Commission had heard argument from one company which had not been put to the other company. This was also rejected on the ground that the Commission had wide and flexible discretion and was not obliged to put every piece of material to all interested parties.[46] Also rejected was an objection that the Commission had decided to disclose information given in confidence.[47]

Most famously, after the Al Fayed brothers had acquired the House of Fraser, which includes Harrods, the Secretary of State in April 1987 appointed inspectors under the Companies Act 1985 to investigate and report on alleged fraud and deceit in the takeover. In July 1988, the Minister sent a copy of the report to the Serious Fraud Office but decided against immediate publication, and, following advice from the Director of Fair Trading, did not refer the takeover to the Monopolies and Mergers Commission. Lonrho plc applied for judicial review for an order requiring the Minister to publish the report and to refer the takeover. Watkins LJ gave the principal judgment in the Divisional Court and upheld the application on the ground that the Minister had not given his reasons for the decision not to make a reference and that this was 'irrational'. But both the Court of Appeal and the House of Lords supported the Minister, Lord Keith saying that the judgments in the Divisional Court illustrated the danger of judges wrongly, though unconsciously, substituting their own views for the views of the decision-maker who alone was charged and authorized by Parliament to exercise a discretion.[48]

45. *R. v. Monopolies and Mergers Commission and Secretary of State for Trade & Industry ex parte Argyll Group* [1986] 2 All ER 257; and see G. Borrie, 'The Regulation of Public and Private Power' [1989] *Public Law* 552.

46. *R. v. M.M.C. ex parte Matthew Brown plc* [1987] 1 WLR 1235; also *R. v. M.M.C. ex parte Air Europe* [1988] 4 BCC 182.

47. *R. v. M.M.C. ex parte Elders IXL* [1987] 1 WLR 1221.

48. *Re Lonrho plc* [1989] 1 WLR 525.

These cases illustrate the importance which the Court of Appeal and the House of Lords attached to the need not to constrain the Commission and the Office of Fair Trading within narrow bounds and to emphasize the width of their discretionary powers. The decisions are in contrast to the attitude of the courts to the powers of the Commission for Racial Equality.

No doubt also the judges have been anxious further to limit the availability of judicial review given its tendency to 'overburden' the courts. But two other examples of the application of these restraints are more serious.

During the 1980s, the group providing most of the applications for judicial review were immigrants.[49]

During the years 1981–4, the number of applications for judicial review from immigrants[50] rose from 157 to 266 per annum. Between 1984 and 1985 the figure almost doubled from 266 to 516,[51] the latter figure representing 59 per cent of the total caseload. Among the reasons for these large numbers are that there is no right of appeal from the Immigration Appeal Tribunal to the courts; that from many decisions by immigration officers adverse to immigrants, an appeal can be made only from outside the United Kingdom; and that from some decisions (such as some exclusions deemed conducive to the public good by the Secretary of State) there are no rights of appeal at all. So judicial review, even on the limited grounds for which it is available, is the only way of having a rejection looked at again.

In February 1986, the Court of Appeal delivered judgment in *R. v. Secretary of State for the Home Department ex parte Swati*.[52] The applicant sought permission to enter the United Kingdom as a visitor for one week. The Immigration Officer refused, saying: 'I am not satisfied that you are genuinely seeking entry only for this limited period.' Leave to apply for judicial review was sought on the ground that this state-

49. See M. Sunkin op. cit. note 20 above.
50. Immigrants is here used to include all those seeking entry to the United Kingdom for any period of time.
51. See M. Sunkin op. cit. The number of applications excluding immigration cases fell from 529 in 1984 to 361 in 1985.
52. [1986] 1 All ER 717.

ment was not a sufficient reason, as required by the regulations, and was itself irrational. The court rejected these arguments but also ruled that those refused entry on the ground that they were not genuine visitors must normally use their statutory right of appeal (available only after they have left the United Kingdom) and not use judicial review. At the same time the Government was seeking to limit the opportunities for Members of Parliament to make representations to Ministers on behalf of those refused entry. This decision in *ex parte Swati* was almost certainly the reason for a sharp decline in the number of applications for judicial review from immigrants in 1986. The number fell from the high point of 516 in 1985 to 409 in 1986.

The decision in *Swati* was reinforced by the Court of Appeal in *Davendranath Doorga v. Secretary of State for the Home Department*.[53] The applicant was refused entry as a student although he had written evidence that the course fees had been paid, that his brother (resident in the UK) would maintain him, and that his employers in Mauritius had given him a year's leave for study. The court held that there was no evidence to suggest that the decision to exclude was unreasonable on *Wednesbury* grounds. Again, it is clear that the courts are taking a very restricted attitude to their powers of judicial review in these cases and are refusing to consider general questions of the fairness of decisions.

Another large group of applicants for judicial review are the homeless. Under the Housing (Homeless Persons) Act 1977,[54] local authorities in certain circumstances become bound to provide accommodation where applicants have a priority need and have not become homeless intentionally. In *Cocks v. Thanet DC*[55] the House of Lords made clear that those aggrieved by local authority decisions must proceed by way of judicial review and could not use procedures available in private law between landlord and tenant. This protected what Lord Bridge called the safeguards built into the judicial

---

53. [1990] IAT 98.
54. Now the Housing Act 1985.
55. [1982] 3 All ER 1135 following *O'Reilly v. Mackman* (above note 21).

review procedure which protected from 'harassment' public authorities on whom Parliament imposed a duty. He referred particularly to the need, under judicial review procedure, to obtain leave to apply on the basis of sworn evidence, on the court's discretionary control of both discovery of documents and cross-examination, on the capacity of the court to act with the utmost speed when necessary and on the court's avoiding the temptation to substitute its own decision of fact for that of the housing authority. As early as 1979, Lord Widgery CJ was emphasizing the limits of judicial intervention in this field.[56]

The Government issued a Code of Guidance which widened the definitions in the Act and was more wide-ranging, to the advantage of the homeless.[57] However Lord Denning was quick to point out that although local authorities had to have regard to the Code, they could depart from it if they thought fit.[58]

In many of the cases arising out of homelessness, local authorities have sought to interpret their statutory obligations narrowly. Especially in London, the dimensions of the social problems far exceeded the available resources both physical and financial. So the courts were called on to decide whether the authorities had correctly interpreted their duties. For example, in 1983 it was said that 'even where the husband had been violent, it would be reasonable for the wife to continue to reside in the matrimonial home but to seek a court order restraining his violence or barring him from the home' and in these circumstances the authority's duty would be 'to advise the applicant so to do, not to accommodate her as a homeless person'.[59] So also, where an impoverished family left their accommodation on receipt of a distress warrant for rent arrears rather than wait for an eviction order, they were held by the House of Lords to have become homeless intentionally and this encouraged

56. *R. v. Bristol City Council ex parte Browne* [1979] 1 WLR 1437.

57. See generally Lorraine Thompson, *An Act of Compromise* (1988).

58. *De Falco v. Crawley Borough Council* [1980] QB 460.

59. *R. v. Wandsworth London Borough Council ex parte Nimako-Boateng* [1983] 11 HLR 95; but see Housing Act 1985 s. 58(3) and *R. v. Broxbourne Borough Council ex parte Willmoth* [1989] 22 HLR 118.

local housing authorities to require such orders before accepting such homeless applicants.[60]

By the end of 1986 there had been 84 reported decisions on the 1977 Act in the High Court and 41 of these had gone in favour of the homeless. But there was to be a change.

In *Puhlhofer v. Hillingdon London Borough Council*[61] a married couple with two young children lived in one room at a guesthouse. No cooking or laundry facilities were provided and no meals except breakfast. They applied to the local authority for accommodation as homeless persons, but were rejected on the ground that they had accommodation. At first instance, the judge held that the accommodation had to be appropriate and that no reasonable authority could have come to that conclusion in this case. But the Court of Appeal and the House of Lords supported the local authority. Lord Brightman said that 'great restraint' should be exercised in giving leave to proceed by judicial review, and that he was troubled at 'the prolific use' of the procedure in these cases. He said:

> The plight of the homeless is a desperate one . . . and commands the deepest sympathy. But it is not, in my opinion, appropriate that the remedy of judicial review, which is a discretionary remedy, should be made use of to monitor the actions of local authorities under the Act save in the exceptional case . . . I express the hope that there will be a lessening in the number of challenges which are mounted against local authorities who are endeavouring, in extremely difficult circumstances, to perform their duties under the [Homeless Persons] Act with due regard for all their other housing problems.

In 1985 there were 66 applications for judicial review and the number was on the decline. Prior to *Puhlhofer*, failure

---

60. *Din v. London Borough of Wandsworth* [1983] 1 HLR 73; but this did not require former licensees to continue in occupation as trespassers pending a court order: *R. v. Surrey Heath Borough Council ex parte Li* [1984] 16 HLR 79.

61. [1986] 1 All ER 467.

to obtain leave to proceed by judicial review occurred in less than 10 per cent of the applications. But following *Puhlhofer* the number of applications halved to 32 in 1986 and the number refused leave rose from 6 in 1985 to 13 in 1986. As Maurice Sunkin says, the decision in *Puhlhofer* 'appears to have led to the introduction of a more stringent test than previously existed'.[62] But the warnings of Lord Brightman seem to have been made more to discourage even the modest number of applications than to respond to excessive use.

In 1986, it was provided that an applicant should not be treated as having accommodation unless it was such that it would be reasonable for him to continue to occupy it. In determining what was reasonable, regard might be had to the general housing circumstances prevailing in the local authority to whom the application was made.[63]

Where an applicant voluntarily left accommodation but had then acquired temporary accommodation, the courts interpreted the legislation so as to entitle the local authority to relate back to the first accommodation and so to find that he was intentionally homeless. And this was applicable where the first accommodation was in another country. So where Bangladeshis spent periods of time in the United Kingdom interspersed with periods in Bangladesh and then brought their families to the United Kingdom, took temporary accommodation, and then applied to be treated as a homeless person, it was held that the local authority was entitled to refuse them. In considering whether it was reasonable for an applicant to continue to occupy accommodation in another country the local authority might take into account the custom and lifestyle in that country. The fact that the authority disregarded certain factors (for example, the limited availability of welfare benefits or the poor prospects for employment) in that country could not ground an application for judicial review as they were not factors which the authority was obliged to take into account. Lloyd LJ referred to Lord Brightman's concern in *Puhlhofer* at the 'prolific use of judicial review' in these homelessness cases.

---

62. Op. cit., at 466.
63. Housing and Planning Act 1986 sect. 14.

Despite the legislative amendments in 1986, that observation, he said, was 'as pertinent now as it ever was'. The Court of Appeal supported this view, Lord Justice Purchas saying that it was 'clearly established' that the circumstances in which the court would intervene by judicial review were 'severely circumscribed', though remitting the cases to the local authority for them to state correctly their reasons for determining that it was reasonable to expect the applicants to continue to occupy their settled accommodation in Bangladesh.[64]

In a remarkable case, very much of our times, the applicants lived in Belfast and had been guilty of criminal and anti-social activities. Their neighbours sought the help of the IRA (which adopted a vigilante role in the area) who told the applicants that, unless they left Northern Ireland within 72 hours, they would all be killed. They came to Hammersmith in London and applied for accommodation as homeless persons. The court held that they were intentionally homeless and so disqualified.[65]

The complexities of these situations are shown by the case of an applicant and his family who left what was described as an 'overcrowded tin or galvanised structure with no basic amenities' in Bangladesh and who were treated as intentionally homeless by one London borough (who considered that it was reasonable for them to continue to occupy that accommodation) but not intentionally homeless by a second London borough who referred the applicant back to the first. Lord Justice Watkins criticised the legislation and doubted whether Parliament had intended it to apply to the housing of immigrants.[66]

It is a condition of an application for judicial review that

64. *R. v. Tower Hamlets LBC ex parte Monaf* [1987] 19 HLR 577 and [1988] 20 HLR 529; but the local authority must have a proper administrative system for considering applications: *R. v. Camden LBC ex parte Gillan* [1989] 21 HLR 114; and see *R. v. Kensington and Chelsea LBC ex parte Bayani* [1989] 21 HLR 580, *The Guardian*, 7 June 1990.

65. *R. v. London Borough of Hammersmith and Fulham ex parte P.* [1989] 22 HLR 21.

66. *R. v. London Borough of Newham ex parte London Borough of Tower Hamlets* [1990] 22 HLR 298; and see *The Guardian* 25 October 1990.

the applicant shall have 'a sufficient interest' in the matter.[67] What this means in practice is very complicated and the caselaw is not clear. Mrs Whitehouse as a television licence holder had such an interest when seeking a declaration that the Independent Broadcasting Authority had acted unlawfully over the screening of the film *Scum*.[68] The Child Poverty Action Group was allowed to challenge the Secretary of State for Social Services over delay in paying social security benefits.[69] Whether a body like the National Federation of Self-Employed and Small Businesses Ltd had a sufficient interest to allow them to challenge the Inland Revenue Commissioners when the IRC made a deal with certain non-payers of tax remains unclear.[70] But Lord Justice Woolf has written that, as a result of this case, usually it is not until the application has been heard on the merits that it can be decided whether the applicant has sufficient interest, and it is rare in cases which may otherwise be meritorious for leave to be refused on the ground of lack of standing.[71] In *Re Friends of the Earth* the applicants sought review of Minister's decision to consent to the construction of Sizewell B nuclear generating plant. It was held that they had a sufficient interest but the Court of Appeal said they had no arguable ground.[72] But in *R. v. Secretary of State for the Environment ex parte Rose Theatre Trust* when the Minister decided not to make an order protecting the site of an Elizabethan theatre, a company of interested individuals was denied the right to challenge this decision, even though this meant that no one was in a position to do so.[73] And when a ratepayer challenged a local authority's conduct of its

---

67. Supreme Court Act 1981 section 31(3).

68. *R. v. IBA ex parte Whitehouse*, *The Times*, 14 April 1984 (see below p. 242.).

69. *R. v. Secretary of State for Social Services ex parte Child Poverty Action Group* [1989] 1 All ER 1047.

70. *R. v. IRC ex parte National Federation of Self-Employed and Small Business Ltd* [1982] AC 617.

71. See 'Public Law – Private Law: Why the Divide? A Personal View' in [1986] *Public Law* at 231.

72. [1988] JPL 93.

73. [1990] 2 WLR 186.

policy to sell council houses and invoked his statutory right to complain to the District Auditor, he was debarred from at the same time pursuing the alternative remedy of applying to the courts for judicial review.[74]

Within the broad and imprecise terms of 'illegality, irrationality and procedural impropriety',[75] it is not easy to forecast what is the extent and what are the limits of judicial review. Where a rating authority had a statutory power, but no duty, to refund rates overpaid by mistake, the House of Lords granted judicial review and ordered repayment where the reasons given by the authority for its refusal to repay were held not to be valid.[76] Where the local ombudsman exceeded his jurisdiction when reporting on a complaint against a local authority the Court of Appeal granted a declaration to that effect.[77] In *R. v. Secretary of State for Education and Science ex parte Avon County Council*, the Minister approved an application from a school for grant-maintained status outside the jurisdiction of the local authority which contended that this rendered the re-organisation of their schools no longer viable. The court quashed the Minister's decision on the ground that he should have considered the school's application in the wider context and not only as it affected the particular school.[78] The judge ordered the Minister to reconsider his decision. He did so and re-affirmed it.

In subsequent proceedings the Court of Appeal held that in such circumstances the court could grant a stay of the Minister's decision.[79] A differently composed Court of Appeal rejected an appeal by the local authority on the substantive questions.[80] Lord Justice Nichols said:

74. *R. v. Westminster City Council ex parte Hilditch*, *The Guardian*, 21 June 1990.

75. See above, p. 125.

76. *R. v. Tower Hamlets LBC ex parte Chetnik Developments* [1988] 2 WLR 654.

77. *R. v. Local Commissioner of the Commission for Local Administration ex parte Eastleigh Borough Council*, [1988] 3 WLR 113.

78. *The Independent*, 15 March 1990.

79. *The Guardian*, 16 May 1990.

80. *The Independent*, 25 June 1990.

An application to the court for judicial review of the Minister's decision was not the appropriate means by which the council should seek to ventilate or pursue its differences of opinion with the Minister.

In *R. v. Inner London Education Authority ex parte Ali*[81] a parent failed to persuade the court that he should be awarded damages for the failure of the respondents to fulfil their statutory duty to provide sufficient schools. For a period of months, several hundred school children in the London Borough of Tower Hamlets – mostly Bangladeshi in origin – had been without places but the court held this did not mean that the respondents were in breach of their duty if they were taking steps to remedy the situation.

The complexity of the social security regulations and the attempts, during the 1980s, by Ministers to limit their applicability resulted in a series of judicial decisions. In 1985 regulations were held to be void as having no statutory authority where their purpose was to force able-bodied young people who lived on supplementary benefit to move from one area to another in search of employment.[82] But where thousands of claimants did not receive repayments to which they were entitled because of errors of local officials the Court of Appeal held that the Minister was not obliged to carry out a fullscale review of files.[83] Nor was he under a duty to appoint a sufficient number of adjudication officers to handle applications within a statutory period.[84]

The Social Security Act 1986, radically changed the law by requiring special or emergency needs, which had previously been dealt with at the discretion of local officers, to be met out of the Social Fund under directions and guidance from the Minister who allocated funds to local offices. The Minister purported to give guidance, the effect of which was, that social fund officers must not make payments which

81. *The Independent*, 15 February 1990.
82. *R. v. Secretary of State for Social Services ex parte Cotton*, *The Times*, 5 August 1985 and 14 December 1985.
83. *R. v. The Same ex parte Child Poverty Action Group*, *The Times*, 8 August 1985 (see last note).
84. See note 69 above.

would result in the budget being exceeded. The court held that the guidance was defective because it was couched in mandatory terms, and inconsistent with the intended flexible nature of the scheme. The court quashed decisions not to give furniture grants in two cases. But, in a third case, the court upheld a Ministerial direction that no money was to be paid out for domestic assistance and the Court of Appeal confirmed this decision.[85]

But where Ministerial powers are drawn more broadly, the courts are much more reluctant to intervene. A group of consultants at Guy's Hospital were unsuccessful in seeking to prevent the Minister from spending money in anticipation of the legislation which would enable hospitals to apply for self-governing status.[86] So were a group of medical general practitioners who claimed that changes in their contracts would seriously damage the health of patients.[87]

When local expenditure was greatly curtailed by Government restrictions on the raising of revenue (rate-capping) many authorities sought ways of raising money by other means. The London Borough of Hammersmith and Fulham entered into a series of transactions with various banks which resulted in considerable losses when interest rates rose. The Court of Appeal held that those transactions were valid so far as they were entered into for the purposes of interest rate risk management and not for trading purposes.[88]

The London Borough of Greenwich sought judicial review of a Government leaflet distributed to every household in England which was explanatory of the community charge or poll tax. The borough argued that the leaflet was misleading because it omitted all reference to the joint liability of spouses and cohabiting couples. The court held that in the

85. *R. v. Social Security Fund Inspector ex parte Sherwin, Stitt and Roberts, The Times*, 23 February 1990; *R. v. Secretary of State for Social Services ex parte Stitt, The Independent*, 6 July 1990.

86. *R. v. Secretary of State for Health ex parte Keen, The Times*, 22 February 1990.

87. See *The Independent*, 14 March 1990.

88. *Hazell v. Hammersmith and Fulham LBC* [1990] 2 WLR 1038; but see decision of the House of Lords, declaring invalid all the transactions, *The Independent*, 25 January 1991.

absence of bad faith (for example, an intention to deceive) the court should not intervene unless the leaflet misstated the law or was manifestly inaccurate or misleading.[89]

The Local Government Finance Act 1988 imposed a duty on local authorities to calculate how much they needed to raise by way of the poll tax. The Act empowered the Secretary of State to put a limit on the amount if in his opinion the amount proposed to be raised was 'excessive' according to principles he determined which were to be the same for all authorities falling within the same class. In June 1990, the Minister proposed to 'cap' nineteen Labour authorities in this way. They argued that the principles he adopted had been politically motivated and should have had regard to the spending needs of each authority. The House of Lords rejected this and held that the Minister was entitled to decide what was meant by 'excessive' and what principles to apply.[90]

One of the more striking interventions by the courts in recent years came when the Court of Appeal overturned the decision by the Secretary of State for the Environment to allow the demolition of listed buildings in the City of London. The Mappin and Webb building adjoins the Mansion House and the Bank of England. Proposals were put forward by the owners during the 1980s for the development of the site and were opposed by Save Britain's Heritage. The published policy of the Secretary of State was that he would not grant consent for the total or substantial demolition of a listed building unless he was satisfied that every effort had been made to continue the present use or find an alternative use. After an inquiry, the Minister granted planning permission and listed building consent for the demolition of the building. The Court of Appeal held that this decision should be quashed because the Minister had not adequately explained his reasons, particularly in failing

89. *R. v. Secretary of State for the Environment ex parte Greenwich LBC*, *The Times*, 17 May 1989.
90. *R. v. Secretary of State for the Environment ex parte Hammersmith and Fulham LBC and others*, *The Independent*, 5 October 1990; but in September 1990 the Court of Appeal held that Lambeth LBC had acted properly in fixing a poll tax in excess of Government limits after taking into account the increased number of non-taxpayers.

to give his assessment of the merits of the existing building.[91] In July 1990, the House of Lords held that a byelaw prohibiting entry to the Greenham Common military bars was invalid because it infringed rights of common.[92]

On the other hand, when the Greater London Council was abolished in 1986, County Hall on the south bank of the Thames became vested in the London Residuary Body which applied for planning permission to use the main block for mixed hotel, residential and general office purposes unconnected with any local government functions. After an inquiry, the Secretary of State disagreed with his inspector and decided that these general office purposes should be permitted. The Court of Appeal held that this decision should be quashed because the Minister had not applied the correct test of competing needs, in this case between those of local government and those of other office users. But the Law Lords unanimously decided that he was obliged to have regard only to 'material considerations' and that the amount of weight to be given to these was a matter for his judgment.[93]

91. *Save Britain's Heritage v. Secretary of State for the Environment, The Times*, 4 April 1990. But the House of Lords later overruled the Court of Appeal and reinstated the Minister's decision, *The Independent*, 1 March 1991.

92. *D.P.P. v. Hutchinson and Smith* [1990] 3 WLR 196.

93. *London Residuary Body v. Lambeth LBC* [1990] 2 All ER 309.

5. Personal rights

Individual freedom

Traditionally, judges are thought of as the defenders of the rights of individuals from attack by public authorities. In recent years this tradition has been upheld only spasmodically.

In 1939 the government took powers by Defence Regulations to detain persons without trial but these powers were expressed in those regulations to be exercisable only 'if the Secretary of State has reasonable cause to believe' that a person had hostile associations. The use of the limiting adjective, one would have thought, clearly empowered the courts to review the reasonableness of the 'cause'. But the House of Lords in *Liversidge v Anderson*[1] held otherwise. This was a considerable abdication by the courts, in circumstances of national emergency, of their controlling jurisdiction.

Yet this decision was also a rallying ground for those who believed that, especially where a man's personal freedom was involved, the powers of the executive should be strictly interpreted. For this was the case in which Lord Atkin, alone against such powerful colleagues as Lords Maugham, MacMillan, Wright and Romer, delivered the most highly influential minority opinion in the English courts of the twentieth century. In the course of his judgment he said:

> I view with apprehension the attitude of judges who on a mere question of construction when face to face with claims involving the liberty of the subject show them-

---

1. [1942] AC 206. See also *Greene v. The Secretary of State for Home Affairs* [1942] AC 284.

selves more executive minded than the executive. Their function is to give words their natural meaning, not, perhaps, in wartime leaning towards liberty, but following the dictum of Pollock CB in *Bowditch v. Balchin*[2] cited with approval by my noble and learned friend Lord Wright in *Barnard v. Gorman*:[3] 'In a case in which the liberty of the subject is concerned, we cannot go beyond the natural construction of the statute.' In this country, amid the clash of arms, the laws are not silent. They may be changed, but they speak the same language in war as in peace. It has always been one of the pillars of freedom, one of the principles of liberty for which on recent authority we are now fighting, that the judges are no respectors of persons and stand between the subject and any attempted encroachments on his liberty by the executive, alert to see that any coercive action is justified in law. In this case I have listened to arguments which might have been addressed acceptably to the Court of King's Bench in the time of Charles I.

Liversidge v. Anderson was a wartime case and the powers of detention without trial (internment) were conferred on the executive under an express statutory provision which authorized the making of regulations 'for the detention of persons whose detention appears to the Secretary of State to be expedient in the interests of public safety or the defence of the realm'.[4] The comparable legislation passed for the purposes of the 1914–18 war contained no express powers authorizing internment but in *R. v. Halliday*[5] the majority in the House of Lords held that general words in the Defence of the Realm Act 1914 were sufficient, a view from which Lord Shaw dissented. In contrast, it was later held by Mr Justice Salter that a similar exercise of powers, this time to take property without payment of full compen-

2. (1850) 5 Ex. 378.
3. [1941] AC 378, 393.
4. Emergency Powers (Defence) Act 1939, section 1(2)(a). See R. J. Sharpe, *The Law of Habeas Corpus* (1976), especially pp. 89–124.
5. [1917] AC 260.

sation, was illegal.[6] Here, as elsewhere, the courts seemed to be more concerned to protect property rights than rights of personal freedom. In *R. v. Governor of Wormwood Scrubs Prison*[7] it was held by the Divisional Court that the internment powers extended to cover the situation in Ireland even after the war was over.

The decision of the majority in *Liversidge v. Anderson* effectively meant that the minister's order authorizing internment could not be questioned because the minister could not be required to show on what basis his order had been made. The general principle that this is the proper interpretation of the words 'If the minister has reasonable cause to believe' has been doubted[8] and two recent decisions in Northern Ireland courts have suggested that improper arrest or a failure to provide the internee with a statement of the material on which the internment was based is sufficient for the internment order to be set aside.[9]

However the majority decisions in *R. v. Halliday* and *Liversidge v. Anderson* were referred to with approval by Lord Denning in *R. v. Secretary of State for Home Affairs ex parte Hosenball*[10] in 1977 where an American journalist lost his appeal against deportation under the Immigration Act 1971. The decision to deport was challenged in the Court of Appeal on the ground that there had been a breach of the rules of natural justice in that the Home Secretary had refused to tell the appellant any of the details on the basis of which the Home Secretary had decided that the appellant was a security risk.

In a remarkable passage Lord Denning MR seemed to accept that the courts had no part to play because the government never erred. He said:

There is a conflict between the interests of national security on the one hand and the freedom of the indi-

6. *National Breweries v. The King* [1920] 1 KB 854.

7. [1920] 2 KB 305.

8. E.g., in *Nakkuda Ali v. Jayaratne* [1951] AC 66 and *Ridge v. Baldwin* [1964] AC 40.

9. *Re McElduff* [1971] 23 NILQ 112; *Re Mackay* [1972] 23 NILQ 113.

10. [1977] 1 WLR 166.

vidual on the other. The balance between these two is not for a court of law. It is for the Home Secretary. He is the person entrusted by Parliament with the task. In some parts of the world national security has on occasion been used as an excuse for all sorts of infringements of individual liberty. But not in England. Both during the wars and after them successive ministers have discharged their duties to the complete satisfaction of the people at large. They have set up advisory committees to help them, usually with a chairman who has done everything he can to ensure that justice is done. They have never interfered with the liberty or the freedom of movement of any individual except where it is absolutely necessary for the safety of the state.

It is well known that unlawful detention may be challenged by means of an application for habeas corpus but the courts sometimes withhold that remedy for political reasons.

Dr Sharpe summarizes his extensive examination of the authorities on habeas corpus and other remedies thus:

This review of the authorities demonstrates that habeas corpus can be an effective remedy to control the exercise of the discretionary power, but that policy considerations may often make the courts reluctant to act. There are several habeas corpus cases which illustrate the ordinary rule of the reviewability of executive action and, most recently, the law of immigration has provided examples. On the other hand it is submitted that the cases which involve emergency powers indicate a reluctance on the part of the courts to use the remedy of habeas corpus to its full potential. Judicial innovation would not have been required to justify intervention in *Halliday* or in *Greene* and *Liversidge v. Anderson*. In each case, accepted principles of constitutional and administrative law were available and applicable. In *Halliday*, and almost certainly in *Greene* and in *Liversidge v Anderson*, the legal arguments weighed against the result reached, and the judges acted on policy grounds.[11]

When it is remembered that habeas corpus is not a discretionary remedy, this amounts to saying that the judiciary, despite all the rhetoric which they pour out in praise of this ancient writ, are willing to deny it to an imprisoned applicant, who in law should be set free, because they consider that the politics of the situation entitle them to do so. This is not what is generally understood to be the function of the courts.

The great weight attached by the courts to claims of national security was shown in the unanimous decision of the House of Lords in *In re the Council of Civil Service Unions* (1984).[12] This was the GCHQ (Government Communications Headquarters) case where the Government, without consulting the unions, introduced with immediate effect new conditions for civil servants at GCHQ the result of which was that they were no longer permitted to belong to national trade unions. The Law Lords held that normally the unions had a legitimate expectation that there would be prior consultations before such a change was made but that the requirements of national security overrode this. The argument first advanced by the Crown before Glidewell J was that previous disruptions caused by trade union activity made the change necessary, although there had been no such disruption during the twenty months preceding the change. The judge ruled in favour of the unions. Before the Court of Appeal, however, the Crown claimed that there had been no consultation because to have consulted would have made disruption more likely. The Law Lords were willing to accept that the Crown had to show there was some evidence to support the claim that the interests of national security must prevail. But it was apparent that they were willing also to accept very slight, even contradictory, evi-

11. R. J. Sharpe, *op. cit.*, pp. 123–4.
12. [1984] 3 All ER 935; compare *Secretary of State for Defence v. Guardian Newspapers Ltd* [1984] 3 WLR 986, see below, p. 278; *R. v. Secretary of State for Transport ex parte Greater London Council* [1985] 3 WLR 574.

dence for this purpose. In 1987, the Divisional Court decided that it was not competent to set aside the Secretary of State's exclusion order made under the Prevention of Terrorism (Temporary Provisions) Act 1976, where he had refused to give his reasons for not revoking the order.[13]

The right to a jury selected at random has been under recent judicial scrutiny. In *R. v. Crown Court at Sheffield ex parte Brownlow*[14] two police officers were charged and committed for trial on counts of assault occasioning bodily harm. On an application by the prosecution, the Crown Court judge ordered that a copy of the panel from which the jury for the hearing would be drawn be supplied to the chief constable and that he supply the accused's solicitors and the prosecution with full details of criminal convictions recorded against any member of the panel. This might have included offences which would not normally disqualify a juror from service. In the Court of Appeal, Lord Denning MR strongly condemned this practice of jury vetting and called it 'unconstitutional'. Shaw LJ echoed this opinion. The majority of the Court of Appeal held, however, that they had no jurisdiction to revoke the judge's order and when the chief constable applied to the judge for revocation, the judge declined to do so but amended his order only so as to exclude spent convictions.

Three months later, in *R. v. Mason*,[15] a differently composed Court of Appeal expressed very different views. Lawton LJ said that if, when a panel was scrutinized, convictions were revealed which did not amount to disqualifications, 'there was no reason why information about such convictions should not be passed to prosecuting counsel' (but not to the defence), who could then ensure that that juror would not be selected to hear the case. 'The practice of the past was founded on common sense. Any juror might be qualified to sit on juries generally but might not be suitable to try a particular case.'

13. *R. v. Secretary of State for the Home Department ex parte Stitt, The Independent*, 3 February 1987.
14. [1980] 2 All ER 444.
15. *The Times*, 4 June 1980.

The abolition of the right of peremptory challenge has made more difficult the selection of multi-racial juries. And the Lord Chief Justice has ruled that judges have no power to interfere with selection to that end.[16]

Police powers

The earlier cases

Police powers and their exercise frequently result in the judiciary drawing and redrawing the lines of what they consider to be permissible and impermissible conduct. In a leading case from the 1930s, a public meeting was held to protest against the Incitement to Disaffection Bill then before Parliament and to demand the dismissal of the chief constable of Glamorgan. Between 500 and 700 people were present. James Sawkins, a sergeant of the Glamorgan County Police, sought admission to the meeting, was told at the door that police officers were not to be admitted, but nevertheless (with other policemen) entered and sat in the front row. At one point Alun Thomas 'laid a hand' on one of the policemen (an inspector) and Sergeant Sawkins pushed his hand away saying: 'I won't allow you to interfere with my superior officer.' Neither Alun Thomas nor Sergeant Sawkins used more force than was reasonably necessary to effect their purposes. Alun Thomas charged Sergeant Sawkins with unlawful assault. The Divisional Court held that a police officer was entitled, as part of his duty of preventing crime, to enter private premises when he had reasonable ground for believing that an offence was imminent or likely to be committed and that Sergeant Sawkins was properly acquitted.[17]

At the end of May 1933, Katherine Duncan of the National Unemployed Workers' Movement addressed a street meeting following which 'a disturbance took place'. On 30 July 1934 she began to address a meeting at the same place, although told by a police inspector that she could not,

16. *R. v. Ford* [1989] 3 All ER 445.
17. *Thomas v. Sawkins* [1935] 2 KB 249.

whereupon she was arrested and taken into custody. It was not alleged that she or any of the persons present at the meeting had either committed, incited or provoked any breach of the peace. The Divisional Court held that she had been properly convicted of wilfully obstructing the police who 'reasonably apprehended a breach of the peace'.[18]

The difficulty and danger of such decisions is that so much discretion resides in the police and neither the courts nor the legislature are willing to lay down any guidelines. This gives rise to suspicion that the police will prosecute one person advocating one set of views while not prosecuting another advocating a different set of views. Certainly this was the impression conveyed when Pat Arrowsmith was convicted of obstructing the highway when addressing a meeting at a place where such meetings were frequently held and where previously no prosecutions had followed. 'That,' said the Lord Chief Justice, speaking without apparent irony, 'of course, has nothing to do with this court. The sole question here is whether the defendant had contravened section 121(1) of the Highways Act 1959.'[19]

The House of Lords has recently approved police conduct which looks like a dangerous modification of such principles. The plaintiff was arrested by a detective constable on suspicion of theft and taken to a police station where she was questioned. She was not charged and she brought an action for wrongful arrest. The judge found that the detective had decided not to interview her under caution but to subject her to the greater pressure of arrest and detention so as to induce a confession. He awarded her £1000 damages. The House of Lords overruled this decision and held that the interrogation of a suspect in order to dispel or confirm a reasonable suspicion was a legitimate cause for arrest so that the fact that the detective, when exercising his discretion to arrest the plaintiff, took into consideration that she might be more likely to confess if arrested did not render the exercise of the discretion unlawful. In practice that may

18. *Duncan v. Jones [1936]* 1 KB 218.
19. *Arrowsmith v. Jenkins [1963]* 2 QB 561.

often be indistinguishable from legalizing an arrest for the purpose of questioning.[20]

Elias v. Pasmore[21] is a leading case on search and seizure. The plaintiffs were the lessees of the headquarters of the National Unemployed Workers' Movement. Walter Hannington (one of the plaintiffs) made a speech in Trafalgar Square in consequence of which a warrant for his arrest was issued. The defendant police inspectors entered the headquarters, arrested Hannington, and seized a number of documents, some of which were used at the trial of the plaintiff Elias on a charge of inciting Hannington to commit the crime of sedition. The plaintiffs claimed the return of those documents, and the question was whether their seizure was lawful, since they had no relevance to the charge against Hannington and no search warrant had or would have been obtained. The court decided that, though the original seizure of the documents was 'improper', it was 'justified' because they were capable of being used, and were used, as evidence in the trial of Elias.

In 1969 police officers enquiring into the disappearance of a woman they believed to have been murdered, searched (without a warrant) the house of her father-in-law. At their request he handed them the passports of himself, his wife and daughter. Subsequently these persons, being Pakistanis and wishing to visit Pakistan, asked for the return of the passports but the police refused. The court ordered their return but in the course of his judgment Lord Denning, summarizing the law where police officers enter a man's home without a warrant, said:

> I take it to be settled law . . . that the officers are entitled to take any goods which they find in his possession or in his house which they reasonably believe to be material evidence in relation to the crime . . . for which they enter. If in the course of their search they come upon any other goods which show him to be implicated in some other crime they may take them provided

20. *Mohammed-Holgate v. Duke* [1984] 2 WLR 666.
21. [1934] 2 KB 164.

they act reasonably and detain them no longer than is necessary.[22]

Two years later in another case, police officers, armed with a warrant authorizing them to enter premises to search for explosives, found none but seized a large number of leaflets and posters, contending that these were evidence of a crime such as conspiracy to pervert the course of justice or to commit contempt of court. The police claimed further that they needed to retain the documents for comparison with other documents purporting to emanate from a criminal organization responsible for causing explosions. The court held that the police were entitled to seize the documents and that they had established they were acting reasonably and were detaining the documents no longer than necessary.[23]

In 1977, the defendant was arrested by officers of the drug squad for stealing a sandwich from a public house. They then searched his lodgings where they found cannabis, and he was charged with possession of the drug. The court held that the entry and search were unlawful but nevertheless that the evidence was admissible.[24] In another case it was confirmed that, save with regard to admissions and confessions and generally to evidence obtained from the accused after the commission of the offence, judges have no discretion to refuse to admit relevant admissible evidence on the ground that it was obtained by improper or unfair means, for example, through the activities of an *agent provocateur*.[25]

The policy choices which are presented to the judiciary were shown clearly in *R. v. Inland Revenue Commissioners ex parte Rossminster Ltd* (1980).[26] One morning at 7 am, at different places, revenue officers armed with search warrants

22. *Ghani v. Jones* [1970] 1 QB 693. Cp. *Frank Truman Export v. Commissioner of Police for the Metropolis* [1977] 3 All ER 431.
23. *Garfinkel v. Metropolitan Police Commissioner*, The Times, 4 September 1971.
24. *Jeffrey v. Black* [1977] 3 WLR 895.
25. *R. v. Sang* [1979] 3 WLR 263. Cp. *Morris v. Beardmore* [1980] 2 All ER 753.
26. [1980] AC 952.

signed, as the empowering statute required, by a Circuit judge, entered offices and private houses and took away masses of documents. The statute was the Taxes Management Act 1970 which provided that if the Circuit judge was satisfied on information on oath given by an officer of the Inland Revenue that there was reasonable ground for suspecting that an offence involving any form of fraud in connection with, or in relation to, tax had been committed and that evidence of it was to be found on premises specified in the information, the judge might issue a search warrant. The statute further provided that a revenue officer might seize and remove any things whatsoever found there which he had reasonable cause to believe might be required as evidence for the purpose of proceedings in respect of an offence referred to above.

These are very wide powers indeed and the Court of Appeal unanimously held that the warrants were defective in that they did not particularize the specific offences. The court also held that the officers could not have had reasonable cause to believe that all the documents might be required as evidence because documents were removed without being examined.

Lord Scarman described the statutory provisions as a 'breathtaking inroad upon the individual's right of privacy and right of property'. But he was part of the majority of the members of the House of Lords who allowed the appeal by the Inland Revenue on the ground that the warrant was strictly and exactly within the authority of the statute. Lord Salmon dissented because the warrant did not recite the essential fact that the Circuit judge had satisfied himself that there were reasonable grounds for suspecting that a tax fraud had been committed.[27]

Tax frauds are unpopular offences amongst those who have not the means (in both senses) for their committal. And it is in the nature of such frauds that drastic and comprehensive action needs to be taken before allegedly incriminating documents are destroyed. It was probably the intention of Parliament that the powers given should be used as they

27. [1980] 2 WLR 1.

were in this case. But also the facts in this case were such that the courts could, without perversity, decide either way. As it was, the eight judges in the Court of Appeal and House of Lords split evenly, with those favouring possible tax fraud detection being more strategically placed than those favouring personal rights of privacy and property.

The general trend of these cases is alarming. It comes very close to giving the police a right to search and to seize documents which have nothing to do either with the warrant (if they have one) or with the original purpose of their investigations. It is an old tradition that general warrants to arrest unspecified persons and to search property at large are illegal and are not justifiable on the ground of the public interest. The tradition is beginning to look less strong than it did. The danger of placing so sharp a weapon in the hands of the government and of the police is very obvious.

Telephone tapping by the police and the security services has been much debated in recent years. In *Malone v. Commissioner of Police for the Metropolis (No. 2)* the courts were given an opportunity, which they did not take, to lay down some principles to govern the activity which has no statutory or other legal authority. Vice-Chancellor Megarry held that there was in English law neither a general right of privacy nor a particular right in relation to telephone communication. The practice has been that all such interceptions are made only on the express warrant of the Home Secretary though how general a warrant may be, how many separate interceptions a warrant may authorize, over how long a period, has never been made clear. The European Convention for the Protection of Human Rights was cited to the court which observed only that it was not part of English law. The Vice-Chancellor rested his refusal to intervene judicially on the general proposition that: 'If the tapping of telephones by the Post Office at the request of the police can be carried out without any breach of the law, it does not require any statutory or common law power to justify it: it can be lawfully done simply because there is nothing to make it unlawful.' But he added: 'Telephone tapping is a subject which cries out for legislation.'[28]

John Cox was a member both of the Campaign for Nuclear Disarmament and of the Communist Party of Great Britain. In 1983, Cathy Massiter, then a member of MI5, was authorized by a warrant of the Home Secretary to tap Mr Cox's telephone on a regular basis. When she later revealed this, during a television programme, he and two other members of the CND (Joan Ruddock and Bruce Kent) sought judicial review of the decision to issue the warrant on the ground that it did not accord with the published criteria for warrants. Counsel for the Home Secretary argued that as it was never admitted, for security reasons, whether or not a particular warrant had been issued, the court should decline jurisdiction and not allow the action to proceed. However, Taylor J would not go so far in the absence of any evidence that to proceed would damage national security. But he found there was no evidence that the Home Secretary had flouted the published criteria, nor any bad faith, nor any grossly unreasonable conduct on the part of the Home Secretary.[29]

The Police and Criminal Evidence Act 1984

The exercise by the police of their powers of arrest, search and seizure, interrogation and charge may be challenged in the courts and so faces the judges with a constantly recurring dilemma posed by the difficulty of their being, at one and the same time, the protectors of personal rights and pre- servers of law and order. Until recently the courts have consistently, though not in every case, lent their support to the police rather than to the individual. Especially in the numerous minor situations where police and public clash, on marches, demonstrations and protests, police evidence has been preferred and the charges of obstruction of the highway or of the police, or of assault on the police, or of

28. [1979] All ER 620.
29. *R. v. Secretary of State for the Home Department ex parte Ruddock* [1987] 2 All ER 518; see now the Interception of Communications Act 1985. In April 1990, surveillance of two prominent members of the National Council for Civil Liberties by MI5 was declared to be a breach of the European Convention on Human Rights.

other more serious offences, upheld. Also on more important occasions, allegations that the police have fabricated evidence or concealed evidence helpful to the defence have not been believed.

In the last few years the attitude of the judges and of juries has changed. So many cases have been disclosed of police misconduct, even corruption, that the reputation of the police for objectivity and fairness has greatly declined. Following the report of a royal commission which reported in 1981,[30] the Police and Criminal Evidence Act 1984 was passed and came into effect on 1 January 1986. This Act, known as PACE, tried to strike a balance between police powers and individual rights. Its provisions and those in the accompanying Codes of Practice made more clear, in particular, many aspects of the relationship between police and suspect in the police station, including the individual's rights of access to lawyers and to family. The Act also sought to clarify important questions relating to the admissibility of evidence in court proceedings. While the police have obtained wider statutory powers, they have also been placed under stricter statutory procedures. What follows concerns a few of the areas where the courts have been required to respond during the first four years or so of the Act's operation.[31]

R. v. Samuel[32] was an important case. The appellant was arrested on suspicion of robbery and burglary. He asked to see his solicitor but this was refused. Section 58 of the Act provides that such refusal can be justified if based on the reasonable belief that the exercise of this right '*will* lead to interference with or harm to evidence' or '*will* lead to the alerting of other persons suspected' or '*will* hinder the recovery of any property obtained as a result of such offence'. After further questioning the appellant confessed to the burglaries and was charged. But he was still denied access

30. Report of the Royal Commission on Criminal Procedure (Cmnd 8092).

31. See *Northern Ireland Legal Quarterly*, vol. 40, no. 4 (1989); and *Criminal Law Review* of July 1990.

32. [1988] 2 All ER 135.

to legal advice. Later he confessed to the robbery, was charged, and then allowed to see his solicitor. The Court of Appeal held that the refusal of access was unjustified and stressed that the use of the word 'will' (which I have emphasised above) must be taken to be deliberately restrictive, thus making it difficult for the police to establish the belief necessary to justify refusal. The conviction was quashed.

This principle was accepted by the Court of Appeal in *R. v. Alladice*[33] but, although there had been a breach of section 58 procedures, the conviction was upheld because there was no suggestion that the confession might have been obtained as a result of the refusal of access to a solicitor and no reason to believe that that fact was likely in all the circumstances to render the confession unreliable. So the confession was admissible. Similarly in *R. v Dunford*, evidence was admitted, despite a breach, when the accused had previous experience of arrest and detention and a solicitor's advice would have added nothing to his knowledge of his rights.[34] In *R. v. Parris*[35] it was said that, although a breach in the required procedures did not necessarily mean that any subsequent statement by a defendant should be excluded, in this case the trial judge had erroneously concluded there was no breach and so never directed his mind to the adverse effect the admission of evidence might have had, consequent on the refusal to allow access to a solicitor.[36]

Another group of cases concerns the conduct of police 'interviews'. In *R. v. Absolam*[37] the appellant, who was on bail for possession of cannabis, was arrested for a different

33. (1988) 87 Cr.App.R. 380.

34. *The Guardian*, 24 May 1990 (Court of Appeal).

35. [1989] 89 Cr.App.R. 68; compare *R. v. Quayson* [1989] Crim.LR 218.

36. For other cases where refusal of access to legal advice led to statements being ruled inadmissible, see *R. v. Paul Deacon* [1987] Crim.LR 404, *R. v. Vernon* [1988] Crim.LR 445, *R. v. Davison* [1988] Crim.LR 442; contrast *R. v. Hughes* [1988] Crim.LR 519 where the accused agreed to be interviewed in the absence of a solicitor having been wrongly informed that no duty solicitor was available. The conviction was upheld.

37. [1989] 88 Cr.App.R. 332; see also *R. v. Kingsley Brown* [1989] Crim.LR 500; and contrast *R. v. Parchment* [1989] Crim.LR 290; *R. v. Sparks*, *The Guardian*, 13 September 1990.

offence and taken to the police station where he was required to report. When the appellant had emptied his pockets, the custody officer asked him to produce any drugs in his possession whereupon he handed over some cannabis which he admitted he was selling. The court decided that these events constituted an interview and that the appellant had been wrongly questioned before being informed of his right to legal advice. His appeal against conviction of supplying cannabis was allowed and a conviction for simple possession was substituted. However, in *R. v. Maguire*,[38] where a juvenile was questioned in a police car following his arrest for attempted burglary and gave incriminating replies, the Court of Appeal decided this was not an interview and so the absence of an appropriate adult (as required by the Code) was not a breach and the statements were admissible. This was an unfortunate decision, especially as there have been allegations that police sometimes deliberately interrogate outside the police station where they can more easily avoid being bound by the rules governing interviews.

The effect of a breach of the rules governing interviews varies according to the circumstances and to the view taken by judges of its significance. Thus in *R. v. Delaney*,[39] a seventeen-year-old educationally sub-normal youth, charged with indecent assault, eventually confessed after lengthy questioning. The interview was not recorded at the time, as it should have been. Nevertheless the judge admitted the statements made by the accused. But the Court of Appeal, speaking of 'flagrant and serious breaches of the Code', struck down the conviction. But in *R. v. Doolan*,[40] the failure to caution and to make a proper record of the interview, while sufficient to have statements excluded, did not vitiate the jury's verdict of guilt, the Court of Appeal finding that the remainder of the evidence was more than enough to justify it.

In *R. v. Fulling*,[41] it was alleged that the police told the

38. [1989] Crim.LR 815.
39. [1989] 88 Cr.App.R. 338; and see *R. v. Foster* [1987] Crim.LR 821.
40. [1988] Crim.LR 747.
41. [1987] 2 WLR 923.

accused that her boyfriend, also a suspect, had been having an affair with another woman and that, being distressed by this news, the accused had confessed in order to get out of prison. The Court of Appeal allowed the confession to stand saying: 'We do not consider that the policeman's remark was likely to make unreliable any confession of the appellant's own criminal activities.' One wonders how any court could come to such a conclusion with any degree of certainty.[42]

In *R. v. Mason*,[43] the accused confessed after he and his solicitor had been falsely told by the police that his fingerprints had been found on a bottle used in starting a fire. The Court of Appeal held that although it was not for the court to discipline the police for misbehaviour, the judge should have excluded the confession.

These and other examples suggest that the courts are anxious to insist that the police act in accordance with PACE and the Codes of Practice as the price they pay for additional powers given by the legislation. In *R. v. Canale*, police notes not made at the time of the interview, made on the wrong form, and not shown to the accused to read and sign, were allowed in evidence by the trial judge exercising his discretion to do so. The Lord Chief Justice, allowing the appeal, said that two police officers had engaged in a flagrant, deliberate and cynical breach of the rules. 'If,' he said, 'which we find it hard to believe, police officers still do not appreciate the importance of [PACE] and the accompanying Code, then it is time they did.' It was reported that, as a result, all Scotland Yard officers had been warned by their seniors of the need to abide by the rules.[44]

Under PACE greater powers are given to the police under new provisions relating to search warrants. Some material held in confidence by journalists may be protected but much may be demanded under statutory special procedure. Where

---

42. Compare *R. v. Harvey* [1988] Crim.LR 241.

43. [1987] Crim.LR 757. But entrapment by police officers posing as private citizens does not necessarily exclude evidence *DPP v. Marshall* [1988] 3 All ER 683.

44. [1990] 2 All ER 187; *The Independent*, 10 January 1990.

photographers from an agency took photographs during communal riots in Bristol, the police demanded their production as likely to be of substantial value to their investigations. This was challenged on the ground that particular photographs were not specified and it was not known whether photographs would be of any use. But the court overruled this objection.[45] So also, after a demonstration of between 10,000 and 15,000 people at Wapping, an investigation was conducted by the police, supervised by the Police Complaints Authority, into allegations and complaints about police behaviour. The investigating officer sought access to films, photographs and other journalistic material. Those who refused argued that they held the material as a result of the operation of the free independent press which would be undermined if they were required to disclose the material. But the judge held that 'there was nothing to put in the scales in the balancing act to weigh against the undoubted benefit likely to accrue to the investigation if the material was obtained'. Accordingly 'it was in the public interest that the material be produced or that access to it should be given'.[46]

But in August 1989, Judge Mohat Singh at Southwark Crown Court refused an application by the police for an order requiring the BBC to hand over a film on alleged rioting by sections of the Bengali community in London's East End.[47] After the demonstrations in and around Trafalgar Square which resulted in violence in March 1990, many newspapers and television companies were ordered by courts to hand over to the police all their published and unpublished film footage and photographs.

Under PACE protection from search and seizure extends to certain communications between solicitor and client and may embrace others where legal proceedings are contemplated. But this legal privilege does not attach to documents

45. [1990] 2 All ER 187; *R. v. Bristol Crown Court ex parte Bristol Press and Picture Agency Ltd.* [1987] 85 Cr.App.R. 190.

46. *Re an application under section 9 of the Police and Criminal Evidence Act 1984, The Independent*, 27 May 1988.

47. *The Independent*, 19 August 1989.

or other items passed to a solicitor for his advice though it would attach to the advice given.[48] Moreover 'items held with the intention of furthering a criminal purpose are not items subject to legal privilege'. The police applied for an order against a firm of solicitors requiring the production of all files relating to the purchase of certain property involving a client who was a member of the suspect's family. The police believed this was part of a laundering exercise whereby the suspect, accused of drug trafficking, was trying to dispose of his assets. The solicitors had no criminal purpose though the client allegedly had. The House of Lords by a majority held that the files were not privileged because the 'intention' did not have to be that of the person holding the documents.[49]

The Wapping demonstration on 24 January 1987 has already been referred to. It took place to mark the first anniversary of the strike of employees of News International. As a result of the inquiry, a number of police officers were alleged to have conspired to pervert the course of justice. The Crown had all the evidence by June 1987 but decided to wait until all the necessary evidence had been collected in the inquiry as a whole before interviewing officers involved in individual incidents. The detailed allegations were served on the officers in February 1988; on 12 October 1988 their files were sent to the Crown Prosecution Service and on 12 January 1989 they were summoned to appear before a magistrate. Police (Discipline) Regulations required the investigating officer 'as soon as is practicable' in writing to inform the officer subject to investigation of the report, allegation or complaint and to give him a written analysis.

A stipendiary magistrate declined to proceed with the committal for trial of these officers on the ground that they had been prejudiced by the delay and that to proceed further would be an abuse of process. The Divisional Court upheld

48. *R. v. Crown Court at Inner London Sessions ex parte Baines and Baines* [1987] 3 All ER 1025. The police must set out in their notice of application a description of the material sought: *R. v. Central Criminal Court ex parte Adegbesan* [1987] 3 All ER 113.

49. *R. v. Central Criminal Court ex parte Francis and Francis* [1988] 3 All ER 775.

this decision.[50] Subsequently the cases against other officers were dropped on the same ground. In March 1990 an application by the Crown Prosecution Service to certify that the decisions raised matters of national importance requiring a clarification by the Law Lords was rejected.

Race relations

The earlier cases

In 1965 the Race Relations Act was passed making discrimination on the ground of colour, race, ethnic or national origins unlawful in certain circumstances. These provisions were expanded by the Race Relations Act 1968. In 1972 came the first of a series of leading cases.

Stanislaw Zesko was born and bred a Polish national and joined the Polish Air Force. In November 1939, after the Nazi invasion of Poland, he escaped to France, came to the United Kingdom, enlisted in the Royal Air Force, and completed three operational tours in Bomber Command. After the war he remained in the United Kingdom, married and for fourteen years lived in the borough of Ealing in conditions of great hardship. He was, said the judge who first heard the case, 'a man of perfect character and integrity and a wholly admirable person'. In 1966, and again in 1968, Mr Zesko applied to be placed on the housing waiting list of Ealing Borough Council. His applications were refused under a council rule that an applicant had to be 'a British subject within the meaning of the British Nationality Act 1948'. A complaint was made to the Race Relations Board which, after investigation, notified the council that its action was one of unlawful discrimination because the Race Relations Act 1968 made unlawful the special treatment of a person on the ground of his national origins. The council applied to the courts for a declaration that its rule was not unlawful. The House of Lords, by a majority of four to one, decided in favour of the council on the ground that 'national

50. *R. v. Bow Street Stipendiary Magistrate ex parte Director of Public Prosecutions, The Independent*, 20 December 1989.

origins' did not mean 'nationality' which was what the council's rule was concerned with.[51]

The approach of the majority was linguistic and formalistic.[52] Viscount Dilhorne argued that Parliament could have used the word 'nationality' and the failure to do so indicated that discrimination on the ground of nationality was meant to be excluded from the Act. It was also argued that to interpret national origins so as to include nationality would extend its meaning in a different context and enlarge the scope of the criminal offence of stirring up hatred under the Act of 1965.

More serious because affecting more people were two decisions about clubs which the House of Lords decided in 1973 and 1974.

In April 1969 Mr Amarjit Singh Shah, who was employed in the Post Office and was a Conservative (having joined the local association in 1966), applied to join the East Ham South Conservative Club. He was proposed and seconded. When his application was considered by the committee, the chairman indicated in reply to a question that he regarded the colour of Mr Shah's skin as relevant and, on the chairman's casting vote, Mr Shah's application for membership was rejected. Mr Shah complained to the Race Relations Board, who issued a plaint against the club. The county court judge rejected the plaint, the Court of Appeal upheld it, and the House of Lords by a majority of four to one rejected it.[53] The Race Relations Act of 1968 provides that it is unlawful for any person concerned with the provision to the public or a section of the public of any services, etc., to discriminate. The majority decided that the club members were not 'a section of the public'.

51. *Ealing London Borough Council v. Race Relations Board* [1972] AC 342.

52. For a discussion of the case see John Hucker, *The House of Lords and the Race Relations Act*, 24 ICLQ 284 (1975).

53. *Charter v. Race Relations Board* [1973] AC 868.

In the second case[54] a member of a dockers' club in Preston took in as his guest Mr Sherrington, a coloured man. Mr Sherrington was told by the secretary to leave ('We do not serve coloured people'). Mr Sherrington was a member of another club in Preston which had no colour bar. Both these clubs, and some 4000 others, were banded together in a union and each member of one club was an associate member of all others in the union. The question was whether associates were 'a section of the public'. The county court judge and the Court of Appeal found for the Race Relations Board. But the House of Lords unanimously found for the club.

How did it come about that the judges who sat in the Court of Appeal and the House of Lords in these two cases differed so markedly? The answer seems to be that they took one of two different 'political' views.

The conservative view is that Parliament should intervene as little as possible in matters about which people differ in large numbers and that statutes should be so interpreted. No doubt motives are mixed when intervention to control racial discrimination is discouraged. But Lord Diplock in the *Dockers' Club* case put it thus, referring to the Race Relations Act:

> This is a statute which, however admirable its motives, restricts the liberty which the citizen has previously enjoyed at common law to differentiate between one person and another in entering or declining to enter into transactions with them . . . The arrival in this country within recent years of many immigrants from disparate and distant lands has brought a new dimension to the problem of the legal right to discriminate against the stranger. If everyone were rational and humane – or, for that matter, Christian – no legal sanctions would be needed to prevent one man being treated by his fellow men less favourably than another *simply upon*

54. *Dockers' Labour Club v. Race Relations Board* [1974] 3 WLR 533; in *Race Relations Board v. Applin* [1975] AC 2598 the House of Lords held that foster parents were concerned with the provision of facilities or services to a section of the public, i.e. the children.

> *the ground of his colour, race or ethnic or national origins.* But in the field of domestic or social intercourse differentiation in treatment of individuals is unavoidable . . . Thus, in discouraging the intrusion of coercion by legal process in the fields of domestic or social intercourse, the principle of effectiveness joins force with the broader principle of freedom to order one's private life as one chooses. [Italics in the original.]

This view begins with the private rights of the individual, including the right to discriminate on the ground of the colour of a man's skin. In interpreting an Act of Parliament, it assumes that those rights are to be diminished to the extent necessary to make sense of the legislation but no further. Therefore within the spectrum of happenings which range from the way a family makes provision for its friends within the home to the conduct of an open market, the definition of 'a section of the public' must be restricted as tightly as possible.

The alternative view does not found itself on this individualist position, does not think primarily of private rights. It makes other assumptions. It seeks to interpret the Race Relations Act in a way which will extend its operation and not restrict it, while recognizing that the Act clearly means to avoid intervention in the domestic sphere and in other private gatherings (certainly including some clubs). It regards racial discrimination not as an individual right but as a social wrong.[55]

One of the most remarkable decisions was *ex parte Selvarajan*[56] where a college lecturer was denied promotion in circumstances which strongly suggested racial discrimination. The Race Relations Board rejected the lecturer's application after following procedures which were flagrantly in breach of the rules of natural justice. But the Court of Appeal, presided over by Lord Denning, refused to interfere.

---

55. On the 'club' cases, see now Race Relations Act 1976.
56. [1975] 1 WLR 1686. For another example of Lord Denning's disregard of serious procedural injustices see *Ward v. Bradford Corporation* [1972] 70 LGR 27.

The CRE cases

The Commission for Racial Equality (CRE) was established by the Race Relations Act 1976 to replace the Race Relations Board and the Community Relations Commission. The statutory duties of the CRE are (a) to work towards the elimination of discrimination, (b) to promote equality of opportunity, and good relations, between persons of different racial groups generally, and (c) to keep under review the working of the Act.

Several attempts have been made in the courts to frustrate investigations instituted by the CRE. As the CRE reported in 1983:

> There have been legal challenges over investigations on such *highly technical procedural matters* as whether terms of reference are too wide; whether the Commission can investigate named persons without a belief that they are acting unlawfully; whether it is reasonable to embark on an investigation; whether natural justice applies as well as the statutory requirements to hear representations; whether the right to make representations under s.49(4) of the Act applies during the course of an investigation if the Commission forms a belief as to unlawful acts; whether it is reasonable to change from a strategic investigation to one based on a belief that unlawful acts have occurred . . . None of these matters actually touch on the fundamental question whether discrimination has occurred and what should be done about it . . . Yet, all this has happened in a system which was itself designed to give the person investigated every opportunity to make representation.[57]

Three decisions in particular have seriously diminished the scope of investigations by the CRE. In July 1978 the CRE informed a company, under section 49(4) of the Act, of their

57. Commission for Racial Equality: *The Race Relations Act 1976 – Time for a Change?* (July 1983). See also G. Appleby and E. Ellis, 'Formal Investigations by the CRE and EOC' in [1984] *Public Law* 236, to which I am indebted.

proposal to investigate and the company submitted eleven pages of representations under that subsection. The CRE, having become satisfied that an unlawful discriminatory act had been committed, told the company, in accordance with section 58, that they were 'minded' to serve a non-discrimination notice and sent a letter containing nine pages of detailed findings on allegations against the company. The company replied by submitting forty pages of further detailed representations. Subsequently the CRE served the non-discrimination notice itemizing the unlawful acts they had found. The company exercised its statutory right of appeal to an industrial tribunal which ordered the CRE to give particulars of every fact found by the CRE in the course of their investigation. The CRE argued that the whole of the lengthy administrative inquiry by the CRE should not be reopened on appeal, especially as the company had had two opportunities of making representations; and that the appeal should be limited to the reasonableness of the requirements in the non-discrimination notice. In February 1982 the Court of Appeal upheld the company's interpretation of the Act. Lord Denning MR, after outlining the facts, said: 'Such is the long procedure which has taken place already. Even so we have only got to this preliminary question: should particulars be ordered or not by the industrial tribunal? The appeal itself to the tribunal is a long way off.' And he concluded: 'I am very sorry for the Commission, but they have been caught up in a spider's web spun by Parliament from which there is little hope of their escaping.'[58]

The second case involved Hillingdon London Borough Council whose area includes Heathrow Airport.[59] In consequence the Council has the responsibility under the Housing (Homeless Persons) Act 1977 of providing accommodation for immigrant families who have made no prior arrangements. A Kenyan Asian family arrived and the Council classed them as intentionally homeless and so not entitled to be rehoused. The chairman of the Council's housing com-

58. *CRE v. Amari Plastics Ltd* [1982] 2 All ER 499.
59. *R. v. CRE ex parte Hillingdon LBC* [1982] AC 779.

mittee arranged for them to be taken by taxi and dumped outside the Foreign Office in support of his view that the responsibility should rest on the central government. At about the same time the Council housed a white family who had just arrived from Rhodesia. Because of this disparate treatment, the CRE told the Council they were embarking on a formal investigation and drew up terms of reference. The Council brought an action to quash the investigation.

Lord Diplock (with whom the other Law Lords concurred) held that it was a condition precedent to the drawing up of the terms of reference that the CRE should form the belief, and should so state in the terms of reference that the named persons (here the Council) might have done or might be doing unlawful discriminatory acts of a kind specified in the terms of reference. The terms of reference drawn up by the CRE stated a belief that the Council might have done or might be doing certain unlawful discriminatory acts in relation to the public or sections of the public as were in need of housing through homelessness. Since that form of words might also include acts done in relation to persons other than ethnic minority families arriving at Heathrow as immigrants, the House of Lords held that, as the CRE had admitted that they had formed no belief as to those other persons, the terms of reference were too wide and so invalid. The fact that the Council knew what the CRE intended to investigate and that the CRE had made this explicit to the Council in a draft press release was not thought to be relevant except as indicating the limits of the CRE's belief.

The most recent of this group of cases was *Commission for Racial Equality v. Prestige Group plc.*[60] In September 1978 the CRE informed the respondent company that they had decided to embark upon a formal investigation of the company to inquire into the employment of different racial groups by the company and its subsidiaries, with particular reference to the promotion of equality of opportunity between such persons as regards recruitment, access to promotion, transfer, training and any other benefits, facilities, services, and terms and conditions of employment. At this

---

60. [1984] 1 WLR 335.

time the CRE had no belief that the company might have committed an act of discrimination. In July 1981 the CRE, having considered information obtained in the course of their formal investigation, gave notice to the company that the CRE were 'minded' to conclude that the company had committed certain specified unlawful discriminatory acts. The company made representations but in November 1981 the CRE decided that the company had committed such acts and served the company with a non-discriminatory notice. After the Lords' decision in *Hillingdon* in June 1982, the company applied to the courts for judicial review claiming that the CRE's entire formal investigation had been ultra vires and void.

The House of Lords held that, on the true construction of sections 49(4) and 50(2)(b) of the Act of 1976, the 'condition precedent' – the belief that the named person (here the company) might be discriminating unlawfully – had to exist in these circumstances as in *Hillingdon* and that this entailed the holding of the preliminary investigation under section 49(4). Since there had originally been no such belief and so no investigation, the non-discrimination notice was ultra vires and void. The CRE argued that in *Hillingdon* the terms of reference did contain a statement of belief whereas in *Prestige* they did not; and that any invalidity was cured by the subsequent formation by the CRE of such a belief. But Lord Diplock (with whom the other Law Lords concurred) said that the CRE could not lawfully continue the formal investigation, once they had subsequently formed such a belief, without first holding the preliminary inquiry.

Lord Denning MR further castigated the CRE in *Mandla v. Dowell Lee*.[61] This was the case where a headmaster refused to admit a Sikh as a pupil unless he cut his hair and ceased to wear a turban. The question was whether Sikhs were a 'racial group' defined by reference to 'ethnic origins' within the meaning of the Race Relations Act 1976. The CRE, said Lord Denning, 'pursued the headmaster relentlessly'. And he expressed 'some regret that the CRE thought it right to take up this case against the headmaster . . . The

61. [1982] 3 WLR 932.

statutes . . . should not be used so as to interfere with the discretion of schools and colleges in the proper management of their affairs.' And Kerr LJ thought that all the CRE had achieved in this case was 'to create racial discord where there was none before' and referred to notes of an interview between the headmaster and an official of the CRE which he said read in part 'more like an inquisition than an interview' and which he regarded as harassment of the headmaster. Oliver LJ suggested that the machinery of the Act had operated against the headmaster as 'an engine of oppression'. The House of Lords overruled the Court of Appeal, found that Sikhs were a racial group and that there had been unlawful discrimination. Lord Fraser said that he thought the Court of Appeal's strictures on the CRE and its officials were 'entirely unjustified'. Lord Templeman agreed that the CRE had not acted oppressively. Lords Edmund-Davies, Roskill and Brandon concurred in their decision.[62]

Immigration

Before 1962 a Commonwealth citizen was entitled to enter the United Kingdom, but the Commonwealth Immigrants Act of that year empowered an immigration officer to refuse admission or to admit only on conditions (including limitation of length of stay).

The law is now primarily to be found in the Immigration Act 1971 (as amended by the British Nationality Act 1981 and the Immigration Act 1988). There is a right of appeal in some cases from the decision of an immigration officer to an adjudicator and to the Immigration Appeal Tribunal. The courts exercise a limited supervision by way of judicial review.

In *Zamir v. Secretary of State for the Home Department*[63] the applicant for habeas corpus was a Pakistani on whose behalf in December 1972 (he was then aged fifteen) an entry certificate was sought so that he might join his father who

62. [1983] 2 WLR 620.
63. [1980] 2 All ER 768.

had been settled in England since 1962. The certificate was eventually granted, in November 1975, on the basis that the applicant was unmarried and dependent on his father. In February 1976 he married in Pakistan. In March 1976 he arrived at Heathrow airport in London, was asked no questions and volunteered no information. He was granted leave to enter for an indefinite period. In August 1978 he was questioned by the immigration authorities and in October 1978 he was detained as an illegal immigrant with a view to his removal from the United Kingdom.

In the House of Lords, Lord Wilberforce, with whom the other Law Lords agreed, said that an applicant for entry to the United Kingdom owed a positive duty of candour on all material facts which denoted a change of circumstances since the issue of the entry clearance. Lord Wilberforce managed to suggest that perhaps the applicant had obtained entry clearance on the basis of a forged birth certificate, though he admitted that this matter had 'not been adjudicated on'. It was, said Lord Wilberforce, for the applicant to show that his detention was unlawful. But this the applicant could not do unless he could show either that there were no grounds on which the immigration officer could legally have detained him or that no reasonable person could have decided as the immigration officer did. To prove these negatives is, of course, virtually impossible. For immigrants the great writ of habeas corpus, which is supposed to stand between the imprisoned individual and the powers of the State, had been effectively neutralized by the judiciary.

Within three years, the House of Lords in a remarkable turnabout reversed its own decision in *Zamir*. The appellant Bohar Singh Khera was born in India in 1956. In 1972 his father was granted leave to enter the United Kingdom for settlement and applied for entry certificates for the appellant and the appellant's mother. In August 1972 they were interviewed by the entry clearance officer in New Delhi. On 5 June 1973, unknown to the UK immigration authorities, the appellant married in India. In December 1974, the appellant and his mother were granted entry certificates. They arrived in the UK in January 1975 and were granted indefinite leave to enter. In November 1978, the appellant's wife applied to join her husband together with two children of the marriage. Enquiries were made, the marriage came to light, and in November 1978 an immigration officer made an order detaining the appellant as an illegal entrant, pending summary removal. The appellant applied to the court for a declaration that he was lawfully in the United Kingdom and had indefinite leave to enter and remain.

It was argued on behalf of the immigration authorities that on one occasion, after the appellant had reached the age of eighteen, he had falsely told a medical officer of the immigration authorities that he was not married and so was guilty of deception on a fact which was material because, as with Zamir, only if he were unmarried and dependent on his father, was he entitled to be admitted for settlement.

The appellant denied that he had made this statement and it appeared that the immigration officer who made the order detaining him had not relied on this evidence and that there was no other evidence outstanding against the appellant.

Lord Fraser, who, with Lord Wilberforce, had also participated in *Zamir*, remarked that the notice of the immigration officer's decision began: 'Having considered all the information available to me, I am satisfied that there are reasonable grounds to conclude that you are an illegal entrant' and he, with Lords Bridge and Scarman, held that this indicated the immigration officer had applied the wrong test. The officer was entitled to order the detention and removal of a person who had entered the country by virtue of an ex facie valid permission only if that person *was* an illegal entrant and in these cases the degree of probability required that this was so on the evidence was high. The Law Lords also agreed that there was no positive duty of candour although silence was capable of amounting to deception.[64]

Why did the Law Lords reverse their own decision so soon and so completely? The *Zamir* decision was badly regarded by several diverse groups, especially on the ruling of a posi-

---

64. *R. v. Secretary of State for the Home Department ex parte Khawaja and Khera* [1983] 2 WLR 321; and see *Ali v. Secretary of State for the Home Department* [1984] 1 All ER 1009 and *R. v. Secretary of State for the Home Department ex parte Awa, The Times*, 12 March 1983.

tive duty of candour. This was seen as unfair and impracticable not only by those who advised immigrants in the UK and abroad, but also by the Home Office and by the lawyers who habitually were concerned with such cases. The apparent reversal of the burden of proof on habeas corpus offended many, including (one suspects) some of the Law Lords themselves. It was recognized that deception took place on a considerable scale but the standard set by Lord Wilberforce was unduly high. In *Khawaja and Khera*, the House of Lords was, save for Lords Wilberforce and Fraser, differently composed and included Lords Scarman, Bridge and Templeman, a more liberal trio than those they replaced. This is reinforced by the history of the cases. On 6 May 1982 an appeal committee consisting of Lords Fraser, Roskill and Brandon dismissed a petition on behalf of Khera for leave to appeal to the House of Lords. On 17 June 1982, Khawaja (whose case was weaker) was given leave by Lords Fraser, Scarman and Bridge. As a result the Khera petition was reheard and leave given. This suggests a crucial change of mind by Lord Fraser between those two dates. And finally, the decision in *Zamir* was being taken to the European Commission of Human Rights and there may have been a wish to avoid yet another decision in Strasbourg critical of the United Kingdom.

Once British governments had decided on strict immigration control, the categories of those to be allowed entry, either temporarily or permanently, fell to be determined. These were governed by Immigration Rules supplementing the immigration statutes and statutory instruments. One situation has resulted in considerable case law.

Typically, a woman who is a British citizen settled in the United Kingdom, with full rights of nationality and citizenship, wishes to sponsor the entry of a man from a non-European country either because he is her husband or because he is her fiancé. Vinod Bhatia[65] was such a fiancé and he applied for entry clearance in Delhi in February 1981. Two years later the entry clearance officer (ECO) rejected

---

65. *R. v. Immigration Appeal Tribunal ex parte Vinod Bhatia* [1985] Imm.AR 50.

his application and one year later his appeal to an adjudicator was dismissed. So he appealed to the Immigration Appeal Tribunal (IAT) which decided against him, by a majority, in October 1984. He applied for judicial review of this decision and his case came before the Court of Appeal in London, in July 1985. Because of the facts, some 200 other cases were said to be awaiting the outcome of his appeal.

Under the Rules, entry clearance is to be refused unless the ECO is satisfied under the following sub-paras: (a) that it is not the primary purpose of the intended marriage to obtain admission to the United Kingdom and (b) that there is an intention that the parties to the marriage should live together permanently as man and wife and (c) that the parties to the proposed marriage have met.

Mr Bhatia's intended wife was Vijay Kumari. She came to the United Kingdom in 1970, married, had a child in 1971 and obtained a divorce in 1978 with custody of the child. Back in Delhi, her parents advertised for a husband and Vinod was selected. Vijay met him in Delhi in 1980. Later Vinod said he did not think his father would have agreed to the marriage had Vijay not been settled in Britain. Vijay herself said she was not prepared to live in India because she wanted her child to be educated in the United Kingdom.

The IAT and the Court of Appeal held that the onus was on the applicant to establish on a balance of probabilities that the three requirements of the Rules under sub-paras (a) (b) and (c) set out above were fulfilled. In this case, there was no dispute about (b) and (c). But the IAT took the view that the Rules presume that the primary purpose is to obtain admission to the United Kingdom and that it is for the applicant to satisfy the ECO that this is not so. The applicant argued that once the genuineness of the intended marriage (that is (b)) was accepted, that was also conclusive of the primary purpose. The Court of Appeal agreed that an applicant who satisfied the ECO on sub-paras (b) and (c) was better placed to satisfy him on (a) also but that it was still possible for the ECO and the IAT to conclude that the primary purpose of the marriage was to gain entry for the applicant. So the Court of Appeal held that the IAT had not misdirected itself in law and that the refusal of Mr Bhatia's application was justified. It is obvious that this gives a wide and subjective discretion to the ECO and it is argued that the requirement that a marriage is genuine (under (b)) is a sufficient safeguard against abuse.

In 1986 *Bhatia* was followed by *Kumar*.[66] In this case, there had been a marriage in India in 1982, the wife being already settled in the United Kingdom. In January 1984, she returned to this country, being pregnant. In February her husband was interviewed in Delhi by an ECO who refused his application for entry. A few days later the wife had a miscarriage. She visited her husband again in India for some time in early 1985 and returned to the United Kingdom where a child was born to her in October. Meanwhile an adjudicator, following or purporting to follow *Bhatia*, dismissed an appeal by Mr Kumar and the IAT refused leave to appeal against that decision. So the matter came to the Court of Appeal for judicial review which was granted.

The Rules for an application by a husband are substantially the same as those for a fiancé save that, for a husband, the ECO must look at the circumstances obtaining when the marriage was entered into, and the events since marriage, such as continuing devotion, may be material as evidence of purpose. In both these cases the marriage or proposed marriage had been arranged by the parents.

In *Kumar* the adjudicator emphasised the arranged nature of the marriage and suggested that this might give rise to an 'ulterior primary reason' to gain admission to the United Kingdom. He also was concerned to separate the requirements of sub-para (a) from (b) and not to 'blur' the distinction between them. The Court of Appeal criticized him on both these points and emphasized the inter-relationship between, in particular, the requirements of those two sub-paragraphs. As the Master of the Rolls said: 'Evidence bearing on one question will often cast a flood of light on the other.'

Both *Bhatia* and *Kumar* were reviewed extensively by the

---

66. *R. v. IAT ex parte Arun Kumar* [1986] Imm.AR 446.

Court of Appeal in *Hoque and Singh*.[67] Both these respondents were husbands of wives settled in the United Kingdom. Mr Hoque was refused leave to remain in this country, and Mr Singh was refused leave to enter, on the grounds of primary purpose. Lord Justice Slade put forward ten propositions of which the most important were those which reinforced the criticisms of the Court of Appeal in *Kumar*. The Court also warned of the danger of treating an admission by the applicant that he sought to obtain admission to or remain in the United Kingdom as evidence that this was the primary purpose of the marriage. On the other hand they disagreed strongly with the view of the judge below in *Hoque* who suggested, on the supposed authority of the Master of the Rolls in *Kumar*, that once it was found that a 'very genuine and soundly based marriage' existed, the requirement in sub-para (a) as well as that in sub-para (b) was satisfied. This, they said, was going too far. Similarly they distanced themselves from similar words used by the judge below in *Singh*. So they reiterated the need for both (a) and (b) requirements to be satisfied.

In both *Hoque* and *Singh* the Court of Appeal ruled that the adjudicator had misdirected himself by not taking into account that the existence of an apparently happy and stable marriage, which had already resulted in the birth of a child, might well throw light on the intentions of the parties when they entered into the marriage. So the cases were returned to the IAT for reconsideration.

In the event, therefore, the Court of Appeal emphasized that if an applicant satisfied the ECO or the adjudicator of the genuineness of the marriage or proposed marriage (that is of the intentions of the two parties to live together permanently as man and wife) this must have an important bearing on the question of primary purpose.[68]

Soon after this decision it was interpreted by Hodgson J as meaning that it placed on the ECO or an adjudicator the obligation to consider the requirements of sub-para (a)

67. *R. v. IAT ex parte Amirul Hoque and Matwinder Singh* [1988] Imm.AR 216. See, similarly, *Choudhury v. IAT* [1990] Imm.AR 211.
68. See also *R. v. IAT ex parte Khatab* [1989] Imm.AR 313.

because otherwise he could not be in a position to see whether, and if so what degree of, illumination was cast on (a) by (b) and (c).[69] And an adjudicator's failure to have regard to material facts may result in a decision of the IAT being set aside or referred back for further consideration.[70]

In *Naushad Kandiya and Aurangzeb Khan*[71] it was contended that it was the duty of an adjudicator in a primary purpose case to make a finding on sub-para (b) before considering sub-para (a) and that in both of these cases he had failed to do so. But the Court of Appeal held that this was not necessary so long as the adjudicator gave adequate reasons for his decision.

Deportation

Any person who does not have the right of abode in the United Kingdom (as most Commonwealth citizens do not) is liable to deportation if (a) having limited leave to enter or remain he does not observe this limitation or (b) the Secretary of State deems his deportation to be conducive to the public good or (c) another person to whose family he belongs is or has been ordered to be deported. There are limited rights of appeal to an adjudicator or the Immigration Appeal Tribunal.

In *R. v. IAT ex parte Cheema*[72] a deportation order was upheld by the Court of Appeal where a marriage was shown to be not genuine but had as its primary purpose the obtaining of admission to the United Kingdom. Lord Lane CJ said:

> Marriage is still, like it or not, one of the cornerstones of our society, despite recent trends of behaviour. If a

69. *R. v. IAT ex parte Bashir* referred to in *R. v. IAT ex parte Sudash Bala Garg, The Times,* 17 March 1989.

70. See *ex parte Garg* (last note); but compare *R. v. Secretary of State for the Home Department ex parte Prajapati* (unreported 14 June 1990) and *R. v. Secretary of State for the Home Department ex parte Salim Bhim* (unreported, 20 October 1989).

71. *Naushad Kandiya v. IAT* and *Aurangzeb Khan v. IAT* [1990] Imm.AR 377.

72. [1982] Imm.AR 124.

person chooses to use a ceremony of marriage or the status simply as a dishonest and deceitful way of avoiding the law . . . then I consider it properly open to the Secretary of State to come to the conclusion that that person's continued presence in this country is not conducive to the public good.

In *Khawaja*[73] Lord Bridge said: 'I cannot suppose that this power [of the Secretary of State] was ever intended to be involved as a means of deporting a perfectly respectable established resident on grounds arising from the circumstances of his original entry'. It had been argued that the Secretary of State's power was meant to cover only highly undesirable persons. The decision in *Cheema* rejected this. So did the Court of Appeal in *Owusu-Sekyere*[74] where Lloyd LJ said there was no reason why the Secretary of State should not deem it conducive to the public good that an immigrant who had deceived the immigration authorities and thereby abused the system should be deported *pour encourager les autres*.

In 1988, the House of Lords decided *R. v. IAT ex parte Patel*.[75] The applicant had been admitted for 'settlement accompanying parents' but had falsely represented that he was unmarried. When this was discovered, he was put on notice that he was liable to be deported. He obtained a re-entry visa when he left to visit India but was refused re-entry on his return on the ground that his exclusion was conducive to the public good. In the lower courts this refusal was quashed because by virtue of *Khawaja* the original deception on entry could not of itself be sufficient. But the House of Lords refused to follow *Khawaja* in this, Lord Bridge eating his words:

I am happily free of any obligation to decide whether what I said in Khawaja was part of the *ratio decidendi* or merely *obiter*. Still less need I attempt to plumb the mystery of precisely what I meant by what I said. I am

73. See above pp. 179–80.
74. *R. v. IAT ex parte Owusu-Sekyere* [1987] Imm.AR 425.
75. [1988] 2 WLR 1165.

at liberty, with the concurrence I believe of all your Lordships, to resort to the more direct and satisfactory expedient, not available in the courts below, of recognising that the opinion I expressed was simply mistaken.

Generally the courts, especially the House of Lords, are much more reluctant to support challenges to the exercise of the Secretary of State's powers to deport than to the exercise of the appellate powers of the immigration authorities. In *Secretary of State for the Home Department v. Zalife Huseyin*,[76] Lord Donaldson MR, expressed his reluctance but held that the wife of a Commonwealth citizen settled in the UK on 1 January 1973 could not be deported even if the marriage was one of convenience.

This reluctance shows itself in the emphasis which courts put, in deportation and asylum cases, on the inherent limitations of judicial review. This is one of the games played by judges, extending and restricting the scope of judicial review like Procrustes fitting victims to his bed. For instance in *Budgaycay*[77] where three Turkish subjects gave reasons, which were untrue, to obtain entry but later sought asylum on political grounds, it was argued that they could not be deported unless and until the courts had rejected their claims to be refugees. But the House of Lords did not accept this, saying that all questions of fact on which the discretionary decision to grant or withhold leave to enter or remain depended must necessarily be determined by the immigration officer or the Secretary of State. Judicial review was strictly limited to *Wednesbury* principles.[78] But their Lordships did accept jurisdiction when the question was whether the Minister had adequately considered what were the consequences of deportation and Lord Templeman spoke of 'a defect in the decision-making process'.[79]

The House of Lords adopted the harder line of interpretation, overruling the Court of Appeal, in *R. v. Secretary of*

76. [1988] Imm.AR 129; see now Immigration Act 1988.
77. *R. v. Secretary of State for the Home Department ex parte Budgaycay* [1987] AC 514.
78. See above pp. 115–16.
79. *Re Musisi* [1987] AC 514.

State for the Home Department ex parte Sivakumaran[80] where six Tamils from Sri Lanka were refused political asylum. The question was whether they had 'a well-founded fear' of being persecuted for reasons of race if they were returned to Sri Lanka. The Court of Appeal held that each had merely to establish that he had what appeared to him to be a well-founded fear but the House of Lords rejected this subjective test and said that he had to demonstrate 'a reasonable degree of likelihood that he would be persecuted', and the Secretary of State could take into account facts and circumstances possibly unknown to the refugee in order to determine whether his fear was objectively justified. On their return to Sri Lanka, two of the Tamils appealed and the adjudicator held that they should be treated as political refugees and granted asylum. The Secretary of State applied for judicial review on the ground that the adjudicator lacked jurisdiction but the Court of Appeal rejected the application.[81]

The case of Viraj Jerome Mendis received much publicity because he obtained 'sanctuary' in a Manchester church. He entered the United Kingdom as a student and overstayed his time for eight years. He had not engaged in political activities in his native Sri Lanka but claimed that his activities in the United Kingdom rendered him liable to persecution if he was returned to that country. The High Commissioner for Sri Lanka wrote an unsolicited letter to the Home Office in London denying that the Sri Lankan authorities had any interest in him or that he would face persecution. The Court of Appeal said it was important to underline the limited role which the courts could play in these cases, echoing Lord Templeman's phrase about defects in the decision-making process though indicating that the courts' scrutiny would be vigorous where life or liberty were at stake. The Court said they placed 'complete confidence' in the assurance given by the High Commissioner whose

80. [1988] 1 All ER 193.

81. *R. v. IAT ex parte Secretary of State for the Home Department* [1990] 1 WLR 1126. In August 1990, the European Commission of Human Rights held that the United Kingdom had violated article 13 of the European Convention in requiring the applicants to pursue their remedies in Sri Lanka (*The Guardian*, 7 August 1990).

letter was proper to take into account and relevant. There was 'material on which the relevant decision makers could properly come to the conclusion that the appellant had no well-founded fear of persecution'.[82]

The Immigration Act 1988 provided that a deportee had no right of appeal to an adjudicator for breach of limited leave or family association except on the ground that on the facts of the case there was in law no power to make the deportation order for the reasons stated in the notice of the decision. Miss Sonia Malhi appealed from a deportation order to the adjudicator on the ground that she had not been allowed an interview before the order was made. But the Court of Appeal held that the adjudicator could not consider this question, and that there was no sign of procedural irregularity or unfairness through the refusal to grant an interview.[83]

Early in 1990, six Lebanese nationals obtained from the Brazilian embassy in Beirut tourist visas to enter Brazil. They landed in the United Kingdom and claimed political asylum. The six had obtained Brazilian visas by deception, never intending to go to Brazil, and they claimed that when this was realised the Brazilian authorities would return them to the United Kingdom. The minister took the view that Brazil was the country which should accept asylum responsibility and directed that they be removed to Brazil. He refused to consider their applications for asylum. They applied for judicial review. Schiemann J said that while it was possible (though doubtful) that the minister's belief that Brazil was responsible was one to which he was entitled to come, no reason had been suggested for him to believe that the Brazilians would share his view and admit the six. It was therefore a belief to which the minister could not lawfully come. His decisions and directions should be quashed.[84] The Government decided not to appeal.

82. *Viraj Jerome Mendis v. IAT and Secretary of State for the Home Department* [1989] Imm.AR 6.
83. *R. v. Secretary of State for the Home Department ex parte Malhi* [1990] 2 WLR 932.
84. *R. v. Secretary of State for the Home Department ex parte Yassine* [1990] Imm.AR 354.

The Secretary of State has powers of deportation under the Immigration Act 1971 which also confers many powers on immigration officers. He authorized certain officials in the immigration department of the Home Office to exercise his powers to deport. It was argued successfully before Lord Justice Woolf that this delegation was not authorized by the Act. But the Court of Appeal, after taking new evidence, held that the immigration officials were not authorized to act 'as such' and were to be regarded simply as ordinary civil servants acting on their Minister's behalf.[85]

Miscarriages of justice

Recent cases, especially those arising out of bombings on the mainland by the IRA, have raised serious questions about the processes of the criminal law. Convictions have been set aside, often after long periods of imprisonment, and doubts have been raised not only about police methods but also about the role of the courts in remedying miscarriages of justice.

Appeals against conviction on serious offences lie to the Court of Appeal (Criminal Division), usually after leave has been obtained. The Court is required by statute to allow an appeal if it thinks (a) that the conviction should be set aside on the ground that under all the circumstances of the case it is unsafe or unsatisfactory or (b) that the judgment of the court of trial should be set aside on the ground of a wrong decision of any question of law or (c) that there was a material irregularity in the course of the trial. In any other case the Court must dismiss the appeal and may do so, in any event, if it considers that no miscarriage of justice has actually occurred. Where the Court allows an appeal it may direct the trial court to enter a verdict of acquittal or it may order a retrial. In addition the Secretary of State may, if he thinks fit, at any time refer a case to the Court of Appeal to be there treated as an appeal.[86] He may also recommend

85. *R. v. Secretary of State for the Home Department ex parte Oladehinde* [1990] 2 WLR 1195; confirmed by the House of Lords [1990] 3WLR797.
86. Criminal Appeal Act 1968 sect. 2, 17.

the Queen to grant a pardon or to remit all or part of the penalty imposed.

In 1969, Widgery LJ in the Court of Appeal said that, in the case before him, no one criticized the summing-up of the trial judge, every issue was before the jury, the jury was properly instructed and so the Court would be 'very reluctant indeed' to intervene. However the Court was now required to consider whether the decision was 'unsafe or unsatisfactory'. That means, he said, that 'in cases of this kind the Court must in the end ask itself a subjective question, whether we are content to let the matter stand as it is, or whether there is not some lurking doubt in our minds which makes us wonder whether an injustice has been done'.[87] However, it is doubtful whether this view is now prevalent. The more common approach seems to be that where the summing-up is impeccable and there are no mistakes of law, the Court of Appeal will not substitute its own opinion for that of the jury in the trial court.

The Court of Appeal may hear fresh evidence where there is a reasonable explanation for this not having been adduced at the trial. In *Stafford v. DPP*,[88] the House of Lords was confronted with two views of how it should consider such evidence. Counsel for the appellant said that the Court of Appeal had asked the wrong question in that they took as the test the effect of the fresh evidence on their minds and not the effect that that evidence would have had on the mind of the jury. Counsel for the respondent said that there was nothing in the Act or in the cases which supported the view that the Court of Appeal should allow the appeal when they did not themselves think that the verdict was unsafe or unsatisfactory, or when they were themselves convinced of the guilt of the appellant but considered that some hypothetical jury might have thought otherwise. Their Lordships decided unanimously in favour of this second view.

Lord Devlin has argued strongly against this decision saying that it meant a person might be convicted of a serious

---

87. *R. v. Cooper* [1969] 1 QB 267; see *Miscarriages of Justice* (1989) a report by Justice, page 49.
88. [1974] AC 878.

offence without having been found guilty by a jury which had heard substantially all the relevant evidence.[89]

We have seen that the Secretary of State may at any time, if he thinks fit, refer a case to the Court of Appeal. In the case of the murder of the Luton sub-postmaster in 1969 he did so on four occasions. On the first occasion, the Court of Appeal quashed the conviction of one of the accused but not of the other two whose convictions the Court refused consistently to reject. Eventually the Secretary of State released the two by remitting the remainder of their sentences in 1980. Of one of the hearings, the Court of Appeal said of the evidence given by the principal witness (Matthews): 'Each of us watched him closely while he was giving evidence. The conclusion which each of us independently has reached in this Court on the vital part of his story is that he was clearly telling the truth.' On this Devlin wrote:

> What was wanted from the Court of Appeal was not confirmation that Matthews appeared from his demeanour to be a truthful witness, whether on essentials or on the whole. What was wanted was an answer, based on a more comprehensive view of the case than the jury could have as well as a more detached one, to the question whether, however convincing Matthews might sound, it was safe to act upon the evidence of an habitual liar, who even at the trial had not come clean, who was an accomplice almost uncorroborated, and who had turned Queen's evidence in the hands of a police officer who was not above suspicion.[90]

Under the Act of 1968, the Court of Appeal had a limited power to order a retrial. Since the Criminal Justice Act 1988, the Court may so order whenever satisfied that it is in the interests of justice to do so. But if the case is very old, this may not be a realistic course.

On 5 October 1974, bombs exploded in two public houses in Guildford killing 5 people and injuring over 60. This was

89. Patrick Devlin, *The Judge* (1979), pp. 148–76.
90. Devlin, *op. cit.*, pp. 170–1.

followed by bombings in Woolwich on 7 November, when 2 died. Other bombings occurred in London.

Three men and a woman – known as the Guildford Four – were charged with the murder of those killed in the Guildford bombings, two of the men being also charged with the murders at Woolwich. In September 1975, all were convicted on the basis of confessions they had made while in police custody and which they retracted in court alleging that the confessions had been extorted. In December 1975, four IRA members were surrounded in a flat in Balcombe Street, London, and when arrested admitted to having been responsible for bombings in and around London over the past year. Subsequently, statements were made by those IRA members that they had been responsible for the Guildford and Woolwich bombings and that the Guildford Four had no connection with those events.

In 1977, the Guildford Four applied unsuccessfully for leave to appeal. The Court of Appeal, said Lord Roskill, 'wholly rejected as unworthy of credence' the evidence of the IRA members that they did not know the applicants and that IRA members alone took part in the Guildford bombings. So, said the Court, the new evidence 'therefore gives rise to no lurking doubts whatever in our minds'.

As the result of statements made by two of the Guildford Four, seven other persons were convicted in 1976 of unlawfully handling nitroglycerine. Six were of or related to the Maguire family and one was a friend of the family. The evidence was almost entirely based on traces which were said to be found on their hands or gloves. Two were sentenced to 14 years' imprisonment, three (of whom one died in prison) to 12 years' and one to 5 years'. The youngest (aged 14) was sentenced to 4 years in youth custody. All applied unsuccessfully for leave to appeal in 1977. The decision was that no member of the Court of Appeal saw any reason for disturbing any of the convictions either on the basis that any of them was unsafe or unsatisfactory or that the learned judge was guilty of any non-direction or misdirection or that his summing-up in any way was unbalanced.[91]

Doubts about the rightness of the convictions of these eleven persons persisted and the Cardinal Archbishop of Westminster, Basil Hume, raised the matter with Mrs Thatcher in 1979. When in 1986 Robert Kee published his book on the case,[92] he found that his doubts were also shared by two former Law Lords (Devlin and Scarman) and two former Home Secretaries (Roy Jenkins and Merlyn Rees). They tried to persuade the Home Office to refer the cases to the Court of Appeal. In November 1986, the matter was raised in the Lords by Baroness Ewart-Biggs, Lord Fitt and Lord Scarman but the Government refused on the ground that there was no factor other than the evidence already examined. In January 1987, the Home Secretary Douglas Hurd told the House of Commons that he could see no grounds for referral. In July 1987, Cardinal Hume, the two former Law Lords and the two former Home Secretaries went as a deputation to see Mr Hurd. In the following month, the Avon and Somerset police were appointed to undertake an enquiry. In April 1988, the first report of that enquiry did not, it is believed, encourage the Home Secretary to refer the case to the Court of Appeal but after further pressure from the Hume deputation, he did so in January 1989, on the basis of new evidence about the effects of drugs on the confession statement of one of those convicted and of new alibi evidence. This by itself might well have proved insufficient. But, at this point, according to Robert Kee, the Crown Prosecution Service pressed the Avon and Somerset to make more inquiries as a result of which documents were found at Guildford which led to the conclusion of police fabrication.

On 19 October 1989, counsel for the Director of Public Prosecutions told the Lord Chief Justice (Lord Lane) and two Lord Justices in the Court of Appeal that the confessions

91. The fullest accounts of the trials and the events concerning the Guildford Four and the Maguire Seven are to be found in Robert Kee, *Trial and Error* (2nd edn 1989).

92. See last note.

in the Guildford case had been found to be the product of fabrications on the part of the Surrey constabulary and that it would be wrong for the Crown to seek to sustain the convictions.

Counsel said there was 'clear prima facie evidence that a total of five police officers seriously misled the court in relation to two of the four appellants'. Notes and records of crucial interviews had been rewritten, altered and suppressed. Lord Lane said of the officers: 'They must have lied'. The evidence of the fabrication by the police was found unexpectedly among the police files at Guildford. The convictions were quashed and the Four were freed.

It was perhaps significant that the Home Secretary decided to pre-empt the consideration by the Court of Appeal. He also set up an enquiry[93] under a former Lord Justice of Appeal (Sir John May) with lay assessors into matters arising from the freeing of the Guildford four, and into aspects of the Maguire Seven, six of whom had by this time served their sentences, the seventh having died in prison. In June 1990, the Director of Public Prosecutions accepted that the convictions of the Maguire Seven were unsafe and unsatisfactory and could not be upheld.[94] In July 1990, Sir John May published his interim report on the Maguire case. His conclusion was that the convictions were unsound.[95] They were referred to the Court of Appeal.

On 21 November 1974, two bomb explosions took place at public houses in Birmingham. Twenty-one people were killed and more than 160 injured. This followed a series of ten or eleven IRA bombings in the West Midlands. At one of those earlier incidents the bomb had exploded prematurely, killing James McDade who was planting it. On the evening of 21 November, six men were arrested, five of them on their way from Birmingham to Belfast to attend McDade's funeral. The sixth man was arrested in Birmingham. According to police evidence, all six made statements admitting

93. 158 HC Deb. col. 271 (19 December 1989).
94. See 174 HC Deb. col. 454 (14 June 1990) for the Home Secretary's statement.
95. HC 556 of 1989–90.

they had taken part in planting the bombs on 21 November, the statements of four being in writing, two being orally made. Those statements which the accused alleged had been forced out of them by the police under torture, violence, threats and intimidation were the foundation of the prosecution case. There was also some disputed scientific evidence. All six were convicted in November 1975 of the murder of the twenty-one who died.

In March 1976, the Six applied for leave to appeal on the grounds that the trial judge displayed excessive hostility to their case, overstepped the bounds of his judicial function in criticism of certain defence witnesses, wrongly allowed certain witnesses to be called by the prosecution in rebuttal, and did not sum up fairly. The applications were refused.

In 1987, following television broadcasts on their case and statements by an ex-police constable that he had seen the Six being ill-treated by the police on 22–3 November 1974, an enquiry was ordered by the Home Office and carried out by the Devon and Cornwall police. Subsequently the Home Secretary referred the case to the Court of Appeal to consider whether any of the convictions should be regarded as unsafe or unsatisfactory. The Court of Appeal (Lord Lane LCJ, Lords Justices Stephen Brown and O'Connor) reported in January 1988: 'The longer the hearing has gone on the more convinced this Court has become that the verdict of the jury was correct. We have no doubt that these convictions were both safe and satisfactory.'

Early in 1990, following the abandonment of the convictions of the Guildford Four, a police investigation was set up into the Birmingham convictions.[96] In August, the Home Secretary referred the case back to the Court of Appeal for the second time. On 14 March 1991 the Court set the six men free.

Three persons had their convictions overturned by the Court of Appeal in April 1990. They had been charged with conspiracy to murder the then Secretary of State for Northern Ireland (Mr Tom King). At their trial, each of the accused chose not to give evidence, but when their counsel

96. See generally Chris Mullin, *Error of Judgment* (1990 edn).

was addressing the jury, the Secretary of State announced the Government's intention to change the law so as to limit the right to silence. The Secretary of State said on television that this change should increase convictions among terrorists. Also, the former Master of the Rolls, Lord Denning, said that the right to silence was a help to the guilty while the innocent would want to give evidence and be cleared. The three were convicted.

The Court of Appeal held that these statements constituted a real risk that the jury might have been influenced and that the judge should have ordered a retrial. At the time when the appellants' notices for leave to appeal were given, the Court of Appeal had no power to order a retrial. So the convictions were quashed and the appellants set free.[97]

97. *R. v. Cullen and others, The Independent,* 1 May 1990.

6. Contempt, confidentiality and censorship

The meaning of contempt

A report stated that the law relating to contempt of court had developed over the centuries as a means whereby the courts might act to prevent or punish conduct which tended to obstruct, prejudice or abuse the administration of justice.[1] Such conduct may take place, in relation to any particular case, before, during or after the trial. Most obviously, if the court makes an order which is disregarded, that is contempt, as happened when trade unions were fined for failing to obey orders of the National Industrial Relations Court; or as happens in matrimonial cases where parties disobey orders not to molest or invade the privacy of other parties.

But, less usually, there may be positive disruption as when, in 1970, a group of Welsh students invaded a court in the Royal Courts of Justice in London and broke up the hearing of a case by striding into the well of the court, shouting slogans, scattering pamphlets and singing. They did this to demonstrate for the preservation of the Welsh language, and those who refused to apologize to the judge were instantly committed by him to three months' imprisonment. On appeal they were bound over for twelve months to be of good behaviour. The members of the Court of Appeal emphasized that the right to protest must be executed within the law. But their judgments also establish, despite statutory law which seemed, as applicable to these

1. Report of the Committee on Contempt of Court (Cmnd 5794) para. 1; and see discussion paper Cmnd 7145; and see 948 HC Deb. col. 1340–50 (25 April 1978).

students, to require that their sentences should be suspended, that the High Court still had power at common law to commit instantly to prison for such contempt.[2]

Prejudicial statements

Clearly the position of an accused person may be adversely and unfairly affected if, before his trial is concluded, publicity about him appears in the press. This may well create prejudice, not least in the mind of any member of the jury. So for a newspaper to describe an accused person of having had an unedifying career as brothel-keeper, procurer and property racketeer is a serious contempt of court – and when this happened in 1967 *The Sunday Times* was fined £5000.[3] In February 1988, News Group Newspapers was fined £75,000 for contempt of court in publishing articles in the *Sun* (one of the Group) about a doctor subsequently privately prosecuted (with finance provided by the *Sun*) and acquitted.[4]

Between 1959 and 1961 a company made and marketed under licence a drug containing thalidomide, as a result of which about 450 children were born with gross deformities.[5] In 1968 and subsequently actions were begun by the issue of writs against the company and some of these were settled out of court. For others, negotiations continued and in September 1972 *The Sunday Times* published the first of a series of articles to draw attention to the plight of the children. The company complained to the Attorney-General that the article was a contempt of court because some actions were still pending. The editor justified the articles and at the same time sent to the Attorney and to the company for comment a second article in draft (for which he claimed complete factual accuracy) on the testing, manufacture and marketing of the drug. The Attorney-General asked the courts to grant

2. *Morris v. Crown Office* [1970] 2 QB 114.
3. *R. v. Thomson Newspapers* [1968] 1 WLR 1.
4. *A-G v. News Group Newspapers* [1988] 3 WLR 163.
5. *A-G v. Times Newspapers* [1974] AC 273.

an injunction to prevent the publication of this second article on the ground that it was a contempt. The Divisional Court granted the injunction but the Court of Appeal refused it. The House of Lords allowed the company's appeal and granted the injunction.

Essentially, the view of the Court of Appeal[6] was that in the unique circumstances of a national tragedy where the public interest required that the issues should be discussed, where the legal proceedings had been dormant for years, and where there appeared no possibility of any action coming to trial, the public interest in fair comment outweighed the possible prejudice to a party. The House of Lords decided against *The Sunday Times* on the ground that the second article might be prejudicial to a subsequent trial. The public interest in proper discussion in the circumstances of this case and the weakness of the parents' situation, unless they could be championed by the press, appeared to carry very little weight with their Lordships whose decision was unnecessary in law and deplorable in practice.[7]

The issue was then taken to the European Court of Human Rights on the ground that the injunction violated Article 10 of the European Convention which protects the right to freedom of expression. The court concluded, by eleven votes to nine, that the injunction did not correspond to a social need sufficiently pressing to outweigh the public interest in freedom of expression and therefore was not 'necessary in a democratic society' for maintaining the authority of the judiciary; and accordingly, was in violation of Article 10.

In response to this finding, the government introduced a bill which became the Contempt of Court Act 1981. Section 5 provided:

> A publication made as or as part of a discussion in good faith of public affairs or other matters of general public interest is not to be treated as a contempt of court under the strict liability rule if the risk of impediment

6. [1973] 1 QB 710.

7. The report of the Committee on Contempt of Court in 1974 (Cmnd 5794) was highly critical of this approach adopted by the House of Lords.

or prejudice to particular legal proceedings is merely incidental to the discussion.

The Act also provided in section 2 that the strict liability rule – which meant liability although there was no intention to interfere with the course of justice – applied only to a publication which created a substantial risk that the course of justice would be seriously impeded or prejudiced.[8]

On 15 October 1980 the *Daily Mail* published an article by Mr Malcolm Muggeridge entitled 'The vision of life that wins my vote' in support of an independent 'pro-life' candidate at a Parliamentary bye-election. She was supported by the Society for the Protection of Unborn Children and took as a main plank in her campaign the stopping of the practice that she asserted was developing in some British hospitals of killing new-born handicapped babies.

The date of publication was also the third day of the trial in the Crown Court at Leicester of a well known paediatrician on a charge of murdering a three-day-old mongoloid baby by giving instructions that it should be treated with a drug which caused it to die of starvation.

The newspaper article made no mention of the trial but it contained the words 'Today the chances of such a baby surviving would be very small indeed. Someone would surely recommend letting her die of starvation or otherwise disposing of her.'

Lord Diplock said that 'substantial' and 'seriously' in section 2 were intended to exclude a risk that was only remote; that the article was clearly capable of prejudicing the jury against the accused; and that it satisfied the criterion in that section. He held, however, that section 5 applied, that the risk of prejudice was merely incidental to the public discussion about the rights and wrongs of the alleged practice of letting deformed babies die, and that the prosecution for contempt therefore failed. The other Law Lords agreed.[9]

However Lord Diplock also commented that the article in this case was 'nearly in all respects the antithesis of the

8. *A-G v. News Group Newspapers Ltd* [1986] 2 All ER 833.
9. *A-G v. English* [1982] 3 WLR 278; and see *A-G v. TVS Television Ltd*, *The Independent*, 7 July 1989.

article which the House of Lords had held to be a contempt of court in *Attorney-General v. Times Newspapers Ltd* (the thalidomide case). In that case, he said, the whole subject of the article was the pending civil actions against the drugs company and the whole purpose of the article was to put pressure on the company in the lawful conduct of their defence in those actions.

Lord Diplock's words make clear that, in his opinion, section 5 of the Contempt of Court Act 1981 does not bring English law into conformity with the European Convention. But indeed his judgment seems to go further. His findings that the article was clearly capable of creating a substantial risk that the course of justice would be seriously impeded or prejudiced reflects a poor view of the independence, fair-mindedness, and intelligence of jurors. Moreover, Lord Diplock's emphasis on 'the whole purpose' of the article in the thalidomide case suggests that, in his view, the limitations in the Act on the strict liability rule might not in any event have availed *The Sunday Times*. Those limitations, including section 5, apply only to unintentional contempts, while 'whole purpose' suggests intention. In the result the Contempt of Court Act 1981, as interpreted by Lord Diplock, may well have made further inroads on the freedom of the press and of publications generally.

An unusual case arose in 1989 when the House of Lords was about to hear argument on an application for judicial review of decisions by the Secretary of State for Trade and Industry to defer publication of an inspector's report and not to refer the matter to the Monopolies and Mergers Commission. While appeal to the Lords was pending, the chief executive of the applicant company (Lonrho) came into possession of a copy of the report, and extracts from it were published in a special mid-week edition of *The Observer* newspaper (a wholly owned subsidiary of Lonrho) which also contained a front-page editorial alleging bad faith on the part of the Secretary of State. The Secretary of State obtained an injunction to prevent publication but too late to stop copies which had been sent to certain persons including (by mistake) four of the five Law Lords due to hear the appeal. The Lords heard and dismissed the appeal and a differently constituted Appellate Committee of the Lords considered whether *The Observer* publication was a contempt of court. That Committee decided that, under Section 2 of Contempt of Court Act 1981 (see above) it was not a contempt because the publication did not in the circumstances create any risk that the course of justice in the appellate proceedings would be impeded or prejudiced.[10] Lord Keith, referring to the decision in the thalidomide case (see above), said:

> How far these passages from the speeches of their Lordships may still be relied upon as accurate expressions of the law is extremely doubtful, certainly in relation to the kind of contempt which is the subject matter of the strict liability rule in sections 1 and 2 of the Act of 1981 . . . Whether the course of justice in particular proceedings will be impeded or prejudiced by a publication must depend primarily on whether the publication will bring influence to bear which is likely to divert the proceedings in some way from the course which they would otherwise have followed.

Confidentiality

Over the last twenty years the courts have developed rules to protect statements made in confidence. This particularly relates to trade secrets, personal relationships, and Government secrets. The courts have been willing to issue injunctions preventing disclosure, as well as giving damages for breach of confidence.

R. H. S. Crossman kept a diary during the six years from 1964 to 1970 when he was a member of the Cabinet. Thereafter he began to collate his records and had completed and handed to his publishers the first volume before his death in April 1974. On 10 May 1974, one of the publishers, who was also a literary executor of Mr Crossman, sent a copy of the typescript of this volume (which dealt with the period

10. *In re Lonrho plc* [1989] 3 WLR 535.

1964–6) to the Cabinet Secretary asking for 'a reasonably quick reading' as publication was planned for that autumn. On 22 June the Secretary said that he could not agree to publication of this volume. He said there were two complementary principles. The first was the collective responsibility of the Cabinet and the need to maintain secrecy to ensure completely frank discussion within the Cabinet and its committees. The second was the personal responsibility of individual ministers. Further correspondence followed and *The Sunday Times* published some extracts from the diaries not all of which had been 'cleared' by the Cabinet Secretary. Then, in June 1975, the Attorney-General brought two actions for injunctions to prevent the publication of the first volume and of further extracts by *The Sunday Times*. The Attorney-General argued that the courts should forbid publication as being contrary to the public interest. He also argued that there was a principle of law that no one should profit from the wrongful publication of information received in confidence. This principle had been recognized as a ground for restraining the unfair use of commercial secrets transmitted in confidence. And in *Argyll v. Argyll*[11] the same principle was applied to domestic secrets passing between husband and wife during marriage. On the basis of the decision in that case, the Lord Chief Justice concluded that when a Cabinet minister received information in confidence the improper publication of such information could be restrained by the courts. In particular, he said:

> The expression of individual opinions by cabinet ministers in the course of cabinet discussions are matters of confidence, the publication of which can be restrained by the court when this is clearly necessary in the public interest.

11. [1967] Ch. 302. In *Fraser v. Evans* [1969] 1 QB 349 the confidential report of the plaintiff, who was a public relations consultant to the Greek government, came into the hands of *The Sunday Times*. The Court of Appeal refused to issue an injunction to prevent its publication on the ground that the person to whom the confidential duty was owed (i.e. the Greek government) was not seeking the protection of the court.

This was a new principle or, at least, the considerable extension of an older principle. When the Lord Chief Justice came to apply this to the case before him, he decided that in view of the lapse of time (nearly ten years since the end of the period covered by the first volume of the diaries) he would not issue the injunctions asked for because he could not believe that publication would inhibit free discussion of the cabinet in 1975.[12]

In the event, therefore, the first volume of the Crossman diaries was published. But more important was the establishment of the new rule of law that the courts have jurisdiction to determine when the public interest requires that ministers shall not be permitted to disclose information. I am not suggesting that there should be no constraints on such publication. But hitherto the constraints, if they have not been imposed by the Official Secrets Acts, have been political. The principle established by this case enables the courts to determine what is in the public interest on a matter which is at the heart of the political system.

In 1981 the majority of Court of Appeal in *Schering Chemicals Ltd v. Falkman Ltd* upheld the granting of an injunction restraining Thames Television Ltd from showing a film about the Primodos drug used in pregnancy testing. Two actions by mothers of deformed children claiming compensation against the manufacturers were due to start some nine months later. This was not a decision on contempt of court but on whether there had been breach of confidence by the producer of the film in respect of confidential information. Shaw LJ, for the majority, said: 'The law of England was indeed, as Blackstone declared, a law of liberty; but the freedoms it recognized did not include a licence for the mercenary betrayal of business confidences.'[13] Lord Denning MR, dissenting, said that he stood as ever for the freedom of the press, including television, except where that freedom was abused as, he said, it was in the *Granada* case. Even if

---

12. *A-G v. Jonathan Cape Ltd*; *A-G v. Times Newspapers Ltd* [1975] 3 All ER 484.
13. [1982] QB 1; for the *Granada* case see below pp. 227–8.

there were abuse in this present case, it was not such as to warrant an injunction operating as a prior restraint.

In *Francome v. Mirror Group Newspapers*[14] the plaintiffs were man and wife, he being the champion National Hunt jockey. Unknown persons tapped telephone conversations to and from the plaintiffs' home and offered the tapes for sale to the *Daily Mirror*, alleging that they revealed breaches by the jockey of the rules of racing. The plaintiffs brought an action for breach of confidence against the *Daily Mirror*, and the Court of Appeal, pending trial, made an order that the newspaper be restrained from publishing any article based on the tapes, that there be a speedy trial and that the newspaper disclose the identity of the unknown persons. On appeal, this order was varied so that disclosure of the identity was not required at this stage.

Ten days later, a differently composed Court of Appeal considered a case where the plaintiff company marketed an electronic computerized instrument known as the Lion Intoximeter 3000, and 60 per cent of their sales were to police authorities for measuring intoxication by alcohol. Two of their former employees leaked copies of the plaintiffs' internal correspondence to the *Daily Express* and the plaintiffs sought an injunction to prevent publication. A conflict of public interests arose because the allegation was that the instrument was not accurate. The court allowed the publication of some of the documents.[15]

Such cases of breach of confidence or of copyright frequently give rise to such conflicts and the courts determine whether the private rights or the public interests should prevail. In *Francome* Sir John Donaldson MR said:

> The 'media' . . . are an essential foundation of any democracy. In exposing crime, antisocial behaviour and hypocrisy and in campaigning for reform and propagating the view of minorities, they perform an invaluable function. However, they are peculiarly vulnerable to the error of confusing the public interest with their own

14. [1984] 1 WLR 892.
15. *Lion Laboratories v. Evans* [1984] 3 WLR 539.

interest. Usually these interests march hand in hand, but not always. In the instant case, pending a trial, it is impossible to see what public interest would be served by publishing the contents of the tapes which would not equally be served by giving them to the police or to the Jockey Club. Any wider publication could only serve the interests of the *Daily Mirror*.

The most famous cases where the protection of confidentiality was claimed deserve a section to themselves.

The Spycatcher cases

The story is complicated and the litigation was conducted over a period of more than four years in Australia, the United Kingdom, Hong Kong and New Zealand.[16] Here, I will concentrate on the hearings in the United Kingdom.

Peter Maurice Wright was a member of the internal security service known as MI5 from 1955 to the beginning of 1976. From 1964, he was in the counter-espionage branch and on the staff of the Director-General as a senior officer. When he retired, he lived in Tasmania and became an Australian citizen. There he wrote his memoirs entitled *Spycatcher* to be published in Australia by Heinemann. The material in the book was not less than ten years old. It included allegations of a plot by members of MI5 to destabilise the Wilson government of the United Kingdom in 1974–6; of a plan by MI6 (the security service concerned with activities outside the United Kingdom) to assassinate President Nasser of Egypt; of regular bugging of foreign embassies, including the French, in London. Wright also alleged that Sir Roger Hollis, one-time Director-General of MI5, was a Soviet spy.

In September 1985, the Attorney-General of the United Kingdom having discovered that Wright intended to publish his memoirs in Australia began proceedings in the Supreme Court of New South Wales seeking to restrain publication.

16. The most useful collection is Michael Fysh (ed.) *The Spycatcher Cases* (1989).

The ground on which the order was sought was that, in making disclosures, Wright would be in breach of the terms of his employment and in particular in breach of his duty of lifelong confidentiality imposed on him by the Official Secrets Act 1911 and declarations which he had signed. On 10 September 1985, the Attorney-General obtained an *ex parte* order in Australia from a court in Australia pending the litigation, and on 16 September the defendant publishers and Wright gave undertakings not to publish until the case had been decided.

On 22 and 23 June 1986, two British newspapers, *The Guardian* and *The Observer*, published articles outlining allegations to be made in *Spycatcher* but denied having seen the manuscript of the book or copies of it. They said the allegations were not new and had been published before. But they wished to be able to publish information in the future deriving directly or indirectly from Wright. The newspapers also argued that breach of confidentiality was permissible if it disclosed wrongdoing and that they should not be restrained from publication, save exceptionally, when the information was of legitimate public interest. On 27 June, the Attorney-General obtained *ex parte* injunctions and on 11 July these were upheld by Millett J pending the full trial. The judge added a proviso that the defendants should be free to publish matters disclosed in open court in Australia. The newspapers appealed but on 25 July the Court of Appeal upheld the Millett injunction citing, amongst other cases, *American Cyanamid v. Ethicon*,[17] *British Steel Corporation v. Granada Television*,[18] *Francome v. Mirror Group*,[19] *Fraser v. Evans*,[20] *Lion Laboratories v. Evans*.[21] Sir John Donaldson MR said:

> Given the special nature of the confidentiality which applies to any aspect of the security service, such publication could not possibly be justified on the evidence at

17. See above p. 106.
18. See below pp. 227–8.
19. See above p. 206.
20. See above p. 204.
21. See above p. 206.

present available and I regard it as in the highest degree unlikely that it could be justified on further evidence which may be available at the trial.[22]

In November and December of 1986, the Attorney-General's application for injunctions in Australia was heard but on 13 March 1987, it was rejected by Powell J in the Supreme Court of New South Wales.

On 27 April 1987, *The Independent* newspaper published an article referring to information in *Spycatcher*, having received a manuscript copy. Two other London papers copied, in part. The Attorney-General moved for contempt of court and this was heard by the Vice-Chancellor (Sir Nicolas Browne-Wilkinson) on 20–22 May. On 2 June, the motion was dismissed on a preliminary point of law of great importance. The parties agreed that it had first to be decided:

> Whether a publication made in the knowledge of an outstanding injunction against another party and which if made by that other party would be in breach thereof constitutes a criminal contempt of court upon the footing that it assaults or interferes with the process of justice in relation to the said injunction.

In other words, while the publication in *The Independent* and the other newspapers was not a breach of the Millett injunction against *The Guardian* and *The Observer*, the Attorney-General argued that nevertheless the publication was one of contempt as it frustrated or impeded the due administration of justice. The newspapers argued that this was to widen the law of contempt and offended the basic principles of natural justice.

The Court of Appeal on 15 July accepted the Attorney-General's argument. Sir John Donaldson MR said:

> I should like to re-emphasize with all the power at my command that this case is not primarily about national security or official secrets. It is about the right of private

22. *A-G v. Guardian Newspapers Ltd and The Observer* (1986) [1989] 2 FSR 23.

citizens and public authorities to seek and obtain the protection of the courts for confidential information which they claim to be their property.

The duty of confidentiality (in these cases, that owed by Wright to the Crown) could be opposed by a claim of a right to publish, whether on grounds of the public interest or otherwise but, pending the trial of the action, 'the balance will normally come down in favour of preserving confidentiality, for the very obvious reason that, if this is not done and publication is permitted, there will be nothing left to have a trial about'.

So the preliminary point of law was decided in favour of the Attorney-General and the case was remitted to the High Court. We return to this below.

Three days before the conclusion of the hearing before the Court of Appeal in July 1987, *The Sunday Times* published extracts from *Spycatcher* and two days before, on 13 July, the book was published in the United States of America, and became available in the United Kingdom. On 18 July, the Attorney-General was granted an injunction, in contempt of court proceedings, against *The Sunday Times* to restrain it from continuing its serialisation of *Spycatcher*.[23]

On 20 July, *The Guardian* and *The Observer* applied for the Millett injunction against them to be discharged on the ground that there had been a material change of circumstance, particularly the availability of *Spycatcher* in the United Kingdom and the earlier failure of the Attorney-General's application in New South Wales. It was agreed that if the Millett injunction was discharged, the Attorney-General's action against *The Sunday Times* would also fail. So the order against *The Sunday Times* was continued to await the decision on the Millett injunction.

Sir Nicolas Browne-Wilkinson V-C on 22 July discharged the injunction against *The Guardian* and *The Observer*. He observed:

It is frequently said that the law is an ass. I, of course, do

---

23. For these and subsequent proceedings see *A-G v. Guardian Newspapers Ltd and others* [1987] 1 All ER 1248.

not agree. But there is a limit to what can be achieved by orders of the court. If the courts were to make orders manifestly incapable of achieving their avowed purpose, such as to prevent the dissemination of information which is already disseminated the law would to my mind indeed be an ass.

At this point, if the drama were being enacted on stage, the curtain would surely fall for the interval. Once *Spycatcher* was published in the United States, and then made available in the United Kingdom, how could publication of articles or extracts be denied? The United Kingdom Government did not seek to prevent publication in the United States, no doubt because they had been advised that the First Amendment to the Constitution of the USA protecting freedom of speech would have precluded the possibility of success in that country. As the audience took their drinks and ate their icecream they would have wondered how the dramatist could develop his story in the second Act.

But the Court of Appeal revived the drama by immediately allowing an appeal. They agreed that the Millett injunction could not continue in its present form but the Vice-Chancellor had made the mistake of not considering some modification of the order. Peter Wright was still in breach of his duty of confidentiality. The common law showed its virility in the words of the Master of the Rolls. Sir John Donaldson said:

> I accept that to the extent that these publications have been read, the information to which they relate has become public knowledge, but not that it has entered the public domain, so losing the seal of confidentiality, because that only occurs when information not only becomes a matter of public knowledge, but also public property.

So Sir John rewrote the injunction to prevent publication of any passage of *Spycatcher* or any words of Peter Wright which 'concerned the British Security Service or its activities or any other security service or its activities' provided that the order should 'not prevent the publication of a summary in very general terms of the allegations made by Mr Wright'.

Off then, poste-haste, to the House of Lords, for a hearing at the end of July. Both sides agreed that the modified injunction 'could not be supported in law and was unworkable in practice', not to say daft. There was much speculation which way their Lordships would jump: to restore the Millett injunction or to take the view of the Vice-Chancellor? Would the Government's pursuit of Peter Wright and the enforcement of his duty of confidentiality be temporarily successful? Or would the Law Lords bring the chase to an end, now that *Spycatcher* was being read by anyone who went to the trouble of obtaining a copy? In the majority, Lords Brandon, Templeman and Ackner came down on the Government's side, with Lords Bridge and Oliver in the minority. The proviso to the Millett injunction permitting the publication of material disclosed in the proceedings in New South Wales was deleted.

For the majority view Lords Brandon and Ackner emphasized that the injunction was temporary, awaiting the full trial of the issues and that the Attorney-General should not be deprived of having the case properly adjudicated. Lords Templeman and Ackner said there was a substantial public interest in maintaining the efficiency of the security service; that the publication of *Spycatcher* would cause grievous harm to individuals and deal a blow to the morale of the service; and that there was ample justification for the continuance of the Millett injunction. Lord Templeman added that if the injunction were discharged an immutable precedent would be created.[24]

Lord Oliver, dissenting, said that as the Vice-Chancellor had properly exercised his discretion in discharging the injunction, appellate courts should not interfere. He also questioned 'both the effectiveness and the appropriateness' of seeking to protect the security service by continuing against the newspaper 'a fetter on disclosure of information

---

24. In October 1989, the European Commission of Human Rights admitted applications from *The Guardian*, *The Observer* and *The Sunday Times* alleging that this decision infringed the European Convention on Human Rights.

which, for good or ill, is now freely obtainable and disclosable by other members of the public'. He added: 'I cannot help but feel that your Lordships are being asked in the light of what has now occurred to beat the air and to interfere with an essential freedom for the preservation of a confidentiality that has already been lost beyond recall.'

These were strong words but Lord Bridge, the other dissentient, went even further. To him the crucial facts were the publication of *Spycatcher* in the United States and the Government's decision not to try to prevent the importation of the book. As the case for maintaining the injunctions could not be any stronger at the trial, the real question was whether the Attorney-General could sustain a claim for permanent injunctions. Lord Bridge questioned whether there was any remaining interest of national security which the Millett injunctions were capable of protecting. Then he said:

> Freedom of speech is always the first casualty under a totalitarian régime. Such a régime cannot afford to allow the free circulation of information and ideas among its citizens. Censorship is the indispensable tool to regulate what the public may and what they may not know. The present attempt to insulate the public in this country from information which is freely available elsewhere is a significant step down that very dangerous road.

On 24 September 1987, the appeal from Powell J's decision in New South Wales was dismissed.

At last in November and December 1987, the full trial of the Attorney-General's case against *The Guardian*, *The Observer* and *The Sunday Times* was heard at first instance, by Scott J.[25] At the end of a long judgment, he refused injunctive relief in the three actions. It must be remembered that the Attorney-General was arguing that it was essential for the future of the security service that the lifelong confidentiality of officers of that service should be enforced; that the newspapers knew that Peter Wright had this duty not to disclose information obtained when he was an officer; that

---

25. *A-G v. Guardian Newspapers Ltd and others (No. 2)* [1988] 2 WLR 805.

they were therefore under a comparable duty not to disclose. Scott J held that the *Guardian* and *Observer* articles reporting the court action in Australia and disclosing other allegations in *Spycatcher*, such as the plot to assassinate President Nasser of Egypt and to destabilise the government of Harold Wilson in the 1960s, were justified as being in the public interest. The wide publication of *Spycatcher* meant that there was no longer any duty of confidence lying on the newspapers.

The Court of Appeal dismissed the Attorney-General's appeal while stressing, as had Scott J, that, depending on the facts of the case, third parties (such as the newspapers) might be bound to respect the confidentiality of information coming into their possession.[26] Certainly the Government had an enforceable right to the maintenance of confidentiality by its confidant. But when information had been generally communicated to the public, the duty of confidentiality could no longer be sustained. The Court of Appeal also accepted that breach of confidence might be justified by countervailing public interests. The Attorney-General appealed and *The Sunday Times* cross-appealed. And so, once again, to the House of Lords where the case was argued in June 1988 and opinions were delivered in October. The appeal and the cross-appeal were dismissed.[27]

On the main issue, the Law Lords held that for the Crown to obtain an injunction to prevent the disclosure of confidential information, damage to the public interest, or a likelihood thereof, must be shown. General publication of *Spycatcher* would not bring any significant further damage to the public interest and so the Millett injunction must be discharged. A third party who comes into possession of confidential information may be under a duty not to disclose it, but this depends on the particular circumstances. The articles in *The Guardian* and *The Observer* had not contained information damaging to the public interest (Lord Griffiths dissenting on this point).

Lord Keith of Kinkel said:

26. See last note.
27. [1988] 3 WLR 776.

The Crown's argument in the present case would go the length that in all circumstances where the original disclosure has been made by a Crown servant in breach of his obligation of confidence any person to whose knowledge the information comes and who is aware of the breach comes under an equitable duty binding his conscience not to communicate the information to anyone else irrespective of the circumstances under which he acquired the knowledge. In my opinion that general proposition is untenable and impracticable, in addition to being unsupported by any authority . . . A communication about some aspect of government activity which does no harm to the interests of the nation cannot, even where the original disclosure has been made in breach of confidence, be restrained on the ground of a nebulous equitable duty of conscience serving no useful practical purpose.

And he referred to the Crossman diaries case where Lord Widgery CJ allowed publication on the ground that it would do no harm to the public interest.

It was, however, held that *The Sunday Times* was in breach of its duty of confidence in publishing its first serialised extract from *Spycatcher* on 12 July 1987; that it was not protected by either the defence of prior publication or the disclosure of iniquity; that imminent publication of the book in the USA did not amount to a justification; and that, accordingly, *The Sunday Times* was liable to account for the profits resulting from that breach.

In May 1989 the remitted case against *The Independent* and others, including *The Sunday Times*, was heard by Mr Justice Morritt. He found them guilty of contempt of court and fined each of the publishers £50,000. The Court of Appeal, in February 1990, dismissed the appeals but discharged the fines. This decision confirmed that it is a contempt of court, as interfering with the course of justice, for a newspaper editor to publish information which he knows is the subject of an injunction against another newspaper.[28]

---

28. *A-G. v. Newspaper Publishing plc and others* [1989] FSR 457.

Disclosure of documents

Official secrets may be protected by the courts under a rule which provides that the Crown may claim that certain documents should not be disclosed to a party engaged in litigation on the ground that the public interest would be harmed by their production. In the leading case of *Duncan v. Cammell Laird*[29] the plaintiffs were the legal representatives or dependants of some of the ninety-nine men who lost their lives when the submarine *Thetis* sank during tests in Liverpool Bay. The defendants were those who had built the submarine. The plaintiffs called for the disclosure of plans, specifications and other documents relating to the construction of the submarine and the First Lord of the Admiralty objected. The objection was upheld by the House of Lords. That the rule applied to a great variety of cases is shown by the decision of the Court of Appeal in *Wednesbury Corporation v. Ministry of Housing and Local Government*[30] when an objection was upheld to the disclosure of departmental briefs for the guidance of, and correspondence with, ministerial inspectors who had held a local enquiry into a proposal by the Local Government Commission that five local authorities should be extinguished and included in larger county boroughs.

As a result of these and other cases, it had come to be assumed that the affidavit of the minister concerned which claimed non-disclosure, so long as it was properly executed, could not be challenged in the courts. If he said that disclosure was not in the public interest, that was the end of the matter. But in *Conway v. Rimmer*[31] the House of Lords held that there might be a clash between the public interest that harm should not be done to the nation or the public service by the disclosure of certain documents, and the public interest in the proper administration of justice. If this were so the court could inspect the documents and might override

29. [1942] AC 624.
30. [1965] 1 WLR 261.
31. [1968] AC 910; and see *Burmah Oil Co. Ltd v. Bank of England* [1980] AC 1198.

the minister's claim – though if the minister's reasons were beyond the competence of the court to assess, the minister's view would have to prevail. The action in the case was brought by a former probationary police constable against his former superintendent for malicious prosecution and the documents included reports made by the defendant on the plaintiff. In the light of the later decision on the Crossman diaries, Lord Reid's comments at one point in his judgment are interesting and left no doubt where his sympathies lay in the perennial conflict between the secretiveness of governments and people's wish to know what is being done in their name:

> Virtually everyone agrees that cabinet minutes and the like ought not to be disclosed until such time as they are only of historical interest. But I do not think that many people would give as the reason that premature disclosure would prevent candour in the cabinet. To my mind the most important reason is that such disclosure would create or fan ill-informed or captious public or political criticism. The business of government is difficult enough as it is, and no government could contemplate with equanimity the inner workings of the government machine being exposed to the gaze of those ready to criticize without adequate knowledge of the background and perhaps with some axe to grind.

One result of this decision may have been that the Crown's claim to non-disclosure is less frequently made than in the past. Recent cases involving disclosures of documents held by Customs and Excise have been decided in opposite directions[32] but one decision of more public interest is disturbing. Under the Gaming Act 1968, certificates of consent have to be obtained from the Gaming Board for the running of bingo halls. R applied and the Gaming Board made certain enquiries with the police. The assistant chief constable of Sussex replied in a letter, a copy of which came into the possession of R, who laid an information against him alleging

---

32. See *Norwich Pharmacal v. Customs & Excise* [1974] AC 133 and *A. Crompton Ltd v. Customs & Excise (No 2)* [1974] AC 405.

criminal libel. As a result the chief constable of Sussex and the secretary of the Gaming Board were both summoned to produce this letter. The Home Secretary objected to its disclosure. The House of Lords held

> that the public interest required that the letters should not be produced, since, if the information given to the Board was liable to be disclosed, it might be withheld and they would thereby be hampered in the discharge of the duty imposed on them by statute to identify and exclude persons of dubious character and reputation from the privilege of obtaining a licence to conduct a gaming establishment.

The argument of the House of Lords was based widely on the public interest, not on the particular position of the Crown. Lord Reid said: 'It must always be open to any person interested to raise the question' of the public interest and it was said that Parliament in passing the Gaming Act must have expected that the Gaming Board would be obliged to receive certain documents which no one would contemplate they had to divulge.[33] The problem in all this is, of course, that such decisions make it extremely difficult, often impossible, for a private citizen to challenge a 'confidential' report made about him by the police or other public authority. The 'proper functioning of the public service' can be bought at too high a price.

A similar reflection inevitably arises from considerations of the grounds given by Lord Denning MR for the decision of the Court of Appeal in *Home Office v. Harman* (1981).[34] Harriet Harman, a solicitor and legal officer of the National Council for Civil Liberties, was acting for a convicted prisoner in his action against the Home Office arising out of his treatment in prison in an experimental 'control unit'. She sought certain documents from the Home Office the disclosure of which was refused on the ground of public interest. But a judge ordered their disclosure. In the action brought by the prisoner against the Home Office, several of these

33. *R v. Lewes JJ ex parte Home Secretary* [1973] AC 388.
34. [1981] 2 WLR 310.

documents were read out in court. Subsequently Ms Harman allowed a journalist to see them. The Home Office brought an action against her for contempt on the ground that documents are disclosed only for the purposes of the specific litigation and that she had no right to show them to a journalist even though they had been made public in court.

In words reminiscent of Lord Reid in *Conway v. Rimmer* (see above) Lord Denning said:

> It was in the public interest that these documents should be kept confidential. They should not be exposed to the ravages of outsiders. I regard the use made by the journalists in this case of these documents to be highly detrimental to the good ordering of our society . . . The danger of disclosure is that critics – of one political colour or another – will seize on this confidential information so as to seek changes in governmental policy, or to condemn it. So the machinery of government will be hampered or even thwarted.

The Court of Appeal upheld the decision of the judge at first instance that Ms Harman was guilty of contempt. The court was obviously influenced by the fact that the journalist had used the documents to write an article condemning the Home Office for what he called 'internal bureaucratic intrigue' surrounding the setting up of the control units.

Ms Harman appealed to the House of Lords which upheld the Court of Appeal but only by the decisions of three Law Lords against two. Lord Diplock, who was joined in the majority by Lords Keith and Roskill, began with a stylistic mannerism of which some of the senior judiciary are apparently fond.[35] He insisted that the case was *not* about freedom of speech, freedom of the press, openness of justice or documents coming into 'the public domain'; nor did it call for consideration of any of those human rights and fundamental freedoms contained in the European Convention on Human Rights. To Lord Diplock the case was only about 'an aspect

---

35. [1982] 2 WLR 338; cf. Lord Wilberforce in *British Steel Corporation v. Granada Television* [1980] 3 WLR at 821: 'This case does not touch upon the freedom of the press even at its periphery.' And see p. 209 above.

of the law of discovery of documents in civil actions in the High Court', and he saw discovery as 'an inroad' upon the right of the individual 'to keep his own documents to himself'. So seen, the obligation not to use a disclosed document for any purpose other than of the litigation did *not* terminate at the moment the document was read out in court. Lord Keith spoke similarly of discovery constituting 'a very serious invasion of the privacy and confidentiality of a litigant's affairs'.

Lord Scarman, joined by Lord Simon in the minority, took a broader view by reference to the European Convention and American law. And he noted that the Home Office took no steps to prevent the documents from being made public once the judge had ordered their disclosure. The Home Office had not appealed against that order or renewed their objection at the trial. So once the documents were read out in open court, in Lord Scarman's opinion, the obligation binding the litigant and his solicitor ceased.

The majority seemed to be unmoved by the manifest absurdities of the position they took up (though Lord Roskill was more hesitant than his colleagues). The journalist could have obtained a transcript of the proceedings in court and so have had legitimate access to the documents. Moreover, only the litigant and his solicitor could be bound by the limitations imposed. Anyone could have taken a shorthand note of the documents when they were read out in court and used the information so acquired as he wished.

Two connected facts seem to have been most influential in the minds of the majority. The first was that these were government documents and governments must not be unduly embarrassed in such circumstances. And the second was the use made by the journalist in attacking the activities of a government department. None of the majority was so explicit as Lord Denning in the Court of Appeal but Lord Keith noted: 'It would be unrealistic not to recognize that (Ms Harman) must have been activated by a desire to advance some aspect of the causes espoused by the National Council for Civil Liberties, which employed her as a legal officer.' It must be very doubtful whether any action for contempt would have been brought by the Home Office had the journalist's article not been critical of the Department.

After the decision, Ms Harman, *The Guardian* newspaper and the National Council for Civil Liberties applied to the European Commission of Human Rights alleging breach of the Convention. In 1986, after the Commission had decided that the complaint was admissible, a friendly settlement was reached and the Government made new provision under the Rules of the Supreme Court. This reads:

> Any undertaking, whether express or implied, not to use a document for any purposes other than those of the proceedings in which it is disclosed shall cease to apply to such document after it has been read to or by the Court, or referred to, in open court, unless the Court for special reasons has otherwise ordered on the application of a party or of the person to whom the document belongs.

This falls short of a ringing declaration in support of the principle that proceedings in open court are public property.[36]

This conflict between the public interest in the proper administration of justice and the protection of documents from disclosure has been the subject of more and more litigation in recent years. In *Neilson v. Laugharne*[37] the plaintiff's house was searched by the police while he was on holiday on suspicion of drug offences but nothing was found. During the search the police noticed that his electricity meter appeared to have been tampered with and, on his return, he was arrested but not charged. He complained to the chief constable who instituted the complaints procedure under the Police Act 1964, which resulted in a decision that there were no grounds for proceedings against the police officers involved. The plaintiff commenced proceedings against the chief constable who refused to disclose statements made during the course of the enquiry into the complaints on the

---

36. See *Bibby Bulk Carriers v. Consulex Ltd* [1988] 2 All ER 820.

37. [1981] 2 WLR 537; and see *Hehir v. Commissioner of Police for Metropolis* [1982] 1 WLR 715.

ground that they were covered by legal professional privilege. The Court of Appeal upheld the refusal. Lord Denning MR said, 'Legal aid is being used by complaining persons to harass innocent folk who have only been doing their duty. The complainants make all sorts of allegations – often quite unjustifiable – and then use legal machinery to try to manufacture a case. We should come down firmly against such tactics. We should refuse to order production.' Oliver LJ rested his decision on the ground that disclosures would inhibit the proper conduct of the enquiry procedure and that the public interest required that the documents should be protected as a class.

The facts in *Williams v. Home Office*[38] are set out above.[39] The prisoner sought documents from the Home Office, some of which were refused on the ground that they came within the class of documents relating to the formulation of government policy and that their production would inhibit freedom of expression between Ministers and inhibit officials from giving full advice to Ministers. McNeill J ordered the disclosure of some of these documents and, citing the authority of Law Lords in an earlier case, rejected the argument about the need to preserve candour between ministers and public servants. But in *Air Canada v. Secretary of State for Trade (No. 2)*[40] a group of airlines which wished to challenge the defendant's approval of substantial increases in landing charges at Heathrow airport were refused disclosure of documents concerned with the formulation of government policy. Three members of the House of Lords upheld this refusal on the ground that the plaintiffs had to show that the information sought was likely to help their case or damage their adversary's in the sense that there was a reasonable probability and not just a mere speculative belief that it would do so; and that the plaintiffs had failed to establish this. The other two Law Lords, while agreeing in the result, held

38. [1981] 1 All ER 1151.
39. See pp. 218–19
40. [1983] 1 All ER 910; see also *Campbell v. Tameside Metropolitan BC* [1982] 3 WLR 74.

that the court should consider disclosures whenever this was necessary for a just determination of the case.

In the Court of Appeal, Lord Denning MR had referred to *Williams v. Home Office*, and to the judge's overruling of the Department's objections to disclosure. Lord Denning said:

> He thought that there was a safeguard in that they could only be used for the purpose of the action . . . His decision was claimed by the advocates of 'open government' to be a 'legal milestone'. But the safeguard proved to be no safeguard at all. The documents were used by a journalist to make severe criticisms of ministers and of higher civil servants who could not answer back. When this was brought to our attention, I said, 'The "legal milestone" will have to be taken up and set back a bit,' see *Home Office v. Harman*. That case is a good illustration of the need for keeping high-level documents secret. Once they are let out of the bag, untold mischief may be done. It is no use relying on safeguards. The documents must not be let out of the bag at all. I trust that today we are setting back the 'legal milestone' to the place where it was before.[41]

Censorship of the media

Most of the cases concern attempts by Law Officers, other ministers or the police to prevent the publication of particular material but one concerned certain local authorities in London who decided to stop taking in their libraries publications of Times Newspapers Ltd, as a gesture of support for employees dismissed by the company during an industrial dispute. The Divisional Court held that this was an abuse of their powers and quashed the decisions. The court held that the ban had been imposed by the local authorities for an ulterior object being inspired by political views which had moved them to use their statutory powers to interfere in an industrial dispute. Lord Justice Watkins said:

41. [1983] 1 All ER 161.

It cannot be other than to all sensible and right-minded people alarming, I think, to see such irresponsible behaviour by persons elected to serve their interest according to clearly stated law and in defiance of impeccably correct advice. There could hardly be a clearer manifestation of an abuse of power, the remedy for which it is for the court and not the Minister to provide.[42]

So also, a Labour-controlled council was held to have abused its powers when it decided to ban the advertising of teaching posts in the *Times Educational Supplement* in order to punish the proprietors for publishing, in *The Sunday Times*, allegedly libellous articles about the council's leader. Costs at the highest level were awarded against the council because of its 'blatant abuse of power' and a 'gross attempt to deceive the court'.[43]

The BBC's programmes under the title of *Rough Justice* were designed to express doubts about convictions in criminal cases. They aroused the wrath of some judges. In January 1986, the BBC suspended two journalists after the Lord Chief Justice (Lord Lane) had accused them of 'outrageous' behaviour and 'investigation by menaces' in putting together a programme about a man found subsequently to have been wrongly convicted. A year later, as the result of a similar programme (*Out of Court*), the BBC was accused by Lord Lane of broadcasting 'a deliberate attack on the integrity and reliability of the system of criminal justice in this country'.

In 1986 the BBC prepared a series of television programmes called *The Secret Society*, the purpose of which, according to its principal author Duncan Campbell, was to examine how Government concealed from Parliament and the public expenditure which should have been disclosed. Under Government pressure, the BBC withdrew the programmes, the first of which concerned a defence project, code-named Zircon. On 21 January 1987, the Attorney-Gen-

42. *R v. Ealing Borough Council and others ex parte Times Newspapers Ltd* [1986] 85 LGR 316.
43. *R v. Derbyshire County Council ex parte Times Supplement Ltd, The Independent*, 19 July 1990.

eral obtained an injunction restraining Mr Campbell and others from disclosing or publishing any information about or included in the programmes. Some Members of Parliament proposed to show the *Zircon* programme in a room in the House of Commons and on 22 January the Attorney-General sought another injunction against them. But the judge refused this on the ground that it was for the House to regulate its own proceedings. So the Speaker issued a direction that the film should not be shown in any room in the House, until the House could decide the matter. On 22 January, the *New Statesman* published an article on the Zircon affair. On 27 January, after debate,[44] the House referred the Speaker's ruling to the Committee of Privileges, on the understanding that it should continue in force until the injunction was lifted or the House decided otherwise. A few days later the police, under warrants, searched the premises of the BBC and the premises of Mr Campbell and others and the *New Statesman* offices in Glasgow and London, and removed films, videotapes and other material.[45] The *Zircon* programme was eventually shown in September 1988. No prosecutions were brought.

Eleven months later, the procedure was repeated. On 3 December 1987, the Government obtained *ex parte* an injunction preventing the BBC from broadcasting a three-part series on Radio 4 on the role of the British security service.

The injunction prevented the BBC from:

> broadcasting or causing or permitting to be broadcast, parts of a radio programme *My Country: Right or Wrong* or in any other way whatsoever, any interviews with, or information derived from, current or former members of the security or intelligence services in the UK relating to any aspect of the work of the said ser-

44. 109 HC Deb col. 206–74. In May 1987, the Committee, by a majority, concluded that the Speaker had acted 'wholly correctly'; the minority wished to record that his action was unconstitutional (see HC 365 of 1986–7.)

45. On 25 February 1987, Mr Campbell gave a detailed undertaking to the High Court and the injunction was discharged.

vices, including their identity as current or former members.

Unlike *The Secret Society* programmes, *My Country* was the responsibility of permanent current affairs producers and editors at the heart of the BBC. The basis of the application for the injunction was that former and serving security service personnel who were to speak on the programme owed the Government a duty of confidentiality. A fortnight later the judge, after a hearing, continued the injunction. Subsequently, after the Government had obtained access to the documents, the injunction was discharged by consent. The programmes were transmitted in 1988. Again there were no prosecutions.

During the hearing of appeals (by persons convicted of IRA bombing) in which the possibility of retrials was argued, the Court granted an injunction to prohibit the broadcast of a television programme in which actors would represent some of those in court and which would be based on excerpts from the appeal proceedings.[46]

On 19 October 1988, the Home Secretary announced[47] that he had issued instructions to the British Broadcasting Corporation and the Independent Broadcasting Authority requiring them not to broadcast material which included any words spoken by a representative of an organization proscribed in Northern Ireland and of Sinn Fein, Republican Sinn Fein and the Ulster Defence Organization. Excluded were words spoken in the course of proceedings in Parliament or by or in support of a candidate at a parliamentary, European Parliamentary or local election. The three named organisations are lawful bodies and Sinn Fein has an elected Member of the House of Commons.

The direction to the BBC was issued under clause 13(4) of the Licence and Agreement and that to the IBA under section 29(3) of the Broadcasting Act 1981, both of which authorize the Home Secretary to require the two bodies to refrain from broadcasting specified matters. Neither the

---

46. *A-G v. Channel 4 Television Co.* [1988] Crim. LR 237.
47. 138 HC Deb. col. 893.

BBC nor the IBA challenged the legal validity of the ban but an action was brought by broadcasters and a member of the public and backed by the National Union of Journalists.[48]

The Court of Appeal rejected the application for judicial review saying that the Home Secretary's decision to make the directives was for him and not for the courts who should intervene only if he took account of irrelevant matters, failed to take account of relevant matters or made a decision which was manifestly outside the wide spectrum of reasonable decisions.

The protection of sources

Journalists have long insisted on their need to be able to protect their sources and not to be required by the courts to disclose the names of those who have provided them with information. In 1963, two journalists who gave evidence to a tribunal of enquiry investigating breaches of security by an Admiralty clerk refused to disclose the sources of the information they published. This tribunal was by statute in a position similar to the High Court where to refuse to answer proper questions is a contempt of court. The Court of Appeal upheld sentences of six and three months' imprisonment.[49]

In 1982, a journalist who refused to reveal the source of his information (which had resulted in the exposure of illegality and corruption at Ladbroke's casinos) was found not guilty of contempt of court because to reveal the source would have served no useful purpose.[50]

The principles governing these cases were reviewed in *British Steel Corporation v. Granada Televison Ltd* (1980).[51] An employee of BSC, without the permission of BSC, supplied Granada with confidential documents, the property of

48. *R v. Secretary of State for the Home Department ex parte Brind* [1990] 2 WLR 787; confirmed by House of Lords, *The Independent*, 8 February 1991.

49. *A-G v. Mulholland* [1963] 2 QB 477.

50. *A-G v. Lundin* 75 Cr. App. Rep. 90.

51. [1980] 3 WLR 774.

BSC. These documents were used by Granada in a televised interview with the chairman of BSC. Subsequently BSC sought an order from the courts requiring Granada to tell BSC who had supplied the information. Granada argued that they should not be obliged to do so, principally because it was desirable in the public interest that press and television journalists should be entitled to protect their sources of information. In the Court of Appeal, Lord Denning MR, who with his colleagues upheld the Vice-Chancellor in ordering disclosure of the name, recognized the interest of journalists. But he found against Granada because he decided that in the circumstances they had not acted 'with a due sense of responsibility'. A majority of the Law Lords agreed with the Court of Appeal. Lord Wilberforce noted that Granada had not disputed that to supply the information was a wrongful act in law. He agreed that journalists had an interest in protecting their sources but the court had to decide, in the particular circumstances, whether that interest was outweighed by other interests to which the law attached importance. He held that BSC had suffered 'a grievous wrong' and to deny them the opportunity of a remedy against their employee would be 'a significant denial of justice'.

Lord Salmon alone dissented. He emphasized that BSC was losing large sums of taxpayers' money and that the employee considered it to be his public duty to reveal the information in the documents. Lord Salmon thought that Granada were right to consider that they had a public duty to disclose any information which exposed the faults and mistakes of BSC. He concluded:

> There are no circumstances in this case which have ever before deprived or ever should deprive the press of its immunity against revealing its sources of information. The freedom of the press depends upon this immunity. Were it to disappear so would the sources from which its information is obtained; and the public be deprived of much of the information to which the public of a free nation is entitled.

In *Secretary of State for Defence v. Guardian Newspapers*

Ltd,[52] a copy of a 'secret' document was passed anonymously to the editor of *The Guardian*. This document was a minute of 20 October 1983, from the Minister of Defence to the Prime Minister. It dealt with parliamentary and public statements to be made on 1 November about, and contemporaneously with, the delivery of Cruise Missiles from the USA to Greenham Common. Six other copies were sent, five to Ministers and one to the Secretary of the Cabinet. On 31 October, *The Guardian* published this minute in full. Not until 11 November – eleven days later – did the Treasury Solicitor write to the editor of *The Guardian* asking for the return of the document and on 22 November he issued a writ claiming delivery of the document from the newspaper. It was accompanied by a notice of motion claiming, as interlocutory relief, immediate delivery of the document. On 15 December, Scott J. ordered the return of the document. This was affirmed by the Court of Appeal the next day and complied with. As a result of a study of the markings on the document, the leak was traced to Miss Sarah Tisdall, a clerk in the private office of the Foreign Secretary and she was subsequently convicted and sentenced to six months' imprisonment. From the decision of the Court of Appeal, *The Guardian* appealed to the House of Lords on the ground that section 10 of the Contempt of Court Act 1981 protected them from being obliged to return the document.

Section 10 provides:

> No court may require a person to disclose, nor is any person guilty of contempt of court for refusing to disclose, the source of information contained in a publication for which he is responsible, unless it be established to the satisfaction of the court that disclosure is necessary in the interests of justice or national security or for the prevention of disorder or crime.

The evidence put forward on behalf of the Secretary of State for Defence was on affidavit, sworn by the principal establishment officer of the Department. And the question was whether the facts stated in the affidavit were sufficient

52. [1984] 3 WLR 986.

to establish that the delivery up of the document was necessary in the interests of national security, it being accepted that the markings on the copy would probably lead to identification of the person who had leaked the document. In the event, three Law Lords thought the facts stated were sufficient and two Law Lords thought they were insufficient.

The majority, faced with an affidavit which did not contain the evidence required to show that disclosure was 'necessary' in the interests of national security, managed to infer facts which could satisfy them. The minority quite sharply found this course impossible. That is hardly a firm basis on which to found the freedom of the Press.

In 1985, a takeover bid of a brewery company was referred to the Monopolies and Mergers Commission. On 8 November, *The Times* published an article by a financial journalist which said that the report of the Commission would recommend that the bid would be allowed without any conditions. This proved to be correct. In October 1986, *The Independent* published an article by the same journalist which accurately forecast that a different bid would be referred to the Commission because the Director-General of Fair Trading was 'understood to have been impressed' by the arguments in favour of a reference and would so advise the Secretary of State. This also proved to be correct. In December 1986, inspectors were appointed under the Financial Services Act 1986 to investigate criminal insider dealings resulting from suspected leaks from the Office of Fair Trading, the Commission or the Department of Trade and Industry. In February 1987, the financial journalist was required to attend before the inspectors and was asked questions about the nature and sources of the information on which the two articles had been based. He refused to answer. Under section 178(2) of the Act, the question for the court was whether his refusal was 'without reasonable excuse'. If so, he could be punished as if he had been guilty of contempt of court. His defence was that his refusal was justified by section 10 of the Contempt of Court Act 1981 or the public interest in the protection of journalists' sources of information.

The House of Lords held that the inspectors had produced

sufficient evidence that it was 'necessary for the prevention of crime' that they should know the journalist's sources of information and that the journalist did not have a reasonable excuse to refuse to reveal them.[53] The journalist was fined £20,000 paid by *The Independent*.

In 1989, while a company was negotiating for a large bank loan, a copy of its draft business plan for the loan disappeared. The next day a journalist was telephoned and given information about the company and the loan. The company applied to the court for an order requiring the publishers of the magazine for whom the journalist worked to reveal the source (known only to the journalist) of the information which could be discovered from the journalist's notes. The publishers were ordered to disclose the notes but the journalist refused to make them available. An order was then made the effect of which was that the journalist should communicate with the source who could deliver the file without identifying himself. The journalist refused to communicate the order. The Court of Appeal gave the journalist the option of handing over the notes in a sealed envelope pending an appeal. The journalist did not accept this. The company sought to commit him to prison for contempt of court.

In the mean time the publishers appealed against the order requiring them to disclose the notes. This appeal was dismissed, the Master of the Rolls saying that the 'interests of justice' referred to in section 10 of the Contempt of Court Act 1981 meant 'the interests in the administration of justice' generally, and in those interests disclosure was necessary in this case. The House of Lords agreed, saying that it was in the 'interests of justice' that persons should be enabled to exercise important legal rights and to protect themselves from serious legal wrongs whether or not resort to legal proceedings in a court of law were necessary to attain those objectives.

Lord Bridge made heavy weather of the position taken by the publishers and the journalist whom he thought might be acting 'under the misguided influence of some members of

53. *Re an Inquiry under the Company Securities (Insider Dealing) Act 1985* [1988] 2 WLR 33.

his profession who see his predicament as providing the opportunity for some kind of an ideological confrontation with the courts'. Lord Bridge's 'unease' was increased by the knowledge that the journalist's litigation costs were being paid by 'another undisclosed source'. He was clearly incensed by the prospect of a journalist being willing, if necessary, to go to prison rather than reveal his sources, and rested his interpretation of section 10 and his decision on the highest principles, referring to undermining 'the rule of law . . . wholly unacceptable in a democratic society . . . sovereignty of the Queen in Parliament . . . [and] of the Queen's courts . . . abdication of the role of Parliament . . . tantamount to conferring an absolute privilege against disclosure . . . paradoxical that a serious challenge to the rule of law should be mounted by responsible journalists' and much else beside. It was held that the potential damage to the plaintiff's business was very substantial and so the necessity for disclosure was established. In the event Mr Goodwin was not sent to prison but was fined £5,000.[54] He was ordered to pay costs said to exceed £100,000. His employer was believed to have backed the case.

Official Secrets

Until 1989, the principal statute was the Official Secrets Act 1911. Section 1 (which is still in force) is concerned with spying but the words are wide enough to cover lesser activities such as demonstrations in 'prohibited places'.[55] Section 2 was so wide that it had been called a 'catch-all' section. It created offences where almost all that needed to be proved was the unauthorized communication or receipt of official information. In 1971, the section was used to prosecute the editor and a journalist of the *Sunday Telegraph* for publishing material from a report on the Nigerian civil war.[56] The

---

54. *X Ltd v. Morgan Grampian (Publishers) Ltd* [1990] 2 WLR 1000.
55. *Chandler v. DPP* (see below p. 243).
56. *R v. Cairns, Aitken and Roberts*; and see J. Aitken, *Officially Secret* (1971).

defendants were acquitted after the judge, in his summing-up to the jury, had suggested that section 2 had reached retirement age and should be pensioned off.

In 1978 when two journalists interviewed a former soldier about the operations of army intelligence seven and more years before, all three were charged under sections 1 and 2. But the judge expressed his view that the use of section 1 in a case not concerned with spying was oppressive and those charges were dropped. The accused were convicted on less serious charges under section 2 but none of them was sent to prison. The whole proceedings reflected judicial dissatisfaction with prosecutions under the Official Secrets Acts.[57] Yet one is left with serious doubts whether the Court of Appeal or the House of Lords would have taken a similar view. These cases are a reminder that not all judges act the same way on all occasions.

In May 1982, an Argentine cruiser, the General Belgrano, was sunk by a British submarine during the Falklands conflict. This gave rise to political controversy in the United Kingdom. In July 1984, the Foreign Affairs Committee of the House of Commons began an investigation into the surrounding events. Clive Ponting, who was an Assistant Secretary in the Ministry of Defence, decided that Parliament was being deliberately misled by ministers and so sent copies of two internal ministry documents to Tam Dalyell MP who passed them to the chairman of the Committee who returned them to the ministry. Subsequently, Clive Ponting was charged under section 2 of the Official Secrets Act.[58]

Section 2 provided that it was an offence for a civil servant to communicate official information to any person other than a person to whom he was authorized to communicate it 'or a person to whom it is in the interest of the State his duty

57. *R v. Aubrey, Berry and Campbell*. See Andrew Nicol, 'Official Secrets and Jury Vetting' in the *Criminal Law Review*, May 1979, p. 281. The soldier John Berry had given the information because he was disturbed at the deportation of Hosenball (see above, p. 153). This was also the case where 'Colonel B' made his appearance and where jury vetting was first, in recent times, disclosed (see above, p. 156). See Crispin Aubrey, *Who's Watching You?* (1981).

58. [1985] Crim. LR 318.

to communicate it'. The prosecution argued that this duty could mean only official duty and that the interest of the State meant what was in the interest of the State according to its recognized organs of government and the policies as expounded by the particular Government of the day. The judge indicated that he agreed with the prosecution and so would have to direct the jury to convict. At this point, the prosecution protested that they wanted a jury verdict, not a direction, and obtained a short adjournment after which the judge withdrew his proposal to direct. The judge summed up strongly in favour of the prosecution but the jury acquitted the accused.

Section 2 was repealed and replaced by the provisions of the Official Secrets Act 1989. It was sought to include in the Bill a general defence that the disclosure was in the public interest particularly where it revealed criminal activity or other serious misbehaviour by public officials. But this was unsuccessful. However, the Act did require that in certain circumstances disclosure had to be shown to be 'damaging'. In *Lord Advocate v. Scotsman Publications*,[59] a former member of the security services was refused authorisation for publication of a book of memoirs. He had 500 copies printed at his own expense and distributed 279 to private individuals before undertaking not to distribute more. One of the recipients handed his copy to a Scottish newspaper which published an article including some information from the book. The Lord Advocate sought to restrain the newspaper. He argued that, although the book and the article did not contain any information the disclosure of which was capable of damaging national security, any unauthorised disclosure of the work of a member of the secret service was against the public interest. The House of Lords held the prosecution had failed to advance a good arguable case. Lord Templeman said that although the Official Secrets Act 1989 was not in force at the time of the publication the courts should exercise their discretion on the principles of that Act including that of the need to show damage. The prosecution failed.

59. [1989] 3 WLR 358.

7. The uses of conspiracy

Introduction

I have already noted the importance of the crime and the tort of conspiracy in relation to trade unions, particularly in the late nineteenth and early twentieth centuries. More recently, criminal conspiracy has acquired a new significance in other fields.

The essence of the crime of conspiracy at common law is an agreement between two or more persons to commit an unlawful act. The crime is the agreement and its execution or non-execution is irrelevant. Moreover the agreement may be inferred: 'A nod or a wink may amount to conspiracy.' But also it is not necessary that the conspirators should ever have met or known each other so long as there was evidence that they were acting in concert. Men may be selected at random from an extensive picket or well-known individuals selected out of thousands who are demonstrating.[1] A single person may be charged with conspiracy 'with persons unknown'.

Moreover the unlawfulness of the act which the conspirators agree to commit is not limited to criminal acts. It extends widely to civil wrongs also, such as trespass to property and beyond that to an ill-defined area where it seems sufficient that the act is immoral or even a matter of public concern.[2] It follows therefore that a person may be convicted of con-

1. See generally Geoff Robertson, *Whose Conspiracy?* (NCCL, 1974); Robert Hazell, *Conspiracy and Civil Liberties* (Occasional Papers on Social Administration, 1974).
2. See below pp. 237–43. This vagueness means that the definition of the crime is for the court to determine.

spiracy to commit an act for which he could not be prosecuted if he acted alone. The charge of conspiracy may also be used to avoid the necessity of some procedural requirement which attaches to the substantive act. Thus for some crimes – such as prosecutions under the Official Secrets Act – the leave of the Attorney-General must be obtained. But conspiracy to commit an offence under those Acts does not require leave. Again, proceedings for certain specific offences – for example under the Obscene Publications Act 1959 – may be prohibited by statute but the prohibition does not cover conspiracy to commit those offences.

For various technical reasons, the rules of evidence apply much less strictly to proof of conspiracy, and it is common for prosecutors to add a charge of conspiracy to charges on the connected substantive offences. This enables the prosecution to indulge in 'plea bargaining', that is, in offering to drop the conspiracy charge if the accused will plead guilty to one or more of the substantive charges. Judges have objected to the adding of the conspiracy charges but in the case of the Shrewsbury pickets the Court of Appeal advanced a dangerous and prejudicial view. 'It is not desirable', said Lord Justice James, 'to include a charge of conspiracy which adds nothing to an effective charge of a substantive offence. But where charges of substantive offences do not adequately represent *the overall criminality* it may be appropriate and right to include a charge of conspiracy.'[3] But how can this notion of 'the overall criminality' be determined?

As has been said, 'a conspiracy count puts the whole lifestyle of the accused on trial'[4] and this can very easily and adversely affect the minds of the jury with matters which are irrelevant to the charges.

Finally, and importantly, the penalties for conspiracy are in effect unlimited. The substantive offence may carry a maximum penalty of a few months' imprisonment. But if the accused is convicted of conspiracy to commit that offence he may be sentenced to many years' imprisonment. Trade

3. *R. v. Jones* [1974] ICR 310 (my italics).
4. Robertson, *op. cit.*, p. 42.

unionists in the nineteenth century were frequently punished in this way. And most recently there has been a revival of the charge of conspiracy to intimidate so that one of the convicted Shrewsbury pickets was sentenced to three years' imprisonment on that charge whereas the maximum penalty for intimidation itself was three months.

The decision whether to prosecute, and if so on what charges, is normally a matter for the Director of Public Prosecutions and the Crown Prosecution Service. In this sense the use of conspiracy in recent years is not the responsibility of the judges. But the extent of their willingness to encourage the development of the common law in this area is strongly influential on decisions about prosecutions and in the success of prosecutions; so we must consider what has been their attitude to the political and social aspects of this crime.

The Criminal Law Act 1977 created a *statutory* offence of conspiracy limited to agreements to commit criminal offences and also provided that the penalty for such conspiracy should be related to the penalty for those criminal offences. The Act abolished the offence of conspiracy at common law except for conduct which tended to corrupt public morals or to outrage public decency but which would not be an offence if carried out by a single person otherwise than in pursuance of an agreement.

Moral behaviour

The Street Offences Act 1959 made it an offence, punishable by fine and, after more than one previous conviction, by imprisonment, for a prostitute to loiter or solicit in a street or public place for the purposes of prostitution. The effect of this statute was to prevent prostitutes soliciting in public. The accused published a booklet, the *Ladies Directory*, in which prostitutes inserted advertisements which they paid for. He was charged with, first, conspiracy to corrupt public morals; secondly, living on the earnings of prostitution; and thirdly, publishing an obscene article. His conviction on all three counts was upheld by the House of Lords.

With one dissentient the Law Lords held, against the vigorous denial by counsel for the accused, that there was an offence known to the common law of conspiracy to corrupt public morals. Viscount Simonds said:

> I entertain no doubt that there remains in the courts of law a residual power to enforce the supreme and fundamental purpose of the law, to conserve not only the safety and order but also the moral welfare of the State, and that it is their duty to guard it against attacks which may be the more insidious because they are novel and unprepared for. That is the broad head (call it public policy if you wish) within which the present indictment falls. It matters little what label is given to the offending act. To one of your Lordships it may appear an affront to public decency, to another considering that it may succeed in its obvious intention of provoking libidinous desires, it will seem a corruption of public morals. Yet others may deem it aptly described as the creation of a public mischief or the undermining of public conduct. The same act will not in all ages be regarded in the same way. The law must be related to the changing standards of life, not yielding to every shifting impulse of the popular will but having regard to fundamental assessments of human values and the purposes of society. Today a denial of the fundamental Christian doctrine, which in past centuries would have been regarded by the ecclesiastical courts as heresy and by the common law as blasphemy, will no longer be an offence if the decencies of controversy are observed. When Lord Mansfield, speaking long after the Star Chamber had been abolished, said that the Court of King's Bench was the *custos morum* of the people and had the superintendency of offences *contra bonos mores*, he was asserting, as I now assert, that there is in that court a residual power, where no statute has yet intervened to supersede the common law, to super-

intend those offences which are prejudicial to the public welfare.[5]

This now famous statement was not universally applauded, many of those who disliked it being of the opinion that Law Lords were not necessarily the most appropriate persons to prescribe codes of moral behaviour (and to make them into rules of law also) for the rest of the community. Lord Reid's dissent was based on an examination of the history of criminal conspiracy (from its origins in the Star Chamber) and on 'the broad general principles which have generally been thought to underlie our system of law and government and in particular our system of criminal law'. He concluded that there was 'no such general offence known to the law as conspiracy to corrupt morals'.

The judgments in the House of Lords were delivered on 4 May 1961. No further prosecutions for conspiracy to corrupt morals were brought until 1965 in which year seventy-seven persons were convicted and this was followed in 1966 by a further forty-five convictions. In 1972, the Lord Chancellor said that most of the thirty-two cases (involving 134 individual convictions) between 1961 and 1971 were for 'blue' films which could not be proceeded against for obscenity unless shown in a private home.[6] So the conspiracy charge was used.

In 1971 three editors of *Oz* were charged with conspiracy to corrupt public morals by producing a magazine containing obscene articles, cartoons, drawings and illustrations; and with contravening the Obscene Publications Act 1964 and the Post Office Act 1953. On the conspiracy charge the jury acquitted them, not being satisfied that they intended to corrupt public morals. On other charges they were convicted and sentenced to imprisonment of fifteen, twelve and nine months. On appeal these convictions were quashed except for that relating to the Post Office Act the sentence for which was automatically suspended. The appeals succeeded because it was held that the judge had misdirected the jury

---

5. *Shaw v. DPP* [1961] 2 WLR 897.
6. See 333 HL Deb. col. 1569; and 839 HC Deb. col 263–4, 427–8. See also *The Law Commission*, Working Paper no. 57, pp. 35–9.

about the meaning of obscene in the Obscene Publications Act.[7] It was particularly in relation to this case that Mr Robertson drew attention, as I have already mentioned,[8] to the fact that the addition of a conspiracy charge enables the whole lifestyle of the accused to be brought before the court and the jury so that the case becomes politically charged in the sense that the accused can be subjected by prosecution counsel to such allegations as advocating dropping out of society, living off the state, and regarding sex as something to be worshipped for itself.

The next year saw the prosecution of another magazine, *International Times*. Three directors were convicted of conspiracy (1) to corrupt public morals and (2) to outrage public decency, because they had published advertisements inviting readers to meet the advertisers for the purpose of homosexual practices. The House of Lords (with one dissentient) upheld the convictions on the first count, on the grounds either that the *Shaw* case was rightly decided, or that even if it were wrongly decided it should stand until altered by Act of Parliament. The Lords (with one dissentient) allowed the appeal on the second count, two of them on the ground that the offence of conspiracy to outrage public decency was an offence unknown to the law, and two of them on the ground that there had been maldirection by the judge; those latter two and the dissentient agreed that there was an offence of that nature.[9]

Lords Morris and Reid took part in the decisions of both *Shaw* and *Knuller*. Lord Reid had dissented in *Shaw* and had held there was no offence to corrupt public morals; but he was not willing to participate in overruling that decision when the same point arose in *Knuller*. He did, however, hold in *Knuller* that there was no offence of conspiracy to outrage public decency. Lord Morris had been with the majority in *Shaw* when upholding the conviction. And in

7. *R. v. Anderson* [1971] 3 WLR 939.
8. See above, p. 236.
9. *R. v. Knuller (Publishing etc.) Ltd* [1972] 3 WLR 143; and see *R. v. Gibson*, *The Independent*, 25 July 1990.

Knuller he was the dissentient to allowing the appeal on the second count.

In the event therefore the decision in *Knuller* reinforced that in *Shaw*. But Lord Diplock in the former case was strongly critical of *Shaw* saying bluntly of that decision that he thought it was wrong and should not be followed. He said that Viscount Simonds's reasoning in *Shaw* had been anticipated in 1591 in Lambard:[10]

> Is it not meet and just, that when the wicked sort of men have excogitated anything with great labour of wit and cunning, so as it may seem they have drawn a quintessence of mischief, and set the same abroach, to the remedilesse hurt of the good and quiet subject; Is it not meet (I say) that authoritie itself also . . . should straine the line of justice beyond the ordinarie length and wonted measure and thereby take exquisite avengement upon them for it? Yea is it not right necessarie, that the most godly, honourable, wise, and learned persons of the land, should be appealed unto, that may apply new remedies for these new diseases?

It was not, said Lord Diplock, compatible with the development of English constitutional and criminal law over the past century that the House of Lords in its judicial capacity should assume the role of 'the most godly' etc. persons and take 'exquisite avengement' on those whose conduct was regarded as particularly reprehensible when Parliament had not found it necessary to proscribe that conduct and no previous precedent for punishing it could be found. As a result of *Shaw*'s case, he said, it would seem that any conduct of any kind which conflicted with widely held prejudices as to what was immoral or indecent, at any rate if at least two persons were in any way concerned with it, might *ex post facto* be held to have been a crime.

In a case in 1973, twenty-one persons were charged with forty-three separate specific offences relating to drugs. And then the forty-fourth count alleged a conspiracy to corrupt public morals in that persons conspired together with other

10. *Lambard Archeion* (1635 edn) pp. 86, 87.

persons unknown to corrupt the morals of such persons as might consume heroin by procuring quantities of heroin and supplying the same to members of the public in, and in the vicinity of Gerrard Street, London, W.1.[11] So it would seem that conspiracy to corrupt public morals may extend, as an offence, beyond the areas of sexual conduct and be used as a net to catch those who may be acquitted on other kinds of substantive charges. It should be added that if persons are convicted of a number of substantive offences the penalties can be severe because made cumulative; and that under the Misuse of Drugs Act 1971 the maximum punishment for the more serious offences (of which there are fourteen) is fourteen years' imprisonment. So it cannot be argued that the conspiracy charge is necessary to ensure that the penalties are severe.

The Independent Broadcasting Authority is under a duty to satisfy themselves that, so far as possible, the programmes broadcast do not offend against good taste or decency and are not offensive to public feeling. Mrs Mary Whitehouse sought judicial review of the manner of the exercise of this duty in relation to the showing of the film *Scum* which portrayed life in borstal institutions. Watkins LJ held that the director-general of the IBA had committed a grave error of judgment in failing to refer the film to all the members of the IBA before authorizing its showing. The judge said that, had the decision been his, he would have been opposed to showing the film. Taylor J agreed that the film was shocking but did not accept Mrs Whitehouse's assertion that it was gratuitous exploitation of sadistic violence for its own sake, and he would have permitted transmission. Nevertheless he agreed that the director-general should not have taken it upon himself to make the decision. He thought that Mrs Whitehouse's more general accusations against the IBA were extravagant and unwarranted.[12] The director-general might well have replied that how he exercised his judgement, within the law, was not a matter which the Court had any

11. See Hazell, *op. cit.*, p. 33; *New Statesman*, 23 February 1973.
12. *R. v. Independent Broadcasting Authority ex parte Whitehouse*, *The Times*, 14 April 1984 (this was not a conspiracy case).

competence to assess. In this respect it presents a nice contrast to the more ambivalent attitude of the Court of Appeal to the exercise of police judgment.

Demonstrations and protests

In 1961, members of the Committee of 100 who sought to further the aims of the Campaign for Nuclear Disarmament took part in organizing a demonstration at an airfield which was a 'prohibited place' within the meaning of the Official Secrets Act 1911 and which was occupied by the US airforce. The plan was that some people would sit outside the entrances to the airfield while others would sit on the runway to prevent aircraft from taking off. The six accused were charged with conspiring to commit and to incite others to commit a breach of the Official Secrets Act, namely, 'for a purpose prejudicial to the safety or interests of the State' to enter the airfield. Their counsel was not allowed to cross-examine or call evidence as to their belief that their acts would benefit the State or to show that their purpose was not in fact prejudicial to the safety or interests of the State. They were all convicted, five of them being sentenced to eighteen months' and one to twelve months' imprisonment. The Court of Appeal and the House of Lords upheld the conviction and sentences.[13]

The accused were not charged with any substantive offence, such as breach of the Official Secrets Acts (approaching or entering a prohibited place). No doubt, proof of conspiracy was easier.

In July 1972 Peter Hain appeared on charges of conspiracy to interrupt visits of South African sporting teams to Britain. The prosecution was brought by a private individual. He was convicted on one of the four counts, and fined £200. The count concerned his running on to a tennis court in Bristol during a Davis Cup match and distributing anti-apart-

13. *Chandler v. DPP* [1962] 3 WLR 694.

heid leaflets.[14] It is not clear how far the conviction amounted to trespass (see below) but that was not the basis of the decision. It may be that any action which is 'a matter of public concern' can found an action for conspiracy. If so 'the agreement to commit an unlawful act' which is the definition of conspiracy may have been extended further.[15]

At present, however, another extension is of greater importance because it was created by a decision of the House of Lords as a deliberate statement of new law. The case concerned some students from Sierra Leone who occupied for a few hours part of the premises of the High Commission of Sierra Leone in London. They brandished an imitation gun and locked some ten members of the staff in a room. No blows were struck. Lord Hailsham said, delivering the opinion of the House of Lords, that the students

> appear to have been reasonably careful to see that no one was seriously harmed, and their motives were *not necessarily* contemptible. They acted from a genuine sense of grievance. The father of at least one of them was, we were told, under sentence of death at the time of the alleged offence, and all appear to have believed that the government in power in their country, *though recognized by Her Majesty's Government here*, was *arbitrary, tyrannical and unconstitutional* [my italics].

The students were convicted of conspiring with other persons to enter the premises as trespassers.

Sit-ins and occupations, by students and factory workers, had for some time been troubling the courts and the legislators. As forms of protest, these were in varying degrees effective, especially if they received publicity and caused embarrassment. Normally they gave rise to no criminal action and the police were reluctant to intervene in what was seen as a private dispute on private property. From the

---

14. *Hain v. DPP*, *The Times*, 28 July–22 August 1972, Robertson, *op. cit.*, p. 16, and Derek Humphry, *The Cricket Conspiracy* (1975).

15. In *Cozens v. Brutus* [1973] AC 854, the House of Lords held that running on to the Centre Court at Wimbledon during a tennis match and distributing anti-apartheid leaflets was not 'insulting behaviour within the meaning of the Public Order Act 1936'.

beginning of student activity, however, there had been some
who urged the introduction of legislation to enable such
demonstrations to be dealt with as criminal.

Lord Hailsham was a Lord Chancellor who chose to sit as
a judge more frequently than is usual. On this occasion, he
delivered the leading judgment with which two other Law
Lords concurred (adding nothing) and the fourth concurred
with a brief speech. Lord Hailsham was a highly political
Lord Chancellor well known for his flamboyance and over-
strained rhetoric. He lumped together in his political
speeches:

> The war in Bangladesh, Cyprus, the Middle East, Black
> September, Black Power, the Angry Brigade, the Ken-
> nedy murders, Northern Ireland, bombs in Whitehall
> and the Old Bailey, the Welsh Language Society, the
> massacre in the Sudan, the mugging in the Tube, gas
> strikes, hospital strikes, go-slows, sit-ins, the Icelandic
> cod war.

The new rule of law he set forth in this case was:

> Trespass or any other form of tort can, if intended,
> form the element of illegality necessary in conspiracy.
> But in my view, more is needed. Either (1) execution
> of the combination must invade the domain of the
> public, as, for instance, when the trespass involves the
> invasion of a building such as the embassy of a friendly
> country or a publicly owned building, or (of course)
> where it infringes the criminal law as by breaching the
> statutes of forcible entry and detainer, the Criminal
> Damage Act 1891, or the laws affecting criminal assaults
> to the person. Alternatively (2) a combination to tres-
> pass becomes indictable if the execution of the combi-
> nation necessarily involves and is known and intended
> to involve the infliction on its victim of something more
> than purely nominal damage. This must necessarily be
> the case where the intention is to occupy the premises
> to the exclusion of the owner's right, either by expelling

him altogether . . . or otherwise effectively preventing him from enjoying his property.[16]

By this simple but considerable extension of the existing law, Lord Hailsham brought within the definition of criminal conspiracy, with its vagueness, and with its almost limitless powers of punishment, demonstrations of all kinds which involved either any entry into a public building or any use of property, whether public or private, which interfered (to however small an extent for however short a time) with an owner's enjoyment of any part of his property. Such an owner would be entitled to call on the police to enter the premises and make any arrests they thought appropriate because a criminal offence would be in the course of commission once two or more people appeared to be combining in such a demonstration. This decision is remarkable even for these authoritarian middle decades of the twentieth century. It also provides a very strong weapon for dealing as criminals with those who squat in empty buildings. In the same case, the only other judge to speak (other than to concur) was Lord Cross. He went further even than Lord Hailsham saying that an agreement by several to commit acts, which if done by one would amount only to a civil wrong, might constitute a criminal conspiracy if the public had a sufficient interest. Such vagueness could lead almost anywhere.

The right to protest was further limited in *Hubbard v. Pitt*[17] in 1975. Lord Denning MR said that, some years before, Islington was 'run down in the world', with houses in a dilapidated condition, tenanted by many poor families. Then property developers stepped in, bought up houses, persuaded tenants to leave, did up the houses and sold them at a profit. Now they were occupied by well-to-do families. A group of social workers who deplored this development conducted a campaign. They accused the developers of harassing tenants and trying to make them leave. The social workers submitted various demands to local estate agents

16. *Kamara v. DPP* [1973] 3 WLR 198.
17. [1975] 3 WLR 201.

which, said Lord Denning, if tenants had been subjected to undue pressure, seemed reasonable enough. In the course of the campaign the social workers picketed the offices of Prebble & Co. About four to eight men and women stood on the pavement in front of Prebble's offices for about three hours on Saturday mornings, carrying placards saying 'Tenants Watch Out Prebble's About' and 'If Prebble's In – You're Out', and handing out leaflets. They behaved in an orderly and peaceful manner and with the full knowledge and agreement of the local police. Prebble & Co. brought an action to stop these activities and Forbes J granted an interim injunction from which the defendants appealed. In the Court of Appeal, two of the Lord Justices rejected the appeal on the technical ground that the interim injunction should be continued until the case was fully heard. As these cases are normally decided on the availability or otherwise of interim injunctions, this was an unrealistic view of the matter. Lord Denning, however, dissented from his two brethren, saying:

> Here we have to consider the right to demonstrate and the right to protest on matters of public concern. These are rights which it is in the public interest individuals should possess; and, indeed, that they should exercise without impediment so long as no wrongful act is done. It is often the only means by which grievances can be brought to the knowledge of those in authority – at any rate with such impact as to gain a remedy. Our history is full of warnings against suppression of these rights. Most notable was the demonstration at St Peter's Field, Manchester, in 1819 in support of universal suffrage. The magistrates sought to stop it. At least twelve were killed and hundreds injured. Afterwards the Court of Common Council of London affirmed 'the undoubted right of Englishmen to assemble together for the purpose of deliberating upon public grievances' . . . The courts . . . should not interfere by interlocutory injunctions with the right of free speech; provided that everything is done peaceably and in good order.

This is the voice of freedom under law. But on a technicality it was overridden by the other two members of the Court of Appeal.

The Central Electricity Generating Board were considering possible sites for a nuclear power station in southwest England and were obstructed, first by farmers and later by protestors preventing them from surveying a site. The chief constable refused to remove the protestors since there was no actual or apprehended breach of the peace nor an unlawful assembly. The Board sought an order from the court requiring the chief constable to instruct police officers or agents to act. The Court of Appeal refused the order. Lord Denning MR, while deploring the activities of the protestors, and expressing the hope that the police would help the Board, said it was of the first importance that the police should decide on their own responsibility what action should be taken in any particular situation and that the decision of the chief constable not to intervene was a policy decision with which the courts should not interfere.[18]

In 1974 Lord Diplock said that on five occasions during the previous three years the House of Lords had had to consider 'the protean crime' of conspiracy under one or other of the various shapes it assumed. The one he was considering was *R v. Withers*[19] in which two husbands and their wives were charged with 'conspiracy to effect a public mischief'. Their actions had been to pretend, for the purposes of their enquiries as an investigating agency, that they were bank employees seeking information from other banks or building societies; and other similar deceptions. The other four cases were *DPP v. Bhagwan*,[20] the *Knuller* and *Kamara* cases and a case argued with *Withers*. Lord Diplock said:

> In each of these five cases what was proved against the defendant at the trial was that he had done something of which the judge and jury strongly disapproved. In each of them what the defendant did was not itself a criminal offence whether done by him alone or in

18. *R. v. Chief Constable of Devon & Cornwall ex parte Central Electricity Generating Board* [1981] 3 WLR 967.
19. [1974] 3 WLR 751.
20. [1972] AC 60.

conjunction with other persons – or, if it was, that was not an offence with which he was charged . . . It would be disingenuous to try to conceal my personal conviction that this branch of the criminal law of England is irrational in treating as a criminal offence an agreement to do that which if done is not a crime and that its irrationality becomes injustice if it takes days of legal argument and historical research on appeal to your Lordships' House to discover whether any crime has been committed even though the facts are undisputed.

In *Withers*, the House of Lords concluded that the law knew no such generalized offence as conspiracy to effect a public mischief. This decision at least stemmed the attempt to spread the tentacles of conspiracy yet further. Viscount Dilhorne said:

The preferment of charges alleging public mischief appears to have become far more frequent in recent years. Why this is, I do not know. It may be that it is due to a feeling that the conduct of the accused has been so heinous that it ought to be dealt with as criminal and that the best way of bringing it within the criminal sphere is to allege public mischief and trust that the courts will fill the gap, if gap there be, in the law. But if gap there be, it must be left to the legislature to fill.

The increased frequency was due, in part, to that climate of opinion which shows animosity to deviations from social and sexual behaviour.

There was, during the middle years of this century, especially amongst younger people, more disregard for conventional behaviour, more changes of sexual and social *mores*, more rejection of mainstream politics, than in any period since the 1920s. And this development was more widely spread amongst all social classes than during that earlier period. The animosity was in reaction to all this.

If the accused in *Withers* had been charged with conspiracy to defraud they might well have been convicted and the convictions upheld by the House of Lords. The prosecution overreached itself in framing the charges as public mischiefs.

But if those charges had been upheld, the way would have been opened to almost limitless charges of conspiracy concerning 'immoral' behaviour. It would be most unwise to regard *Withers* as a turning of the tide.[21] Indeed, in *R. v. Soul* (1980)[22] two women were convicted of conspiring to effect a public nuisance, namely to effect the escape of a patient at Broadmoor, detained there by reason of diminished responsibility after a conviction for manslaughter. The limits of public nuisance are so ill-defined that public mischief may be included within its scope.

21. For views of the Law Commission on conspiracy see Working Papers nos. 50, 54, 56, 57, 63.
22. [1980] Crim. LR 233.

Part Three

Policy

The courts hold justly a high, and I think, unequalled pre-eminence in the respect of the world in criminal cases, and in civil cases between man and man, no doubt, they deserve and command the respect and admiration of all classes of the community, but where class issues are involved, it is impossible to pretend that the courts command the same degree of general confidence. On the contrary, they do not, and a very large number of our population have been led to the opinion that they are, unconsciously, no doubt, biased. [Hon. Members: 'No, no', 'Withdraw' and interruption.]

The Secretary of State for the Home Department (Mr W. S. Churchill) on the second reading of the Trade Unions (No. 2) Bill, 1911 (26 HC Deb. col. 1022).

The habits you are trained in, the people with whom you mix, lead to your having a certain class of ideas of such a nature that, when you have to deal with other ideas, you do not give as sound and accurate judgments as you would wish. This is one of the great difficulties at present with Labour. Labour says 'Where are your impartial Judges? They all move in the same circle as the employers, and they are all educated and nursed in the same ideas as the employers. How can a labour man or a trade unionist get impartial justice?' It is very difficult sometimes to be sure that you have put yourself into a thoroughly impartial position between two disputants, one of your own class and one not of your class.

Lord Justice Scrutton in an address delivered to the University of Cambridge Law Society on 18 November 1920 (1 *Cambridge Law Journal*, p. 8).

I know that over 300 years ago Hobart CJ said the 'Public policy is an unruly horse'. It has often been repeated since. So unruly is the horse, it is said (per Burrough J. in Richardson v. Mellish *[1924]) that no judge should ever try to mount it lest it run away with him. I disagree. With a good man in the saddle, the unruly horse can be kept in control. It can jump over obstacles. It can leap the fences put up by fictions and come down on the side of justice . . .*

Lord Denning MR in *Enderby Town Football Club v. Football Association Ltd* [1971] 1 Ch. 591.

So far as this country is concerned, hitherto every judge on his appointment discards all politics and all prejudices. The judges of England have always in the past – and I hope always will – be vigilant in guarding our freedoms. Someone must be trusted. Let it be the judges.

Lord Denning MR in the Richard Dimbleby Lecture, 1980.

The call today is for more 'open government'. It is voiced mainly by newsmen and critics and oppositions. They want to know all about the discussions that go on in the inner circles of government. They feel that policy-making is the concern of everyone. So everyone should be told about it.

Lord Denning MR in *Air Canada v. Secretary of State for Trade (No. 2)* [1983] 1 All ER 161.

When I started in practice one of the qualities that many of the judges had was eccentricity; it was part of their character. But we are now so leavened into a mould of similarity that eccentricity no longer exists.

Lord Ackner during the committee stage of the Courts and Legal Services Bill on 29 January 1990 (515 HL Deb. col. 96).

8. Judicial creativity

In the first chapter I referred to the importance of the creative function which judges perform both in the development of the common law and in the interpretation of statutes. All the cases in this book are examples, greater or smaller, of this function.

It was common at one time for judges to deny that they had any creative function at all or, more precisely and more positively, to assert that, in the development of the common law, all they did was to declare it. Lord Reid, one of the outstanding Law Lords of this century, has said:

> Those with a taste for fairy tales seem to have thought that in some Aladdin's cave there is hidden the Common Law in all its splendour and that on a judge's appointment there descends on him knowledge of the magic words Open Sesame. Bad decisions are given when the judge has muddled the password and the wrong door opens. But we do not believe in fairy tales any more.[1]

Nowadays, however, the argument still persists in relation to the interpretation of statutes. When a particular interpretation – for example of the Race Relations Acts – is objected to, it is common for the interpretation to be defended on the ground that all the judges can do is to apply the law as made by Parliament and not to improve it.[2]

But if the statute is open to more than one interpretation then the judges are supposed to discover, by looking at the

---

1. 'The Judge as Law Maker' in 12JSPTL 22 (1972).
2. See, for example, Lord Hailsham in a letter to *The Times* on 25 October 1974.

whole of the law on the matter, including the statute itself, what was the intention of Parliament and to interpret accordingly. At this point strong disagreement may arise, even within the court itself. If the court decided that, for example, it was the intention of Parliament to exclude Conservative clubs or dockers' clubs from the operation of the Race Relations Act 1968, some critics will say that so widespread an exception, applying to clubs with such extensive membership, is wholly contrary to the spirit and the intention of that statute. And they will go on to say that the courts are showing a restrictive attitude on a matter of social policy and politics.

On the other hand there will be those who say that the Race Relations Acts mark a serious intervention and a considerable regulation of personal relationships. Therefore, they will argue, such regulation should be kept to a minimum and Parliament should be assumed to have intended that the intervention should not be extended beyond the most explicit provision.[3]

A similar division of opinion can be seen where other forms of regulation arise – for example, in the interpretation of the legislation about the control of the use of land. Wherever private rights are regulated, whether of property or of persons, there will be those who say that the regulation should be kept to a minimum and those who say that it must not be so restricted as to weaken its application.

But the difficulty lies deeper than disagreements about the so-called 'intention of Parliament'. First, if particular judges or particular courts consistently interpret certain types of legislation either widely or narrowly they will gain the reputation either of being 'liberal', 'progressive', 'socialist' et cetera, or of being 'restrictive', 'reactionary', 'conservative' et cetera. Secondly, many people will simply disbelieve the judges who say that they are concerned only with ascertaining the intention of Parliament. And this disbelief is strengthened when judges express opinions, in the course of their judgments, which seem to show where their sympathies lie.

Similarly Lord Diplock drew attention to the way the

---

3. Cp. Lord Diplock in the *Dockers' Club* case; see above, p. 172.

law of conspiracy had developed because 'what was proved against the defendant at the trial was that he had done something of which the judge and jury strongly disapproved' although he had done nothing illegal or, if he had, was not charged with it.[4]

Lord Denning has said:

It is plain that Parliament intended that the Supplementary Benefit Act 1966 should be administered with as little technicality as possible. It should not become the happy hunting ground for lawyers. The courts should hesitate long before interfering by certiorari with the decision of the appeal tribunals . . . The courts should not enter into a meticulous discussion of the meaning of this or that word in the Act. They should leave the tribunals to interpret the Act in a broad reasonable way, according to the spirit and not to the letter: especially as Parliament has given them a way of alleviating any hardship. The courts should only interfere when the decision of the tribunal is unreasonable in the sense that no tribunal acquainted with the ordinary use of language could reasonably reach that decision.[5]

How creative judges should be in either their development of the common law or their interpretation of statutes has long been argued by the judges themselves. Lords Diplock, Devlin and Reid are three most distinguished recent contributors to the debate.[6]

Lord Diplock in 1965 was a Lord Justice of Appeal. He chose to talk about tax law which, he said, he was not interested in reforming – 'It no more lies within the field of morals than does a crossword puzzle.' But judicial decisions interpreting tax law affect all like cases and so the legislative content of such decisions is most obvious, especially as most

4. See above, p. 241.

5. *Ex parte Moore* [1975] 1 WLR 624. Cp. *R. v. Ebbw Vale and Merthyr Tydfil S. B. Appeal Tribunal ex parte Lewis* [1981] 1 WLR 131.

6. Lord Reid on *The Judge as Law Maker* (1972) see above note 1; Lord Devlin on 'Judges and Lawmakers' in 39 MLR 1 (1976); Lord Diplock on 'The Courts as Legislators' (Holdsworth Club, University of Birmingham 1965).

cases concern transactions which Parliament had not anticipated or thought about at all. In many such cases Lord Diplock accepted that judges had to adopt a narrow, semantic and literal approach answering the question, what do the words mean? Not what did the users of the words intend? But he thought the danger was that the courts tended to apply the same criteria to statutes of a different kind which contained clear indications of general principle or policy which, in his view, ought to qualify the sense in which particular words or phrases were understood.

To Lord Diplock, 'Law is about man's duty to his neighbour.' He saw the fashioning of these rules of human conduct as the proper field of judge-made law and referred with approbation to 'the bold imaginative judgments delivered by a great generation of judges between the 'sixties and the 'nineties of the last century'. This courage and imagination he found lacking in judges of the first half of this century but thought there was evidence of recent change for the better.

Lord Diplock's view of the amorality of tax law underwent a change. Tax avoidance schemes frequently entail a series of transactions and transfers and until 1981 it had been assumed that the courts had to consider each step in the series but could not view the legality of the purpose of the whole series overall. Then in *Ramsay v. Inland Revenue Commissioners*[7] and *IRC v. Burmah Oil Co. Ltd*,[8] the House of Lords took a different view. As Lord Diplock said in the latter case:

> It would be disingenuous to suggest, and dangerous on the part of those who advise on elaborate tax avoidance schemes to assume, that *Ramsay*'s case did not mark a significant change in the approach adopted by this House in its judicial role.

In *Furniss v. Dawson*,[9] the Dawsons wished to sell their shares in the family company to WB company. They incor-

7. [1981] STC 174.
8. [1982] STC 30.
9. [1984] STC 153.

porated an Isle of Man company and exchanged their shares in the family company for shares in the Isle of Man company which immediately sold those shares to WB. The Dawsons claimed that by this device their liability to capital gains tax was deferred. In simple terms the question was whether the momentary control exercised by the Isle of Man company should be disregarded. If so, there would be no deferment. The Special Commissioners for Tax, the High Court judge, and the Court of Appeal all decided in favour of the Dawsons but the House of Lords unanimously allowed the Crown's appeal.

This decision aroused much concern in certain quarters and the complaint was made that the courts were engaging in unacceptable legislative activity. In April 1985, Lord Templeman (who did not adjudicate in *Furniss v. Dawson*) said in a conference speech: 'while tax avoidance is not, by definition, an illegal activity, a tax avoidance *industry* of the scale that developed in the 1970s had to be destroyed. The origins of the new approach by the Courts had to be seen as a reaction to the growth and activities of this industry.'[10] That seems to leave no doubt that the House of Lords saw themselves as charting a new approach to tax avoidance schemes.

The Law Society in 1985 published a pamphlet 'Tax Law in the melting pot' and this was followed the next year by comments from the policy unit of the Institute of Directors curiously entitled 'Abolishing the rule of the threat of law' which spoke of a recent 'trend in the House of Lords to usurp the function of Parliament and to re-mould legislation by a disregard of rights conferred by legislation'; and included for good measure the text of the Bill of Rights (1688). In 1988, the Law Society published a report by a special committee of tax law consultative bodies. This referred, inaccurately, to 'the common law doctrine that the courts, when making findings on matters of law, do not make new law but merely declare what the law is and always has been'. This suggests that the author of this section of the report was a pre-war Oxford graduate but the whole dis-

10. *Fiscal Studies* Vol. 6 No. 3 (1985) p. 51.

cussion reveals how sharply professional and business interests will, on occasion, react to innovative judgments from their Lordships.[11]

As usual with those who wish to stop the judges making rules in their field, emphasis is placed by the special committee on the need for certainty, and on the slow and expensive process of litigation. All this is no doubt true but while there are tax statutes, there will be continuous attempts to persuade the courts to interpret them in the way most favourable to taxpayers. In past years the courts have accepted many tax avoidance devices. In the 1980s they began to look behind the form to the substance.

In 1972, Lord Reid wrote of 'the real difficulty' about judges making law.

> Everyone agrees that impartiality is the first essential in any judge. And that means not only that he must not appear to favour either party. It also means that he must not take sides on political issues. When public opinion is sharply divided on any question – whether or not the division is on party lines – no judge ought in my view to lean to one side or the other if that can possibly be avoided. But sometimes we get a case where that is very difficult to avoid. Then I think we must play safe. We must decide the case on the preponderance of existing authority.

This caution extended even to those cases where there was 'some freedom to go in one or other direction'. 'We should', continued Lord Reid, 'have regard to common sense, legal principle and public policy in that order', and he made it clear that the first two criteria were unlikely to leave much scope for the application of the third.

Lord Devlin's position was more elaborate but in the end closer to Lord Reid's than to Lord Diplock's. He distinguished 'activist' from 'dynamic' law-making. The first meant keeping pace with change in the consensus; the

---

11. Cases subsequent to *Furniss v. Dawson* include *Inland Revenue Commissioners v. Challenge Corporation* [1986] STC 548, *Bird v. Inland Revenue Commissioners* [1987] STC 168 and *Craven v. White* [1988] STC 476.

second meant generating change in the consensus. And he said that the consensus in a community consisted of those ideas which its members as a whole liked or, if they disliked, would submit to. So he argued that the law had been used cautiously in the field of race relations with some success; but not so cautiously in the field of industrial relations without success. For Lord Devlin the social service which judges rendered was the removal of a sense of injustice and for this both impartiality and the appearance of impartiality were essential. Lord Devlin is clear that the judge should never be a dynamic law-maker.

The discussion about how creative judges should be, how far the approach to statutes should be literal and semantic, or seeking 'the intention' of Parliament, and other variants on the same theme, has been continuing for many years. Yet it has been and is a somewhat unreal discussion. While in certain circumstances and on some specific issues particular judges can be shown, from the record of their decisions, to belong more to the creative or more to the conservative school, it is very doubtful whether either tendency follows from one or other general judicial position. Lord Diplock is not regarded as a more creative judge than was Lord Reid, and Lord Devlin was thought of by some as a more creative judge than either.[12]

All this leads to the conclusion that, as one might expect, judges like the rest of us are not all of a piece, that they are liable to be swayed by emotional prejudices, that their 'inarticulate major premises' are strong and not only inarticulate but sometimes unknown to themselves. The judges seldom give the impression of strong silent men wedded only to a sanctified impartiality. They frequently appear – and speak – as men with weighty, even passionate, views of the nature of society and the content of law and of their partial responsibility for its future development.

Individualistic strains could, of course, exist alongside a consistent attitude to creativity or its opposite. What is lacking however is any clear and consistent relationship between the general pronouncement of judges on this matter of

12. Lord Devlin retired from the bench in 1964 at the age of fifty-eight.

creativity and the way they conduct themselves in court. Lord Simonds was Lord Chancellor in 1951–4 and is often quoted as the exemplar of the conservative view. Thus in one case he said that he would not 'easily be led by an undiscerning zeal for some abstract kind of justice or ignore our first duty, which is established for us by Act of Parliament or the binding authority of precedent'.[13] Yet it was he who in the previous year had discovered that there was an offence known to the common law of conspiracy to corrupt public morals, a view which caused no little surprise in legal and political circles.[14]

For a time Lord Simonds and Lord Denning carried on a public dispute, the latter making a strong plea for the creative function. Lord Denning, like Lord Simonds, is a reminder that creativity is neither good nor bad but that thinking makes it so. When he supported the action of the college governors in changing the rules of discipline to enable them to dismiss the woman student who was found to have a man in her room, he was certainly acting 'creatively'.[15] When he sought to protect the rights of demonstrators to protest outside the offices of the estate agents in *Hubbard v. Pitt* he was refusing to be bound by an earlier procedural decision which his colleagues on the bench thought binding on them. And he did so on strong liberal principles. The view taken by Lord Denning can be seen as either creative (refusing to be bound by the earlier decision) or conservative (maintaining the traditional right of individuals to 'free speech', as he put it).

I am arguing that the public position adopted by judges in the controversy about creativity is not consistently reflected in their judgments and that more important are their reactions to the moral, political and social issues in the cases that come before them.

The law reports abound with references to the duty of the courts to abide by the provisions of Acts of Parliament. But

---

13. *Scruttons Ltd v. Midland Silicones* [1962] AC 446.
14. *Shaw v. DPP*; see above, pp. 237–9.
15. *Ward v. Bradford Corporation* [1972] 70 LGR 27.

that does not help in deciding how to deal with ambiguities or obscurities. In *Chandler v. DPP*[16] Lord Reid said:

> Of course we are bound by the words which Parliament has used in the Act. If those words necessarily lead to that conclusion then it is no answer that it is inconceivable that Parliament can have so intended. The remedy is to amend the Act. But we must be clear that the words of the Act are not reasonably capable of any other interpretation.

The 'conclusion' referred to was that Parliament in passing the Official Secrets Act in 1911 intended that a person who deliberately interfered with vital dispositions of the armed forces should be entitled to submit to a jury that government policy was wrong and that what he did was really in the best interests of the country. Lord Reid continued:

> The question whether it is beneficial to use the armed forces in a particular way or prejudicial to interfere with that use would be a political question – a question of opinion on which anyone actively interested in politics, including jurymen, might consider his own opinion as good as that of anyone else. Our criminal system is not devised to deal with issues of that kind. The question therefore is whether the Act can reasonably be read in such a way as to avoid the raising of such issues.

Lord Reid concluded that it could be read 'in such a way' and that the submissions about government policy were rightly excluded.

The problem in *Charter* (the Conservative Club case) and the *Dockers' Club* case[17] was where to draw the line between 'public' and 'private' in interpreting the Race Relations Act of 1968. In both cases Lord Reid extended the notion of what was private far beyond the domestic sphere. And he said in *Charter*:

> I would infer from the Act as a whole that the legislature

16. [1962] 3 WLR 694; see above, p. 243; and cp. *R. v. Ponting*, above pp. 233–4.
17. See above, p. 172.

thought all discrimination on racial grounds deplorable but thought it unwise or unpracticable to attempt to apply legal sanctions in situations of a purely private character.

The three members of the Court of Appeal and one member of the House of Lords disagreed with Lord Reid and with the majority in the Lords. It is difficult to believe that the judges in these cases did not consider the effect their views would have on race relations. It is difficult to believe that such considerations would be regarded as improper by the ordinary layman. It was, after all, what the Act of Parliament was concerned with.

Similarly, are we expected to assume that the House of Lords did not take into account or were ignorant of the effect of their decision in *Rookes v. Barnard?*[18] The realities were referred to by Lord Devlin. He said:

> But there is one argument, or at least one consideration, that remains to be noticed. It is that the strike weapon is now so generally sanctioned that it cannot really be regarded as an unlawful weapon of intimidation; and so there must be something wrong with a conclusion that treats it as such. This thought plainly influenced quite strongly the judgments in the Court of Appeal . . . I see the force of this consideration. But your Lordships can, in my opinion, give effect to it only if you are prepared either to hobble the common law in all classes of disputes lest its range is too wide to suit industrial disputes or to give the statute a wider scope than it was ever intended to have.

The Court of Appeal had held that the tort of intimidation did not include a threat to break a contract. The Law Lords, including Lords Devlin and Reid, held that it did. And so a crucial section of the Act of 1906 received an interpretation nearly sixty years later which challenged the right to strike and had to be corrected by another statute.[19] Lord Devlin

18. See above, pp. 84–5.
19. Trades Disputes Act 1965.

warned their Lordships of the dangers of the courts inter fering in 'matters of policy' in this branch of the law although this was certainly the consequence of their decision. Again, creativity or its opposite is not the issue.

One group of decisions well illustrates the difficulties. We have seen that in *Shaw v. DPP* (1961)[20] the House of Lords invented a new crime called 'conspiracy to corrupt public morals'. This was certainly a creative decision and one which Lord Reid dissented from in that case. He said:

> Notoriously, there are wide differences of opinion today as to how far the law ought to punish immoral acts which are not done in the face of the public . . . Parliament is the proper place, and I am firmly of the opinion the only proper place, to settle that. When there is sufficient support from public opinion, Parliament does not hesi tate to intervene. Where Parliament fears to tread it is not for the courts to rush in.

Nine years later the House of Lords in a judgment deliv ered by Lord Diplock and concurred in by the other Law Lords (including Lord Reid) allowed the appeal of Mr Bhagwan[21] who had been convicted of a conspiracy to evade immigration control although he had not committed any wrong. The House of Lords could certainly have followed the lead given in *Shaw*'s case – Lords Morris and Hodson sat in both cases – but preferred to distinguish it and Lord Diplock used words which seemed to seek to diminish the importance of *Shaw*'s case.

Then in 1972 came the decision in *Knuller*[22] (the *IT* case). The Court of Appeal followed *Shaw*'s case and upheld the convictions of conspiracy to corrupt public morals. The House of Lords (Lord Diplock dissenting) upheld the Court of Appeal on this count. Lords Morris and Kilbrandon did so on the ground that *Shaw*'s case was rightly decided. Lord Reid (with Lords Morris and Simon) did so on the ground

20. See above, pp. 237–9.
21. *DPP v. Bhagwan* [1972] AC 60.
22. See above, pp. 240–1.

that even if it were wrongly decided it must stand until it was altered by Parliament.

Lord Reid said:

> I dissented in Shaw's case. On reconsideration I still think that the decision was wrong . . . But I think that however wrong or anomalous the decision may be it must stand and apply to cases reasonably analogous unless or until it is altered by Parliament . . . Parliament alone is the proper authority to change the law with regard to the punishment of immoral acts.

It is a logical but curious position to adopt. Lord Reid said in *Shaw*'s case that the House of Lords should not there act creatively but his advice was not regarded. But when the opportunity arose in *Knuller* to reverse the decision in *Shaw*'s case, Lord Reid refused to do so because that also would be to act creatively in an area where the courts should not do so.

Lord Diplock had no such qualms. He said:

> My Lords, this appeal raises two questions of outstanding importance . . . The first is: whether the decision of the majority of this House in *Shaw*'s case upon the count which charged a conspiracy to corrupt public morals was right. I think that it was wrong. The second is: ought it to be followed even if it was wrong. I think that it should not.

Since 1966, the House of Lords has considered itself not bound by its own decisions.[23] But it is reluctant to overrule them as this, it is argued, would introduce more uncertainty into the law. As Lord Reid said elsewhere:

> I would venture the opinion that the typical case for reconsidering an old decision is where some broad issue is involved, and that it should only be in rare cases that we should reconsider questions of construction of statutes or other documents. In very many cases it

23. See [1966] 1 WLR 1234.

cannot be said positively that one construction is right and the other wrong . . . Much may depend on one's approach. *If more attention is paid to meticulous examination of the language used in the statute the result may be different from that reached by paying more attention to the apparent object of the statute so as to adopt that meaning of the words under consideration which best accord with it.*[24]

The words I have emphasized indicate how the differences between the more literal and the more creative approaches may lead to different conclusions.

When judges get carried away by their personal convictions of where rightness and justice lie and stray too far from the established rules of the common law or the words of statutes, they create uncertainty. If those convictions are held on issues which are political, broadly or narrowly so, then they will arouse animosity as well as support. And if the political issues are serious and large, as are those of industrial relations, judicial pronouncements begin to lose their authority and their legitimacy.

The considerable conflict that surfaced in late 1979 and early 1980 between the Court of Appeal and the House of Lords over the interpretation of industrial relations law flowed from differing views about the creative function of the judiciary and not from differing views about the undesirability of that law. The Court of Appeal pursued its policy of interpreting the legislation restrictively so as further to control and curtail the activities of trade unionists. But the House of Lords refused to adopt a similar role and began to emphasize the danger to the administration of justice of so positive and so political a stance.[25] At the same time, some of them made no secret of their distaste for the legislation.

The conflict became acute when the Court of Appeal held in *Duport Steels v. Sirs* that the extension of the steel strike to the private sector was not 'in furtherance' of a trade dispute. In view of the recent decision of the House of Lords

24. *Jones v. Secretary of State for Social Services* [1972] 1 All ER 145.
25. See above, pp. 93–9.

in *Express Newspapers v. McShane*, the Court of Appeal's interpretation of the phrase was positively perverse, and was a challenge which their Lordships could not ignore. Nor did they. Lord Diplock said:

> When the meaning of the statutory words is plain and unambiguous it is not for the judges to invent fancied ambiguities as an excuse for failing to give effect to its plain meaning because they themselves consider that the consequence of doing so would be inexpedient or even unjust or immoral . . . It endangers continued public confidence in the political impartiality of the judiciary, which is essential to the continuance of the rule of law, if judges, under the guise of interpretation, provide their own preferred amendments to statutes which experience of their operation has shown to have had consequences that members of the court before whom the matter comes considers to be injurious to the public interest.

The prose may be convoluted but the meaning is clear. Lord Scarman said:

> My basic criticism of all three judgments in the Court of Appeal is that in their desire to do justice the court failed to do justice according to law. Legal systems differ in the width of the discretionary power granted to judges but in developed societies limits are invariably set, beyond which the judges may not go. Justice in such societies is not left to the unguided, even if experienced, sage sitting under the spreading oak tree.

Lord Scarman then distinguished common law where society has been content to allow the judges to formulate and develop the law. Even in this, their 'very own field of creative endeavour', the judges bound themselves by the doctrine of precedents. But in the field of statute law 'the judge must be obedient to the will of Parliament in its enactments'. And in the *Express Newspapers* case Lord Scarman said: 'It would need very clear language to persuade me that Parliament intended to allow the courts to act as some sort of backseat driver in trade disputes.'

This is to put the matter boldly – deliberately so, no doubt, to make the argument stick. In practice, judges are often most reluctant to be creative in the development of the common law though it is precisely there that Lord Denning had been at his most creative during his long judicial life. And judges are often not reluctant at all to interpret statutes in a way which Parliament could not have intended. But I think Lord Scarman is here rebuking Lord Denning for applying his common law instinct for creative developments to statute law where, according to Lord Scarman, it has much less justification.[26] The distinction is a valuable contribution to the debate (which will continue as long as the present system lasts) about the proper limits of judicial creativity.

26. 'The choice', Lord Denning has said on statutory interpretation, 'is a matter of policy for the law: which gives the more sensible result? It is not a semantic or linguistic exercise.' (*R. v. Crown Court Sheffield ex parte Brownlow* [1980] 2 All ER 444 at 451.)

9. The political role

The traditional view

In the traditional view, the function of the judiciary[1] is to decide disputes in accordance with the law and with impartiality. The law is thought of as an established body of principles which prescribes rights and duties. Impartiality means not merely an absence of personal bias or prejudice in the judge but also the exclusion of 'irrelevant' considerations such as his political or religious views. Individual litigants expect to be heard fairly and fully and to receive justice. Essentially, this view rests on an assumption of judicial 'neutrality'.

This neutrality is regarded as more than impartiality between the parties. It means, also, that the judge should not advert to matters which go beyond those necessary for decisions in the case before him. On this view the judge is not to take into account any consequences which might flow from his decision and which are wider than the direct interests of the parties. He must act like a political, economic, and social eunuch, and have no interest in the world outside his court when he comes to judgment.

Where the issues are simple and the dispute limited to the interests of the two parties, the judge may fulfil his traditional function. Divorce, the meaning of a contract between businessmen, a personal claim for injury sustained in a road accident, the buying and selling of a house – for these the traditional view often suffices. But less simple

---

1. As in the foregoing parts of this book, I am speaking in this part primarily of judges of the High Court, the Court of Appeal and the House of Lords.

issues can easily emerge. If there are children of the marriage which is to be dissolved, if the purpose of the contract is contrary to public policy, if the accident was caused by dangerous driving, if the seller is a bankrupt, then other persons and even the State itself may be involved. And their interests may have to be taken into account.

Moreover, these are all civil cases. But if the proceedings are for alleged crimes, then the state is almost always directly concerned and considerations again arise which go beyond the individuals themselves.

A more sophisticated version of this traditional view sees the judiciary as one of the principal organs of a democratic society without whom government could be carried on only with great difficulty. The essence of their function is the maintenance of law and order and the judges are seen as a mediating influence. Democracy requires that some group of persons acts as an arbiter not only between individuals but also between governmental power and the individual. In criminal matters this governmental power will be exercised through the police and the prosecution service to bring a wrongdoer before the court. It will ensure that the order of the court is enforced, that prisons are provided, that fines are paid. But there must be some body, other than the government, which hears the case, makes the decision, and decides the sentence. By this means the daily use, by the government and its agencies, of *force* is legitimated and so made acceptable to society at large.

Judges then, in this view, operate as an essential part of the democratic machinery of administration. They take their place alongside the other two great institutions of Government and Parliament, more passive than they, but indispensable. No doubt there is something of a dilemma in the judiciary's position as both upholders of law and order and protectors of the individual against a powerful executive. But this is explained in terms of checks and balances or countervailing power and so what might be an inherent contradiction dissolves in a cloud of words which nevertheless, be it noted, defines the function of the judiciary in *political* terms.

In these terms, therefore, the judiciary may come into

conflict with the Government of the day. Formally, this conflict can arise only where the Government acts 'illegally'. But it is the judges who, particularly in their creative and interpretative function, determine whether Governments or their agents have so acted. Thus they set limits to the discretionary powers of Governments and to the rights of individuals, especially when these two forces conflict. Where and how they set those limits has been the theme of this book.

Governments have extensive powers and, with adequate Parliamentary majorities, can add to them without too much difficulty. This being so, it is well that judges should be willing to ensure that government bodies do not seek to act beyond those powers. And no doubt the existence of the courts and of opportunities to bring before them dubious exercises of governmental power is some deterrent to any public servants who may be inclined to stretch their powers beyond legal limits. So also where statutes lay down procedures to be followed before powers are exercised, the courts should insist that those procedures are followed and may even add their own gloss to ensure that governmental bodies do not act unfairly or in bad faith. How far beyond those elementary propositions of principle the judges should go, how far they should exercise their own wide powers further to control governmental activity, is the crucial political question.

The myth of neutrality

I have said that, traditionally, impartiality is thought of as part of a wider, judicial neutrality. Judges are seen essentially as arbiters in conflicts – whether between individuals or between individuals and the State – and as having no position of their own, no policy even in the narrowest sense of that word.

In denying such neutrality, I am not concerned to argue that judges, like other people, have their own personal political convictions and, with more or less enthusiasm, privately support one or other of the political parties and may vote accordingly. That, no doubt, is true but political partisanship in that sense is not important. What matters is the function they perform and the role they perceive themselves as fulfilling in the political structure.

Neither impartiality nor independence necessarily involves neutrality. Judges are part of the machinery of authority within the State and as such cannot avoid the making of political decisions. What is important is to know the bases on which these decisions are made.

Lord Devlin put this most clearly when he wrote immediately after the industrial dispute of 1972 and when the five dockers had just been released from prison (see above, p. 89). He made a distinction between consensus and non-consensus law, by consensus meaning a result which people generally were 'prepared to put up with'. 'Most law', said Lord Devlin, 'is in fact based on this sort of consensus. It is what gives the law its stability and saves it from change after every swing of the pendulum.' The Industrial Relations Act 1971, continued Lord Devlin, was not based on consensus and he asked what was the position of the courts with regard to such law. Lord Devlin then said:

> The question would not need to be asked if in Britain the role of the courts was in accordance with theory. In theory the judiciary is the neutral force between government and the governed. The judge interprets and applies the law without favour to either and its application in a particular case is embodied in an order which is passed to the executive to enforce. It is not the judge's personal order; it is substantially the product of the law and only marginally of the judicial mind. If its enforcement is resisted or evaded, the judge is no more concerned than if he were an arbitrator.
>
> British judges have never practised such detachment. The reason may lie in their origin as servants of the Crown or perhaps in the fact that for a long time the law they administered was what they had made themselves. A mixture of the two has left the High Court with the power to enforce its order in civil cases by treating disobedience as contempt itself.

In the criminal law the judges regard themselves as at least as much concerned as the executive with the preservation of law and order. Then there is what can best be described as the expatiatory power. Whereas under most systems the judgment is formal, brief and to the legal point, the British judge may expatiate on what he is doing and why he is doing it and its consequences; and because of his prestige he is listened to.

These high powers make the British judiciary more than just a neutral arbitral force. On the whole their wise and cautious deployment has enabled the judiciary to use its reputation for impartiality and independence for the public good. But it is imperative that the high powers should not be used except in support of consensus law. If the judges are to do more than decide what the law means, if they are also to speak for it, their voice must be the voice of the community; it must never be taken for the voice of the government or the voice of the majority.

So, he argued, non-consensus law should not be enforceable by the courts and he criticized the way the Industrial Relations Act involved the courts in making orders for the enforcement of strike ballots and cooling-off orders. 'The prestige of the judiciary,' concluded Lord Devlin, 'their reputation for stark impartiality to be kept up in appearance as well as in fact, is not at the disposal of any government: it is an asset that belongs to the whole nation.'[2]

The distinction drawn between consensus and non-consensus law is not easy to sustain. Every government passes a number of politically controversial statutes – commonly about ten in each session – which contain much that is objected to by a large section of the electorate. Tax provisions, privatisation, police powers, local government finance, industrial relations, education reform, race relations, all these are obvious recent examples. If Lord Devlin means to limit non-consensus legislation only to those measures which people generally are not 'prepared to put up with'

2. *The Sunday Times*, 6 August 1972.

then his list will be very short indeed. If he means to extend it to include those major areas of controversy just exemplified then the list will be much longer. Is he saying that the enforcement procedures of the courts should not be used where, for example, council tenants refuse to pay rents, or councillors refuse to pay sums surcharged on them after an auditor's examination, or a member of the National Front refuses to remove a sign from his property which is in breach of the Race Relations Act, or a parent keeps his child away from a comprehensive school, or Welsh students disrupt court proceedings?

Surely Lord Devlin is trying to have it both ways. If the judiciary is more than 'a neutral arbitral force' – and I agree that it is – then it is most obviously so in controversial matters where its 'deployment' of power is highlighted. When the public interest is involved, judges become active and cannot suddenly become coy about enforcing laws – if necessary by their own procedures – which they believe to be politically controversial. Judges are in the business of upholding the law and that means they are part of the machinery for enforcing party political law as much as other 'consensus' legislation. Moreover, Lord Devlin is wrong if he believes that trade union distrust of the judiciary flows from the fact that the enforcement of the order for committal to prison of the dockers was effected by court officials rather than by other public servants. It was the order of the court that mattered, not the method of its enforcement.

Nevertheless, when all this is said, the importance of Lord Devlin's analysis rests in his denial of the neutrality of the judiciary in matters like the criminal law and, I would add, inevitably whenever judges set limits, as they frequently do, to governmental powers and individual rights in circumstances where statutes and common law give guidance which is inadequate or imprecise.

The public interest and its application

At this point the traditional views become inadequate as descriptions of what judges do. The judges determine (where doubts arise) the limits of governmental powers and of individual rights. But as the law has not provided them with full indications of where those limits are to be drawn, they must have regard to some concept on which they can base their judgments.

The higher judiciary comprises some hundred persons, but the truly effective number of policy-makers in the Divisional Court, the Court of Appeal and the House of Lords is about fifty. *These judges have by their education and training and the pursuit of their profession as barristers, acquired a strikingly homogeneous collection of attitudes, beliefs and principles, which to them represent the public interest.* They do not always express it as such. But it is the lodestar by which they navigate.

I use 'the public interest' because that is the phrase most used by the judges themselves when they choose to be explicit. Sometimes they speak of 'the interests of the State' but this carries a somewhat narrower meaning and suggests either the interests of the United Kingdom internationally or the interests of good government. 'The national interest' is synonymous, in judicial usage, with State interests. I take 'the public interest' to embrace both these other phrases but also to include the interest of the people at large, especially when contrasted with the interests of sections of the people.

What is or is not in the public interest is a political question which admits of a great variety of answers. On important issues, especially where there are only two or three possible alternative courses of action, personal opinions easily become part of group opinions. Indeed, as conventional rhetoric, political parties always claim that their policies, and not those of their opponents, best serve the public interest. Another truism is that I will be inclined to identify my interests with those of the public. If I am chairman of General Motors I will be inclined to think that what is good for General Motors is good for the nation. But my own interests, as I see them, will not be limited to my obvious economic interests. They may include, for instance, the continuing stability of the society in which I live, or the continuance of those surrounding circumstances which may give my life meaning.

Clearly then what the Government proposes to do may, or may not, in my opinion, promote the public interest. To accuse the Government of not acting in the public interest is the oldest political criticism.

Judges in the United Kingdom are not beholden politically to the Government of the day. And they have longer professional lives than most ministers. They, like civil servants, see governments come like water and go with the wind. They owe no loyalty to ministers, not even that temporary loyalty which civil servants owe. Coke said that Bracton said that the King ought to be under no man but under God and the law.[3] Judges are also lions under the throne but that seat is occupied in their eyes not by the Prime Minister but by the law and by their conception of the public interest. It is to that law and to that conception that they owe allegiance. In that lies their strength and their weakness, their value and their threat.

By allegiance to 'the law' judges mean the whole body of law much of which has its origins in the judge-made common law. 'The law' also means the rule of law and here the allegiance is to the philosophical ideal that we should be ruled by laws and not by men. If that means that power should not be exercised arbitrarily or on the whim of rulers and their officials but should be dependent on and flow from properly constituted authority and from rules written down and approved by some form of representative assembly, it is an admirable and necessary, if partial, safeguard against tyranny. The proposition can hardly be taken further because, in modern industrial society, it is impossible to avoid vesting considerable discretionary power in public officials if only because laws cannot be adequately framed to cover every eventuality.

The direct involvement of judges in the political process may not have become greater during the 1980s but it has certainly become more open. The replacement of Lord Hailsham by Lord Mackay meant the end of the artificial and patronising rules which in effect required judges to obtain the Lord Chancellor's consent before they expressed any

3. *Prohibitions del Roy* (1607) 12 Co. Rep. 63.

extrajudicial opinions. More importantly, it is desirable that their policies on sentencing and their views on the treatment of prisoners should be publicly discussed and that they should publicly take part in this discussion. The conflicts which have arisen as some judges have sought to ensure that the 'management' of their courts does not interfere with the administration of justice have shown the limitations and dangers both of consultation and of participation.

None of this, however, prepared the general public or the legal profession for the remarkable outburst of anger from many of the most senior judges when they first learnt of the reforms proposed by Lord Mackay early in 1989, nor for the continued opposition by (especially) Lords Donaldson and Ackner when the proposals were debated in Parliament. The profession did not expect to be put to the sword by a Conservative Government. Many of the lawyers, those on the bench and those appearing before it, seem to have regarded this interference with their practices as a breach of the trust which they had thought bound together political leaders and lawyers in unspoken allegiance. Their reaction was the measure of their outrage.

We must wait to see how the reforms, when implemented, will change the rôle of the judiciary. Certainly the statutory provisions which enable the four senior 'designated judges' to veto schemes for widening rights to audience in the higher courts gives them a new political function. The main criterion which the judges will be required to apply is whether the scheme is 'appropriate in the interests of the proper and efficient administration of justice'. With so wide and vague a remit, one wonders whether justice is not too serious a matter to be left to judges.

When the Green Papers on the Mackay proposals were published, observations were made by a group of judges appointed by the Judges' Council. They admitted that 'in the normal way' it was not appropriate for judges collectively to propound their views on proposed reforms of the law or the legal system. But this was an exceptional situation. Their general view of the Papers was expressed thus:

There is a serious risk that the long-term collective

effect of these proposals would impair the competence, integrity and trustworthiness of advocates; that as a result, in due course the quality of judges would be reduced; that discipline would be more difficult to enforce and, therefore, less effective to maintain standards; and that the quality of service provided by small firms of solicitors would be lowered, and even jeopardised, by depleting their choice of specialist advocates.

The way the designated judges exercise their powers will be crucial. Certainly they have the opportunity greatly to limit the impact of the proposals on the Bar. But if they do so, this will be seen by many as a political manoeuvre to protect the profession in which they have all been bred.

The judicial conception of the public interest, seen in the cases discussed in this book, is threefold. It concerns, first, the interest of the State (including its moral welfare); secondly, the preservation of law and order, broadly interpreted; and, thirdly, the promotion of certain political views normally associated with the Conservative Party.

The interests of the State

The interests of the State, as the basis of judicial law-making, are most obvious in cases where there are national dimensions. The civil liberty cases like *Liversidge v. Anderson, Greene, Halliday* and others (see above, p. 152) are examples, and it is significant that the so-called libertarian principles which are said to lie behind habeas corpus and other such remedies have seldom proved strong enough to prevail over the interests of the State. The decisions of the House of Lords in the *Guardian Newspapers* and the *GCHQ* cases of 1984 show how difficult it is to rebut overriding claims by Ministers that actions are necessary in the interests of national security (see above, pp. 230, 155).

But the interests of the State, or the national interests, are invoked more widely as the basis for judicial policies. The exercise of judicial legerdemain which sprang the five dockers from prison in 1972 was certainly motivated by the imminence of a probable general strike (see above, p. 89). So also the national interest in the administration of justice was appealed to – unconvincingly – by the judges when they decided to stifle further discussion by *The Sunday Times* of the thalidomide scandal (see above, pp. 199–200).

The power of the Crown to claim that documents ought not, in the public interest, to be disclosed, conflicts directly with the political claim that the public has a right to know unless strong evidence is adduced to the contrary. In *Conway v. Rimmer* (see above, pp. 216–17) the House of Lords shifted their interpretation of where the public interest lay a little towards the interest of the public. But Lord Reid swept aside in the grand bureaucratic manner a few democratic rights when he said that the most important reason for preserving secrecy for government documents was that their disclosure might 'create or fan ill-informed or captious public or political criticism' from those 'without adequate knowledge of the background and perhaps with some axe to grind' (see above, p. 217). This undue protectiveness towards governmental institutions was markedly emphasized by the House of Lords in *British Steel Corporation v. Granada Television* (see above, pp. 227–8) and by the House of Lords in *Home Office v. Harman* (see above, pp. 218–19). In the former case Lord Wilberforce made a significant distinction when he said: 'There is a wide difference between what is interesting to the public and what it is in the public interest to make known.' So also, the Lord Chief Justice in the Crossman diaries case (see above, p. 204) may have introduced his judicial colleagues to new and dangerous opportunities for the exercise of their conception of the nature and extent of the public interest and have established a new legal principle of confidentiality under which the views of ministers and former ministers could be suppressed without resort to the Official Secrets Acts.

Only rarely can freedom of speech be claimed as an absolute value. Always there are claims to be made for its modification in the interests of national security, confidentiality, protection of reputation, fair judicial proceedings, the prevention of disorder or crime. The test of a legal system is the extent to which and the circumstances in which these specific interests are to prevail over the general principle. In the USA, the First Amendment to the Constitution which protects freedom of speech is given very high priority especially where attempts are made to prevent publication. But in the United Kingdom 'the fundamental importance to society in general of freedom of expression seems to be considered almost as background to the specific interests that are said to require restrictions'.[4] Lip service is paid by the courts to the general principle but the claims of the specific interests prevail.

In *Spycatcher* (see above, pp. 207–15), the claim was essentially that of confidentiality, the Government not being prepared to put to the test the opposing arguments of any threat to national security. And for many months the courts in the UK suppressed publication in the press on this ground. The crucial decision was that of the majority of the House of Lords on the continuation of the interim injunction and we have seen how the minority as well as the majority expressed themselves. Those who put their faith in the incorporation into UK law of the European Convention on Human Rights, should read Lord Templeman's view. It was put to him that the question for the House was whether interference with the freedom of expression constituted by the continuation of the injunctions was, in the words of the Convention, 'necessary in a democratic society in the interests of national security, for protecting the reputation or rights of others, for preventing the disclosure of information received in confidence, or for maintaining the authority or impartiality of the judiciary'. Lord Templeman said that the continuance of the injunctions 'appears to be necessary for all these purposes'.[5] Publication was eventually allowed only when the book was so widely available that further restraint had become absurd.

The *Spycatcher* litigation exposed the political bias of some of the most senior members of the judiciary in the most blatant way. The case was pursued by the Government with great vigour both in this country and in Australia long after any useful purpose could be achieved. Before it was concluded, the action had become an abuse of the judicial

---

4. *Freedom of Expression and the Law*, published by JUSTICE (1990).
5. *A-G v. Guardian Newspapers Ltd* [1987] 3 All ER 316.

process. And for much of the time a majority of the judges sitting in the Court of Appeal and the House of Lords gave support to the Government in circumstances which grossly interfered with the right and duty of the national press to report matters of the greatest public concern. In October 1990, the European Commission on Human Rights found that the injunctions imposed on the *Guardian* and *Observer* were in breach of the European Convention.

So also, the attitude of the courts to exposures of miscarriages of justice by the press and broadcasts, to programmes like *The Secret Society* (see above pp. 224–5), *My Country: Right and Wrong* (see above pp. 225–6), to the restrictions on interviews with Sinn Fein (see above pp. 225–6), to disclosures of sources of information by journalists (see above pp. 227–32), to the Ponting prosecution (see above pp. 233–4), to all these and others, the judges have consistently (though not in all cases unanimously) preferred the claims of the specific interests to the general principle.[6] The deep conservatism of the judiciary is shown in these cases. It is often an attitude of mind rather than a conscious political position. No doubt an argument can be made, on the grounds of national security or otherwise, for such censorship of the media and against whistle-blowing. But the basis of the judicial attitude seems to be primarily that anything which the Government considers should be kept secret in what the Government asserts is the public interest should not be published or made known. It is an attitude not of subservience but of complicity, almost amounting to conspiracy. The idea that matters of public concern should be made public, save in the most extreme circumstances where national security is truly at risk (and none of these cases comes near that category) is not entertained by Her Majesty's Judges. It rarely seems to occur to them that they might have a positive duty to support publication, especially when to do so is embarrassing to Her Majesty's Government.

The serious charge to be laid against the judiciary is that they rarely do more than pay lip service to the fundamental freedoms. That is why the outburst by Lord Bridge in *Spy-*

---

6. On this and other aspects see K. D. Ewing and C. A. Gearty *Freedom under Thatcher* (1990).

catcher where he spoke of totalitarianism (see above p. 213) seemed so remarkable. For once an English judge hit the table hard, almost as if he were one of the great liberal judges of the Supreme Court of the USA. The shock was considerable. But the mood passed and the impulse died. It was followed by the failure in the *MorganGrampian* case to protect the principle against the claims of commercial interest.

We have noticed the confusion that surrounds the so-called offences of outraging public decency, and of corrupting public morals, and the claimed power of the courts, in the rhetorical periods of Lord Simonds 'to enforce the supreme and fundamental purpose of the law, to conserve not only the safety and order but also the moral welfare of the State' (see above pp. 237–8). No doubt there are activities, falling within these general descriptions, which should be offences. There must, however, be considerable doubt whether their definition should be left to the particular whims and prejudices of the judiciary.

Law and order

The public interest is seen as a reflection of social discipline. Lord Devlin said, in the passage already quoted (see above, p. 273), 'the judges regard themselves as at least as much concerned as the executive with the preservation of law and order.' One of the greatest political myths is that the courts in this country are alert to protect the individual against the power of the State. Sometimes, it is true, they will intervene to help the weakest, as some of the immigration cases show. But minority groups, especially if they demonstrate or protest in ways which cause difficulty or embarrassment, are not likely to find that the courts support their claims to free speech or free assembly. The judges see themselves as occupying a key position in the struggle to enforce the law, and are always conscious of the dangers which they believe will follow if they do not support the powers of the police.

Demonstrations, if properly organized and controlled by the police, are acceptable by the judiciary as being within the framework of law and order. But individual demonstrators are always likely to be viewed with considerable disfavour by the courts. Although very different in kind, two of the most repressive decisions handed down in recent years were those in *Kamara* (see above, pp. 244–6) and in *Hubbard v. Pitt* (see above, pp. 246–8). Lord Hailsham's extension of the criminal law to cover peaceful sit-ins and occupations as a method of demonstration in the first of these cases, and the Court of Appeal's finding for the estate agents against peaceful demonstrators in the second, mark once more the willingness of the judiciary to extend the rather special judicial conception of where the public interest lies into the areas of political controversy. We have seen that angry but non-violent demonstrators had injunctions issued against them during the miners' strike.[7]

Sometimes the views of the judiciary outrun those of the Government.[8] In June 1973, the House of Lords ruled that the powers to detain and remove illegal entrants contained in the Immigration Act 1971 were retrospective[9] and so deprived many Commonwealth citizens in the UK of their status and made them liable to be detained and deported. In April 1974 the Home Secretary announced that he would not exercise this new judge-made power. In effect he declared an amnesty. The next step by the courts was to declare in 1976 and 1977 that, contrary to previous belief, illegal entrants included those who had secured entry by deception whether by the entrant himself or by someone acting on his behalf with or without his knowledge.[10] The Home Secretary responded in November 1977 by announcing that he would not use the retrospective powers where entry had been obtained by deception. The Home Office policy was that for deception to amount to illegal entry, the deception practised on an immigration officer had to be deliberate, material, and positive (the last meaning a clear failure to disclose information sought or a clearly misleading

7. *Thomas v. NUM (South Wales area)*: see above p. 107.

8. See Minutes of Evidence taken before the Home Affairs Committee subcommittee on race relations and immigration (HC 89 of 1980–1).

9. *R. v. Governor of Pentonville Prison ex parte Azam* [1974] AC 18.

10. *Khan v. Secretary of State for the Home Department* [1977] 3 All ER 538; *R. v. Secretary of State for the Home Department ex parte Hussain* [1978] 1 WLR 700.

misrepresentation as to the truth). Failure to volunteer information was not considered to be deception. Then came the *Zamir* decision[11] which conflicted with the Home Office view. The Home Office responded by saying that they intended to interpret the judgment narrowly and that it was unlikely to lead to significant changes of policy or practice. The Home Office would not consider a person to be an illegal entrant unless satisfied that he realized or should have realized that the facts he failed to disclose were material.

The heart of this interaction is that whatever interpretation the courts may give to the definition of 'illegal entrant', it is for the Home Secretary to decide whether to take any action in each case. Every year the Home Office allows a substantial proportion of illegal entrants to remain indefinitely.

The *Zamir* decision was therefore wholly contrary to administrative policy and imposed a far harder line on dealing with immigrants than the Home Office had been practising. Indeed if that decision had had to be followed by deportation in each case, gross and manifest injustice would have resulted and it is significant that in the *Jayakody* case[12] the Home Office supported an appeal by an immigrant on the question of the materiality of the information withheld. Lord Wilberforce's language in *Zamir* showed his own approach.

> At the very lowest an intending entrant must not practise a deception . . . deception vitiates the permission to enter . . . an alien seeking entry . . . is seeking a privilege.

We may assume that by the time the House of Lords came to consider *Khawaja and Khera* they had realized that the Home Office policy made more sense and was more just. And so they reversed their decision in *Zamir*. But the whole story demonstrates again how maladroit and clumsy is the approach adopted by the courts when faced with the difficult

---

11. See above, pp. 179–80.
12. *R. v. Home Secretary ex parte Jayakody* [1982] 1 **WLR** 405.

task of interpreting legislation designed to confer discretionary powers on administrative authorities.[13]

The more recent immigration cases exemplify the kind of choices that courts must make. Perhaps the most important are those which turn on the interaction between the primary purpose not being to obtain admission and the genuineness of the marriage. Under the rules, to be successful, applicants must show both. But if a would-be immigrant can show the genuineness of the marriage, why should he be obliged to prove also that his primary purpose in entering the marriage is not to obtain admission to the UK? Indeed if the intention to marry is 'genuine', how can the primary purpose be ulterior? So the courts could have argued. But instead we have the opposite in *Bhatia* (see above, pp. 181–3), in part reversed in *Kumar* (see above, p. 183). *Hoque and Singh* (see above, p. 184) supports *Kumar* but still leaves open the ambiguity. It would, however, be unfair to suggest that the courts have positively supported the policy of the Government as expressed in rules which are designed to limit the number of Asian and other non-white immigrants. Several of the decisions in the courts show concern at the injustice of this policy and it was this attitude which, as we have seen, so angered the Treasury Solicitor's Department that the attempt was made to subvert the decision in *Khatab* (see above, p. 184, note 68) amongst others.

Again in the recent deportation cases, we must regret that Lord Bridge concluded in *Patel* (see above, pp. 186–7) that he had to retract his earlier interpretation of Parliamentary intention and to entrust the Secretary of State with the largely untrammelled discretion he claimed. Effectively the Law Lords similarly abandoned supervision of the proper exercise of State power in *Budgaycay* (see above, p. 187), *Sivakumaran* (see above, p. 188) and *Oladehinde* (see above, p. 190, note 85). *Yassine* (see above, p. 189, note 84) was politically a more realistic decision but may not remain an authority if the Court of Appeal hear a similar case in the

---

13. For a recent decision that seems closer to *Zamir* than to *Khawaga and Khera* see *R. v. Secretary of State for the Home Department ex parte Durojaiye, The Times*, 22 March 1989.

future. Government policy is to discourage refugees and the courts, by limiting their powers of judicial review, have supported this.

The legislation governing immigration, deportation, and also homelessness, sets the frame within which judicial interpretation operates. The criticism that can validly be made is that the courts take a limited view of their role within this frame. The suspicion is that they became alarmed at the extent of the use being made in these cases and deliberately moved the goalposts so as to restrict this use. Certainly, they showed few signs of wishing to adopt a more liberal interpretive approach to these minority groups, whom they appear to regard more as problems of law and order than as disadvantaged individuals.

But by far the most important aspects of law and order are the powers of the police and the exercise of those powers. Today, as we have seen (above, pp. 163–70), many of the problems have centred around the Police and Criminal Evidence Act 1984. Before 1 January 1986, when the Act came into operation, the judges' Rules laid down what was the proper practice for the police to follow when dealing with suspects. The Rules had not the force of law, though breach of them might have legal consequences for the prosecution. They were not always followed and often the courts seemed not to be assiduous in their enforcement. When PACE came into operation with its statutory rules and code of practice, it seems that the police did not fully appreciate that they were now operating under a new dispensation. It also took the courts some time to decide what the rules and the code meant when applied to particular situations. The decision in *Samuel* (see above, pp. 164–5) showed that failure to allow access to legal advice could be fatal to the conviction but *Alladice* (see above, p. 165) in effect went the other way. Moreover, the disregard by the police of the rules did not mean that they were guilty of an offence; so the 'rights' were not directly enforceable. The Lord Chief Justice presided over the Court of Appeal in *Alladice* and some attributed the difference to him, but the Act itself had left the issue open by not conferring a positive right to legal advice.

Nor were the police happy, being uncertain of their rights and the limits of their investigatory powers. Some resorted to various devices to avoid the rules. So, for example, suspects were questioned at times and in circumstances which might avoid the procedures applicable to 'interviews'; arrests were delayed to avoid the full protection of the Act; detainees were not always told of the existence of duty solicitors; the existence of statutory rights was communicated too quickly, incomprehensibly or incompletely. Then in *Canale* as we have seen (above, p. 167) the Lord Chief Justice sought to impose his authority.

We have seen the courts claim that it is no part of their function to discipline the police for misbehaviour (see above, p. 167). But it is clear that the failure of the police to apply the procedures provided in PACE and the Code has forced a revision of this judicial attitude. The judges' criticism, sometimes heavy, of police practice has no doubt had consequences within the force. How far these will result in better observance by individual police officers remains to be seen. Continuous pressure from the courts may well be essential.

PACE itself does not seem adequately to protect confidential material. Judicial interpretation has to some extent undermined the efficacy of the new safeguards. It is surprising that the courts ruled there was no implied contractual duty on the bank in *Taylor*'s case to inform its client that information about his account had been passed to the police.[14] And the courts seem to have assumed, almost without question, that all police demands for press photographs should be met even though this may amount to general unspecific search warrants. The requirement that the material sought by the police must be shown to be 'of substantial value' to the investigation has proved to be no safeguard – so easily have the courts been satisfied. The decision in *Francis and Francis* (see above, p. 169) has been criticized as interfering with the privileged relationship between solicitor and client. Other increases of police powers on arrest and road blocks seem to have led to a large increase in

---

14. *Barclays Bank v. Taylor* [1989] 3 All ER 563; and see *Criminal Law Review* of July 1990.

arrests, followed by the release of a third of these without charge or caution. On the other hand the taping of interviews, where it takes place, may result in an improvement in relationships between police and public.

In the result, PACE has begun uncertainly and the courts have not yet managed to introduce consistency in its application. This may well be because the judges have not yet arrived at positions based on principles which will enable them to strike an acceptable balance between police powers and personal liberty. This failure is strikingly emphasized when gross miscarriages of justice are revealed.

The abandonment by the Crown of the convictions of the Guildford four and the Maguire seven was a serious blow to the system of criminal justice. The reputation of the police suffered generally, especially when associated with other events resulting in the removal from criminal investigation of many officers of the West Midlands force.[15]

The Guildford case began to look like the collapse of an appellate structure designed, it had been supposed, in part, to prevent miscarriages of justice.

The system relied on a police force which investigated, charged and prosecuted, though the final decision on prosecution for serious offences rested with the Director of Public Prosecutions.[16] Counsel are then employed to present the case against the accused in the way most likely to result in a conviction. The police should not, of course, suppress evidence favourable to the accused but are not always wholly assiduous in passing information to the defence lawyers. The trial judge sits with a jury who are the sole deciders of questions of fact. From a conviction, application may be made for leave to appeal. The Court of Appeal is reluctant to differ from the trial jury on a question of fact and the right to introduce fresh evidence is limited. As we have seen, the Court of Appeal, following *Stafford*, makes its own

15. See, for example, *R. v. Khan*, *The Independent* 2 March 1990, where the Court of Appeal quashed a conviction, based on alleged admissions, as being unsatisfactory.

16. Since 1986, the Crown Prosecution Service has operated under the control of the DPP.

evaluation of fresh evidence rather than asking whether the jury would have convicted had they known of it.

Once the application or the appeal has been dismissed the case is closed, save in the highly exceptional circumstance of a further appeal being allowed on a point of law to the Law Lords.

We have seen how difficult it is to persuade the Home Secretary to have the case re-opened by referring it back to the Court of Appeal. The overriding reason for this reluctance is, once again, because to allow re-opening is to question the validity of the system. So the Home Secretary has to be firmly convinced that there is some fresh information or consideration of substance which might suggest that the conviction is unsafe or unsatisfactory.[17] If all that can be shown is that, on reflection, the trial and appeal courts probably made a mistake in coming to their decision, a reference is not likely to be made. In the past the Home Office has sometimes seemed unduly sensitive to the known distaste of the senior judiciary for the referral procedure.

It is also clear that the Court of Appeal is traditionally most reluctant to quash a conviction, or order a retrial, on a referral. The Court seems to believe that the general public will be likely to lose faith in a system that admits any errors. But of course when the error is made manifest, as in the case of the Guildford four, the failure to rectify the error earlier is seen as a far greater condemnation of the system.

The danger of admitting the possibility of error has been written firmly into English jurisprudence by the infamous words of Lord Denning when rejecting civil proceedings sought by the Birmingham six:

> If the six men win it will mean that the police were guilty of perjury, that they were guilty of violence and threats, that the confessions were involuntary and were improperly admitted in evidence and that the convictions were erroneous. That would mean the Home Secretary would either have to recommend they be par-

17. See *R. v. Secretary of State for the Home Department ex parte Pegg*, *The Guardian*, 19 July 1990.

doned or he would have to remit the case to the Court of Appeal. This is such an appalling vista that every sensible person in the land would say: 'It cannot be right that these actions should go any further'.

There is now a widespread view that the Court of Appeal is not an appropriate body, under the rules it has adopted for itself, to correct miscarriages of justice and indeed that it does not regard this as its task, so long as the rules of law and of evidence were applied at the trial.

Recently there seems to have been some tension between the Lord Chief Justice and the Home Office. Lord Lane is known to dislike reopening cases which have already been disposed of by the system. Both the pardon given by the Home Secretary in the Luton case after abortive references to the Court of Appeal, and the pre-empting of the decision of the Court in the Guildford case by the DPP, suggest that the inutility of the Court in dealing with references has been recognized.

In the most difficult and most political cases of IRA bombings, especially those on the mainland where public opinion runs so strongly, the judicial system is put under strain. The police are under great pressure to show that they can make arrests and obtain convictions. Ministers want results. And the judicial system is not expected to impede the process. For the police this means that any leads which look at all promising will be pursued vigorously. (It has been suggested that the Special Branch drew the attention of the police to one of the Guildford Four as a possible suspect.) Interrogations follow and confessions are obtained. The police may become convinced they have the culprits and then fabricate evidence; or they may do so anyway. The prosecution lawyers will act on the evidence put before them by the police. They will not do so slavishly and they will draw attention to the weaknesses of what they are expected to present. But, under the adversarial system, it is their job to present the case against the accused as strongly (one hopes, also, as fairly) as possible.

The judge in these cases is also under pressure. The police have spent many hundreds of man-hours in their investigation and they have arraigned the accused for trial. The evidence has been presented by both sides. The case against the accused is certainly not positively weak. They appear to have confessed to the murder of innocent persons. Their defence is that the confessions were beaten or bullied out of them. Remembering the words of Lord Denning and of others, it is not surprising that judges prefer to believe police officers rather than the accused, some of whom may have previous convictions, or have been on drugs, or live in squats. So it is not surprising that the judge's summing-up to the jury seems rather to support the argument of the forces of law and order.

Robert Kee in his book[18] on the trial of the Guildford Four, seems to me to indicate strongly that Mr Justice Donaldson (as he then was, Lord Donaldson MR as he now is) summed up impeccably but unfairly in favour of the prosecution. What he said could not be faulted but there was much that he could have said, favourable to the accused, which he did not. Surprisingly, Donaldson J. was also the judge at the trial of the Maguire Seven. And Robert Kee, it seems to me, makes the same criticism of him in that case.

In his interim report on the Maguire case (above p. 195) Sir John May was critical of the conduct of the trial under Sir John Donaldson. Sir John May said he did not think that the jury were adequately directed about the effect of an exhibit which cast doubt on the Crown's argument that the scientific tests showed the accused must have handled nitroglycerine. Sir John May added that in his opinion certain Crown evidence on the results of tests was inadmissible.

On the Maguire appeals, Kee is more direct in his opinion. 'Lord Justice Roskill', he says, 'seemed almost to go out of his way to give Mr Justice Donaldson the benefit of any doubt . . . His judgment in fact reads more like an opportunity seized to reinforce the case against the Maguire Seven than a balanced hearing of the appellants' complaints.' Roskill LJ also presided over the appeal of the Guildford Four. Robert Kee found him unduly dismissive of evidence which favoured the accused.

18. *Trial and Error* (2nd edn 1989); see above p. 194.

Behind this lies a deeper consideration. In the trials both of the Guildford Four and of the Maguire Seven, three men were appointed under the judicial system to prosecute and adjudicate: Sir Michael Havers, later to be Conservative Attorney-General and then Lord Chancellor; Mr Justice Donaldson, later to be Lord Donaldson and the Master of the Rolls; and Lord Justice Roskill, later to be Lord Roskill.

To the accused at these two trials, these three must have appeared as a formidable team before whom they were unlikely to have a fair and impartial hearing. Much was said about the two trials being separate and distinct but it must have seemed to the Maguires in particular that their case was wholly prejudiced by previous trial of the Guildford Four. It was Anne Maguire's nephew who, as one of the Guildford Four, had allegedly implicated her and she was originally charged with murder until it was realized that there was no evidence to support this. But the Maguire Seven were from the beginning inevitably associated with the Guildford Four and their trial. Any expectation they had of the prosecution objectively presenting facts and legal argument and of the judges as independent arbiters being alert to ensure that proof of guilt was clearly established beyond reasonable doubt must have been difficult to sustain.

The certainties expressed by the Court of Appeal in the case of the Birmingham Six – 'the longer the hearing has gone on the more convinced this Court has become that the verdict of the jury was correct' (see above p. 196) – were upended when in March 1991 the Six were finally set free by the Court of Appeal.

The promotion of political views
The third aspect of the public interest is, I have suggested, the promotion of certain political, conservative views. First there are the trade union cases. We have seen (see above, pp. 77–81) that the prevailing view of the senior judiciary in the late nineteenth and early twentieth centuries was, in conflict with much of the governmental view of the time, that the growing power of the trade unions should be strictly controlled by law. The judges were seeking to undo some of the effects of earlier legislation and Lord Halsbury, as

Lord Chancellor, led them to some success in this attempt. When, over half a century later, the judges and the unions once more came into conflict, the government had adopted the judicial view which was shown in the picketing cases, *Rookes v. Barnard*, and the culmination in *Heaton*'s case and the imprisonment by the NIRC of the five dockers (see above, pp. 87–9). Nor is the view unpopular. But when the economic consequences of the continued detention of the dockers and the threat of a general strike became clear, then what was in 'the public interest' was seen to have changed dramatically, and the dockers were released. The president of the NIRC imprisoned the dockers expressly in defence of the rule of law when to ignore their challenge would be to 'imperil all law and order', on which 'our whole way of life' was based. A few days later he released them – also, expressly, in defence of the rule of law – having been provided by the House of Lords with a flimsy justification for so doing (see above, p. 89).

So the National Industrial Relations Court in 1972 forced the judiciary to take up a position on the government's side of industrial disputes which divided the country (see above, pp. 87–93). But, especially here, the distinction must be observed between the interests of the government of the day and the judiciary's view of the public interest. Certainly, the two interests coincided for the judges enabled the government to escape from a situation which would probably have brought it down and would have presented the trade union movement with a considerable political victory. The judges, we may assume, were not concerned to save that particular Conservative government. They were concerned, however, both to preserve the authority of governments and to avoid economic chaos. That was where they saw the public interest to lie. The price they paid was the increase in distrust between themselves and the trade union movement. So they may have mistaken the public interest. But that is a political comment about a political choice.

In the conflict between the Court of Appeal and the House of Lords in 1979–80 (see above, pp. 93–7) the difference in views of the law, as I have said, did not reflect any difference about its undesirability. In *NWL Ltd v. Woods* Lord Diplock talked of the possibility of wage demands bringing down 'the fabric of the present economic system'. In *Express Newspapers v. McShane* he said that the consequences of applying the subjective test in interpreting 'furtherance of a trade dispute' 'not surprisingly have tended to stick in judicial gorges',[19] and in *Duport Steels v. Sirs* he said that the immunity given to trade unionists was:

> intrinsically repugnant to anyone who has spent his life in the practice of law or the administration of justice . . . It involves granting to trade unions a power, which has no other limits than their own self-interest, to inflict by means which are contrary to the general law, untold harm to industrial enterprises unconcerned with the particular dispute, to the employees of such enterprises, to members of the public and to the nation itself . . . [20]

even though the 'immunity' was, as Lord Scarman said, in substance that given by the legislation of 1906.

In the same case Lord Edmund-Davies called the outcome of the statute 'unpalatable to many', and Lord Keith referred to trade unionists as 'privileged persons' who could 'bring about disastrous consequences with legal impunity'.[21]

Similarly, Lord Denning MR in the Court of Appeal said:

> There is evidence of the disastrous effect which the action will have, not only on all the companies in the private sector, but on much of British industry itself . . . our competitors will clap their hands . . . there is a residual discretion in the courts to grant an injunction restraining such action as in this case, where it is such as to cause grave danger to the economy and the life of the country, and puts the whole nation and its welfare at risk.[22]

19. [1980] 2 WLR at 97.
20. [1980] 1 All ER at 541; and see Wedderburn's article referred to below at note 53.
21. Ibid. at 548, 550.
22. Ibid. at 535, 536, 538.

Why, then, did the House of Lords not support the Court of Appeal? To have done so in *Express Newspapers v. McShane* would not have been difficult. It is not manifestly absurd to interpret 'in furtherance of a trade dispute' as implying an objective test and the gap between Lord Wilberforce's approach and that of Lord Denning (see above, pp. 95–6) is not large. To have supported the Court of Appeal would certainly have brought the judiciary into even sharper confrontation with the trade unions and to have further diminished in certain quarters what Lord Diplock in *Duport Steels* called 'that voluntary respect for the law as laid down and applied by courts of justice'. Lords Keith and Scarman expressed similar fears.

Moreover these decisions were taken at a time when the newly elected Conservative government were embarking on their legislative reforms of trade union law, the Employment Bill being published at the beginning of December 1979. Their Lordships may well have concluded that it would be wiser to leave such highly contentious political matters to the professional politicians. At the same time, some of their Lordships did not hesitate to push the Conservative government in what they saw as the right direction. Their criticism of the powers which the existing legislation gave to trade unionists could hardly have been stronger and Lords Diplock, Salmon and Edmund-Davies in *Duport Steels* made quite clear that they hoped the law would be changed. To the layman it must have seemed that members of the senior judiciary were publicly throwing their weight behind the Conservative government.

The Law Lords were, in these cases, moving sharply and clearly to restrain Lord Denning and the Court of Appeal from developing a policy of restricting trade union activity. The Law Lords saw the need, in the public interest, of avoiding an open conflict between the courts and the trade unions. The disagreement between the Court of Appeal and the House of Lords presented a clear difference of tactics. Both courts were agreed that trade union power should be curbed, and in this their political position was identical. But on the question of how far the courts should intervene, the

Law Lords preferred discretion to valour. But they knew the Employment Bill would do the job for them.

During the 1980s, the Thatcher Government continued to develop anti-union legislation, making illegal a number of union practices. The courts, as we have seen (above, p. 107), became deeply involved in the miners' strike of 1984 and the punitive effect of injunctions, fines and sequestration of assets became severe. The attitude of the courts even to those demonstrations and picketing which did not result in violence was to seek to curtail union activity. Certainly there was violence by both strikers and the police. Later, during the dispute over the National Dock Labour Scheme, the Court of Appeal went beyond previous limits in granting an interim injunction so that what it called a difficult question of law could be considered subsequently at the full trial. Had this question been decided in favour of the employers, it would have meant that since 1947 dock workers had had no sanction to strike. The House of Lords prevented what would have been a manifest injustice and a display of political bias remarkable even in the context of industrial relations. Nevertheless the consequences were negligible as the Government Bill abolishing the scheme was passed before further action could be taken. So the Lords' decision was no great blow in support of the right to strike. However, also in 1989, the attempt by British Rail to have the NUR ballot declared invalid on grounds which would have made the holding of a legal ballot almost impossible also failed (see above, p. 111).

Industrial disputes arise out of the conflict of interest between owners, employers and managers on the one side and the employed wage-earners on the other. Each side has some bargaining weapons. Government legislation in the 1980s has been directed to strengthen the employers and weaken the employed. Inevitably, because that is their function and their role, whether they like it or not, the courts have been drawn into the conflict and, by the nature of the legislation, have been required to make political decisions. As Wedderburn has said, the courts see an industrial dispute as essentially one where the enjoyment of private 'property' is being interfered with. It is on this basis that they are so ready to grant interim injunctions, the effect of which is greatly to diminish the workers' bargaining power by wholly suspending the right to strike.

In the 1980s, employers have seemed much more intent on testing the extent to which the courts were prepared to go in restraining union activity, particularly in their interpretation of the more recent legislation. The rejection of injunctions by the House of Lords in the Dock labour Scheme and NUR cases (see above p. 109) carried echoes of the restraints placed on Lord Denning's enthusiasm which we have already noticed. On both occasions there was a pulling back from the brink when perhaps the Law Lords sensed that to uphold the employers would have amounted to a denial of the right to strike in most circumstances. Not for the first time in industrial relations, their Lordships have required Parliament to take the next steps. So far they have rarely been disappointed. A good example of the restrictive gloss which the courts sometimes attach to statutory words was given by Lord Donaldson MR in *P.O. v. U.C.W.* (see above p. 111) when, on balloting, he said:

> Where over a long period of continuous action there has been a significant change in the relevant workforce, any call for industrial action following a ballot should be expressly limited to those who were employed by the employer and given an opportunity of voting at the time of the ballot.

This raises the question of what the courts are supposed, in constitutional theory as well as political practice, to be doing in disputes between employers and trade unions. Are they to be arbitrators of last resort? If so, on what basis, taking what factors into account? Once again, Lord Templeman's comments in his interview with Hugo Young give a possible indication.[23] He said, speaking generally of cases coming to the courts (including the House of Lords) that judges were of two kinds: those who ask what is the point of law and those who ask what are the merits of the case.

23. Radio 4 on 13 April 1988.

He adds, however, that even in the House of Lords 'Merits have influence on every case.'

So to ask what is the judicial role in industrial disputes is always to oversimplify, both because there will always be at least two possible interpretations of statute or common law and because individual judges will put different weight on the two considerations: law and merits. What may be true is that in the highly 'political' area of such disputes, merits counts for more than law. For in these cases, more than in any others, the consequences of judicial decisions are likely to be far-reaching.

Another policy dispute arose out of the challenge to poll tax capping (see above, p. 149) which was seen by some commentators as a genuine test of the courts' attitude to the exercise of Ministerial powers. It was argued that Parliament did not intend 'in-year' capping which forced local authorities to revise spending targets already budgeted for and embarked on; that the Minister was under a duty to consult and to base any restrictions on the particular circumstances of each authority; and that he should be obliged to give reasons for his decisions.

The rejection of these arguments exemplifies once again the wide range of discretion enjoyed by the courts in such cases. As a matter of course, the standard reply was given: as Lord Donaldson MR said in the Court of Appeal 'In relation to statutes the only duty of the judiciary was to interpret and apply them.' Innumerable cases from *Liversidge v. Anderson* (above p. 151) through *Padfield* (above p. 116) to the interpretations of the Contempt of Court Act 1981, show how easily the courts can subvert the intentions of Parliament when they think it appropriate to do so. The fact was that the courts, faced with a political decision of such magnitude as that presented by the poll tax capping were not prepared to use their muscle. And Lord Donaldson effectively admitted this when he began his judgment by reference to another stand-by: the doctrine of the separation of powers. The House of Lords was even more dismissive.[24]

24. *R. v. Secretary of State for the Environment ex parte Hammersmith and Fulham LBC, The Independent,* 5 October 1990.

On the other hand, there are groups of cases where the courts come down quite heavily on the exercise of Ministerial powers. Those affecting regulations on social security (see above p. 147) are examples. Often they are cases where Ministers deliberately seem to push the exercise of their powers beyond their natural limits. In the radio interview with Hugo Young on 13 April 1988, Lord Templeman spoke of 'bullying' by Ministers and local authorities who 'throw their weight about too much'. The comment is revealing because it suggests that the senior judiciary needs to have evidence of positive oppression on individuals not easily able to withstand such treatment. This seems to fall far short of Lord Atkin's famous claim that judges should 'stand between the subject and any attempted encroachments on his liberty by the executive, alert to see that any coercive action is justified in law'.[25]

Why, for example, should the courts not take a more robust line in cases like *R. v. ILEA ex parte Ali* (see above p. 147)?

It was, no doubt, easiest to duck the issue, to fall back on the proposition that the failure to provide school places for scores of Asian children in east London, although a statutory duty cast on the local education authority, is not one to be enforced at the instance of a parent whose son has been denied schooling for over twelve months. The Education Act 1944 requires local education authorities to ensure that schools in their area are sufficient in:

> number, character and equipment to afford to all pupils opportunities for education offering such variety of instruction as may be desirable in view of their different ages, abilities and aptitudes, and of the different periods for which they may be expected to remain at school, including practical instruction and training appropriate to their respective needs.

In another context it is easy to imagine the courts insisting that that duty was mandatory and should be fulfilled. So to rule would, of course, have been deeply embarrassing to the

---

25. *Liversidge v. Anderson* [1942] AC 206; see above p. 152.

Government whose refusal to provide adequate funds was the cause of the crisis.

Again, in *R. v. Secretary of State for Social Services ex parte Stitt* (see above p. 148) the domestic help was necessary to enable an unemployed man with a wife and six children to take an offered place on an employment training scheme. It was refused because of a blanket Ministerial direction excluding all payments for this purpose. The Court of Appeal expressed concern that Parliament should have given the Minister such wide powers and Lord Justice Purchas thought it might be 'an unwelcome feature of a dominating executive in a basically two-party democracy'. He suggested that Parliament must have been asleep when it permitted such 'wholly exceptional and, it might be thought by some, objectionable powers' to be given to Ministers without any Parliamentary fetter or supervision. The Court of Appeal could have used the familiar formula for the exercise of judicial authority: that Parliament 'could not have intended' the power to be exercised in this way. But it chose not to do so and merely to wring its hands.

Three case studies

If it is agreed that the senior judiciary, especially those who sit in the Court of Appeal and the House of Lords, are required from time to time to decide where the public interest lies (or which of two conflicting public interests should prevail) and that, in this sense, they cannot be neutral but must make political choices, the question is how well they perform this difficult task. It has been part of the argument of this book that they are inevitably, as are the rest of us, to a considerable extent conditioned by their social background, by their experiences and by their professional careers as barristers. But they are also constrained by the system within which they work.

The senior judiciary are, of course, well aware of the importance of their role in government. They are better informed about policy and its development than most of those who are neither ministers nor senior civil servants.

Their ears are close to the ground of politics, whether it concerns industrial relations or race relations, immigration policy, police powers or national security. On many matters their policies (or views of where the public interest lies) accord with those of the government of the day because they are part of that consensus. If the political differences between the major political parties were more divergent, and a party of the right or of the left, holding what would now be regarded as extreme views, were elected, the senior judiciary would be faced with critical choices. But this is not, and is not likely to be, the case.

At the same time, the senior judiciary are men of great ability and strong opinions. Their assessment of the public interest does from time to time differ from that of the central Departments and local authorities whose decisions and actions they are called on to judge. And they are not greatly knowledgeable in the processes of administration. Nor, despite their sensibility, are they necessarily fully aware of current developments in policy or administration. These two factors – the independence of their assessments and their lack of knowledge – explain how, from time to time, they come to decisions that seem eccentric.

Three recent examples are illustrative. The first is the *Bromley v. GLC* litigation over the Fares Fair policy.[26]

Bromley v. GLC

It may be that the Court of Appeal and the Law Lords deliberately intervened to control the collectivist policies of the administration at County Hall because they disapproved of those policies. But in addition and perhaps more significantly, they seem not to have understood what they were doing, because they did not grasp the nature of the problem of London Transport. The administrative build-up to the Fares Fair Policy had its roots in the mid-1960s; and professional administrators, not only in London, had been grappling with the problems over a long period. It was for that reason that those administrators were stupefied and dismayed by what seemed to them to be arbitrary and wholly

26. See above, pp. 128–36.

unrealistic sets of reasons advanced by the Court of Appeal and the House of Lords for upsetting an attempt to solve the financial, administrative, social and economic problems of London Transport.

The judgments delivered in the Court of Appeal and the House of Lords in *Bromley v. GLC* demonstrate how ill-suited is judicial review to the examination of administrative policies. They show how the narrow approach of the courts to the interpretation of statutes leads to a misunderstanding of the purpose of legislation. When this is combined with the application of a broad principle ('the fiduciary duty') to the examination of the exercise of administrative discretion, the mismatch becomes almost total. We do not know to what extent the members of the two courts sought to inform themselves of the recent developments in transport policy, other than by looking at the legislation of the 1960s. Lord Wilberforce, as we have seen,[27] while recognizing that there existed 'discussion on the political level', concluded that 'the only safe course' was to try to understand 'the contemporary language' by which he meant the words of the Act of 1969. Lord Diplock was again the exception, refusing to accept, in the absence of clear words, that the GLC was prohibited from operating a system of deficit financing deliberately created.

The crisis in urban transport received popular recognition in the publication in 1963 of Colin Buchanan's *Traffic in Towns*. This was followed in 1966 by the white paper on *Transport Policy*.[28] This emphasized the 'severe discomforts' brought by the growth of road traffic: congestion, the misery of commuter travel, noise, fumes, danger, casualties and the threat to the environment; and the need to plan, as a whole, for the related needs of industry, housing and transport.[29] The paper drew attention to the mutually contradictory objectives of providing adequate services and self-financing.

27. See above, p. 132.
28. Cmnd. 3057. On the development of transport policy in the 1960s see J. Dignan, 'Policy-making, Local Authorities and the Courts' in 99 *Law Quarterly Review* (1983) 605, to which I am much indebted.
29. Car and motorcycle licences in the London Transport area rose from 1.7m in 1960 to 2.3m in 1966.

In January 1968, the London Transport Joint Review was published and was followed in July by the white paper *Transport in London*.[30] The Review found that the major factor underlying London Transport's recurrent financial deficit was the imbalance between peak and off-peak demand. The Review was somewhat ambiguous about the need for financial viability, but it certainly envisaged some form of grant and emphasized the social benefits of controlling the level of fares while providing proper services. *Transport in London* went further in emphasizing the need of the transport system to take account of 'the social as well as the economic needs of the country'. Subsidization through the local rates was one of the means adopted by the Transport Act 1968 for conurbations outside London and this was intended to enable the transport authorities to achieve, in part, the purpose of developing transport as a social service.

The Transport (London) Act 1969 was seen by ministers as taking this approach further. For the first time in London, the responsibility for transport was given to a directly elected local authority acting through an Executive appointed by itself. Comparison has been made with a nationalized industry operating the day-to-day management under the general directions of a minister. But the control by the GLC over the LTE was much tighter than that of a minister over the coal, gas or electricity authorities. The GLC was not merely empowered but required by section 1 'to develop policies, and to encourage, organize and, where appropriate, carry out measures'. The LTE existed to implement policies of the GLC (section 4(1)) and to act 'in accordance with principles laid down or approved by the GLC' (section 5(1)). Additionally, the GLC might give the LTE general directions in relation to functions which the GLC was under a duty to perform (section 11(1)). There were also other more detailed provisions emphasizing the powers of the GLC. Above all, the GLC's primary duty was to promote 'the provision of integrated, efficient and economic transport facilities and services for Greater London'. Finally, the LTE was required to submit to the GLC for their approval the

30. Cmnd 3686.

general level and structure of the fares to be charged and
the GLC might 'direct the Executive to submit proposals for
an alteration in the Executive's fare arrangements to achieve
any object of general policy specified by the Council in the
direction' (section 11(3)).

As Dignan has written:[31]

If one examines in this way the detailed legislative history of the 1969 Act and its closely related predecessor,
enacted in the previous year, it will be seen that the
Labour Government had clearly embarked on a radical
new policy for urban transport, one which entailed profound implications for the local state in terms of its
functions, its powers and its responsibility. It was not
just that the government's novel response to a whole
series of interrelated problems represented a substantial
break with earlier transport policies; rather, it marked
a decisive shift from one kind of legislative framework
to another, consistent with . . . a transition from a
gesellschaft to a bureaucratic-administrative infrastruc-
ture.

Separate from the social and political background which
shaped the transport of the late 1960s was an administrative
development of significance. It was a period of 'planning,
programming and financing'.[32] The approach at this time,
not only for public transport, was, first, to determine what
was to be achieved; second, to produce a programme for
this end; and third, to determine how it was to be financed.
This does not mean that the cost was irrelevant. On the
contrary, it was an important element in determining what
was to be achieved and how it was to be achieved. But
finance was used as a tool of measurement. Once it was
decided what transport policy, for example, should be and
how it was to be implemented, the question of the method

31. See note 28 above.
32. I am much indebted to a paper by Mr Stonefrost, then Comptroller
of Finance and later Director-General of the GLC, presented to the Oxford
University Faculty of Law and SSRC Centre for Socio-legal Studies on 2
March 1983; and to Mr Fitzpatrick, former Solicitor to the GLC.

of financing (by fares, by grants, by taxation) was determined as seemed most appropriate. The principle, beloved of market economists, that the consumer should pay the full cost unless some very special case could be made out for some form of subsidy, was not seen as of great significance. As Mr Stonefrost wrote:

> To hold out a presumption that an undertaking can 'break even' or 'make a profit' when such an assumption is implicitly known to be impracticable on current policies in the accounting period in question is to contribute to irresponsibility. Management needs to be set realistic financial possibilities. In public administration in the late 60s debts were cleared on several public services, realistic planning and management targets were established, and, if subsidy was known to be necessary, its size and the conditions applying to its availability were set in advance as a necessary precondition to set out and to test management performance.

The House of Lords, like the Court of Appeal, had a clear policy choice in interpreting the 1969 Act.[33] By choosing to set the words of section 7 (dealing with the financial accounting arrangements between the GLC and the LTE and the financial duties of the LTE) over the policy provisions of sections 1 and 5 (the grants section) and by invoking the concept of the fiduciary duty, the courts were able virtually to ignore social and economic factors which had produced the Act. Why did they make this choice?

For the members of the Court of Appeal, one reason seems to have been their annoyance with the way in which the GLC majority group implemented their manifesto commitment. Five days after the election in May 1981 the leader of the GLC instructed the chairman of the LTE to submit proposals for the 25 per cent reduction in fares to a meeting on 1 July. Lord Denning held that the GLC had no power to make resolutions to enforce a 25 per cent cut which 'was a completely uneconomic proposition done for political motives – for which there is no warrant'. Similarly Watkins

33. See above, pp. 131–3.

LJ had 'no doubt whatsoever that the large reduction of fares the LTE was ordered to introduce by the GLC arose out of a hasty, ill-considered, unlawful and arbitrary use of power . . . and the ratepayers of this great city, who are unlikely to gain anything from it (many of them will in fact be at a loss), will bear the cost of what seems to many to have been an astounding decision'. With a nice touch of judicial arrogance he added: 'Those who come newly to govern people and who act in haste in wielding power to which they are unaccustomed would do well to heed the words of Gladstone . . . "The true test of a man, the test of a class, the true test of a people is power. It is when power is given into their hands that the trial comes."' Oliver LJ also found the procedural hurdle ('perhaps rather a technical one') impossible for the GLC to surmount.

In the House of Lords these arguments hardly featured and were certainly not crucial. There, with all the emphasis on 'economic', on the need for the GLC to act in a 'business-like' manner, the reason for the choice seems to have been primarily the Law Lords' strong preference for the principles of the market economy with a dislike of heavy subsidization for social purposes. Their decisions were in the tradition of individual rather than social, private rather than collective, enterprise. They appeared to think there was something unseemly in a policy change of these dimensions. Lord Keith, referring to the power of the GLC in section 11 to direct the LTE to submit proposals for an alteration in the fare arrangements to achieve 'any object of general policy' specified by the GLC, said that that phrase 'clearly' was 'confined to the field of transport policy'. Such a limitation, very difficult to justify from the language of the Act, shows how far their Lordships were from understanding the statutory intention. Whether or not their Lordships were politically biased, their habits of thought determined their decision.

Bromley v. GLC raises all the questions about the nature, the function, and the limits of judicial review. The whole method of adjudication as presently adopted by the courts is inappropriate to the consideration of political decisions affecting the distribution of costs between the tax and rate-paying public, on the one hand, and the users of public services, on the other. As Mr Stonefrost said, in the paper to which I have referred, as he reflected on the judicial process in this case:

> The process itself was more in the nature of an intellectual marauding over a wide area of hunting territory rather than an ordered, structured, predictable and prepared process. Some issues were dealt with comprehensively and with full intellectual rigour. But others were not and it was not possible to predict which of many issues a member of the Court might concentrate upon at any one time. The basic judicial process of adversarial advocacy, punctuated courteously but irregularly, unpredictably and frequently by important court questions and interjections working from a mound of papers within a necessarily highly concentrated but limited time scale, contrasts sharply with an administrative policy decision which may be an important final expression of widespread political struggle and practical pressures over a very long period of time.

The second example is the treatment by the Court of Appeal and the House of Lords of the Commission for Racial Equality.[34]

The courts and the CRE

In *Hillingdon*, Lord Diplock took the view that the terms of reference defined the scope of the investigation and that the terms as drawn were wider than the 'belief' and so invalid; and that this was so even though the CRE had made clear from the beginning that their investigation would be limited to the area of their belief about the treatment of immigrants only.

Lord Diplock's interpretation was clearly not one to which he was driven by the words of section 49(4). He chose a narrow and over-literal meaning and so unnecessarily frustrated the main purpose of the Act. Nor could it be said that the alternative interpretation would have caused injustice to

34. See above, pp. 174–8.

the Council. 'Belief' in this context is understood, even by Lord Diplock, as a very modest state of consciousness. In *Prestige* he said that the CRE 'should in fact have already formed a suspicion that the persons named may have committed some unlawful act of discrimination and had at any rate *some* grounds for so suspecting, albeit that the grounds upon which any such suspicion was based might, at that stage, be no more than tenuous because they had not yet been tested.' If 'belief' may properly be as weak as that, no measurable hardship can come from drawing terms of reference a little widely especially when they do not name any person other than one to whom justifiable suspicion is directed.

As we have seen, it was in *Hillingdon* that Lord Diplock first laid down that 'belief' about a named person was a condition precedent to the drawing up of terms of reference. In *Prestige* he repeated and applied this. 'We have always taken the view', said the CRE in 1983, 'that the CRE is entitled to carry out formal investigations whether there are grounds for suspecting an unlawful act or not,' and they regarded the Court of Appeal's contrary opinion in *Prestige* (which was to be confirmed by the House of Lords) as 'a severe, and in our view wrong, constraint on the discretion of the Commission'.[35] The strategy of the CRE in relation to formal investigations – which had had considerable success – is having to be rethought, as in the view of the CRE they can now only investigate a named organization – 'and all organizations have names' – if they already have reason to believe that it may be discriminating unlawfully.[36]

Here again, Lord Diplock in *Prestige* made his choice. The words of sections 49 and 50 of the Act are fully capable of being interpreted as meaning that a named-person investigation need not be directed to uncovering discrimination, although in such a case the CRE would have no coercive powers. Of course the distinction between a named-person investigation and a general investigation is frequently not

35. See above, pp. 176–7.
36. CRE *Annual Report* for 1983 at p. 3.

clear because the latter is often sparked off by specific complaints.

Again, the judicial interpretation of sections 49(4) was far from obvious. This subsection was, as Lord Denning MR pointed out in *Hillingdon*, a drafting blunder. Lord Hailsham had moved an amendment as a new clause to the Bill to a similar effect with the intention of ensuring that a person named would have the right to be heard *during the course* of a formal investigation. The government rejected his formulation and produced one of their own. But this was tacked on as subsection (4) to the previous clause (now section 49) and so fell under the terms of subsection (1) which requires compliance with subsections (2)–(4) before the CRE could embark on a formal investigation. In *Prestige*, unlike *Hillingdon*, no 'belief' was expressed in the terms of reference, and it was not until the investigation was well advanced that the CRE came to a belief that Prestige were committing discriminatory acts. So, CRE argued, subsection (4) applied only to the start of an investigation when in the terms of reference a belief had been stated about a named person.

Moreover subsection (4) refers to a named person having the right to make representations with regard to 'it' in a context where 'it' could mean the proposal to investigate or the discriminatory act itself. If it were interpreted to mean the latter, then the obligation on the Commission before embarking on the investigation would be limited to offering an opportunity to make representations about the act during the course of the investigation, which is what Lord Hailsham (and we may assume the government) meant.

Both these interpretations were rejected by Lord Diplock although both of them would have promoted the purposes of the statute without causing injustice.

We have already seen how Lord Diplock, in 1974 in the *Dockers' Club* case, saw legislation seeking to deal with racial discrimination as a restriction on the liberty of the citizen.[37] In these cases involving the CRE his emphasis is the same. As the CRE said in 1983: 'It may be that judges will never be able to accept the fact that Parliament has

37. See above, p. 172.

entrusted the CRE with sweeping investigative powers to work towards the eradication of a great social evil being carried out covertly.'[38] Individual grievances were left, under the Act of 1976, to individuals to redress. The CRE was given 'a major strategic role in enforcing the law in the public interest'.[39] The idea of a public authority invested with the power to investigate, to adjudicate and to decide, while providing persons affected with opportunities to make representations, was too much for the senior judiciary, reared in the tradition of private rights, to accept. Lord Denning MR expressed their horror.

> I would draw attention to the immense powers already granted by Parliament to the statutory commissions. They can conduct 'formal investigations' by which they can interrogate employers and educational authorities up to the hilt and compel disclosure of documents on a massive scale. They can take up the cause of any complainant who has a grievance and, in his name, issue a questionnaire to his employers or educational authorities. They can use his name to sue them, and demand full particulars in the course of it. They can compel discovery of documents from them to the same extent as in the High Court. No plea is available to the accused that they are not bound to incriminate themselves. You might think that we were back in the days of the Inquisition. Now we come to the most presumptuous claim of all. They demand to see documents made in confidence, and to compel breaches of good faith – which is owed to persons who are not parties to the proceedings at all. You might think we were back in the days of the General Warrants.

Laker Airways

The decision in the *Laker Airways* case[40] provides a third example of the inadequacies of the judiciary when faced with

---

38. See above, note 36.
39. The Home Secretary (Mr R. Jenkins) during the second reading debate on the Bill (906 HC Deb. col. 1558, 4 March 1976).
40. See above, pp. 121–2.

administrative processes with which they are unfamiliar.[41] In 1960 the Air Transport Licensing Board was created by statute primarily to decide whether the Board should issue to an airline an 'air service licence' without which the airline could not operate. Under the Act and regulations, the Board was required to hold hearings and the procedure was highly judicialized. There was a right of appeal to the minister from a decision of the Board and he appointed a Commissioner to hear the appeal and to make recommendations which the minister could accept or reject. The minister also had to enter into agreements with foreign states in relation to traffic rights and fare levels. In addition the minister gave general non-statutory guidance to the Board on policy matters. The working relationship so constructed between the Board and minister did not make for rational policy-making and G. R. Baldwin concluded that the Board provided 'an unadventurous blend of the judicial with the managerial and of expertise with independence'.[42]

In 1967 the Select Committee on Nationalised Industries recommended drastic changes.[43] So did the Edwards Committee which in 1969 recommended the setting up of a much stronger agency and favoured the use of written policy guidance from the minister. Such guidance should be set down in 'terms sufficiently clear to be generally understood and if necessary to stand the test of judicial interpretation'. The Labour government published a White Paper[44] which emphasized the need for a new Civil Aviation Authority (CAA), the essential feature of whose status would be the separation between policy formulation (which would be for ministers to determine) and the detailed application of policy (where the CAA would have a wide discretion). This was the Authority set up by the Conservative government under the Civil Aviation Act 1971. As we have seen, the minister was now statutorily empowered to issue written policy guid-

41. See G. R. Baldwin, 'A British Independent Regulatory Agency and the "Skytrain" Decision' [1978] *Public Law* 57, to which I am indebted.

42. See last note.

43. HC 673 of 1966–7.

44. Cmnd. 4213 (1969).

ance and to hear appeals. The first guidance comprised twenty-two pages of general policy. In 1974 the new Labour minister conducted a review of policy to which the CAA submitted detailed reports and in July 1975 he proposed a number of policy changes to be incorporated in the new guidance. One of these changes was that the new policy would in general rule out long-haul scheduled competition. British Caledonian and British Airways would be given protected spheres of interest and Laker's Skytrain would not be allowed to operate. The new guidance was issued in March 1976.[45]

The crucial question in the litigation was therefore whether the minister's power of 'guidance' entitled him to overrule the CAA. And this, in turn, depended on the purpose of the legislation in relation to the minister's powers generally over the CAA. The Court of Appeal, in the usual judicial manner, based itself on semantics. 'The word "guidance"', said Lord Denning, 'does not denote an order or command.' Roskill LJ said: 'it is not unreasonable to think, in spite of certain dictionary definitions of guidance . . . that the draftsmen intended a different result to follow according to whether it was guidance or a direction that was to be given.' And Lawton LJ said: 'The word "guidance" has the implication of leading, pointing the way, whereas "direction" even today echoes its Latin roots of *regere*, to rule. When the Secretary of State exercises his statutory powers to direct he does indeed rule. He is in command: he is more than a guide.' To all this the answer is that, as the history of the matter shows, it was the minister who was intended to determine policy by his guidance and that competitiveness or monopoly on long-haul routes was essentially a matter of policy.

G. R. Baldwin's summary seems irrefutable.

The judges of the Court of Appeal strove to protect the CAA's discretion and to cut down the Minister's discretion. In doing so they conceived of the CAA as a traditional body with 'quasi-judicial' functions. They

45. Cmnd 6400.

saw it as a court giving licences with rights to be protected by legal due process and as a judicial body deserving protection from executive interference. They failed to see the significance of the CAA as a new form of multi-faceted agency of government, attempting to combine judicial and executive methods in a delicately balanced legal framework whilst acting in a politically contentious area. In attempting to preserve for the CAA an independent judicial status the judges sought to achieve the impossible. No one expected the CAA to be fully independent of government, in the manner of a court. As was pointed out in the Court of Appeal, the Government could always control the agency in ways other than by using guidance. The Court of Appeal decision damaged a system of balance based on compromise because the system of control fitted no neat jurisprudential category.

It might be asked 'Why is it that the intentions behind the 1971 Act were not communicated to the judges?' The answer appears to be that the 1971 Act was based on a new conception of the relationship between the independent agency and government, a conception which the judges, with more old fashioned views concerning 'quasi-judicial' tribunals and ministerial powers, were unable to accept. The decisions are explicable perhaps, as the product of a period in which the courts (and some judges in particular) demonstrated a distinct eagerness to increase their review of executive powers and discretion. They were certainly disruptive.

A similar comment may be made of the decision in *Padfield*.[46] The reason why the minister was empowered rather than required to refer a complaint to the committee of investigation was to enable him to decide that the complaint was a matter of policy and so appropriate for determination by the Milk Marketing Board and himself. By requiring him to set up the committee and refer the complaint to it, the House of Lords misinterpreted the statute. The result was that the minister referred the complaint to the committee which

---

46. See above, p. 116.

recommended certain changes in the scheme. Whereupon the minister rejected the recommendation and the absurdity of the Lord's decision was demonstrated.[47]

These examples show that, under their present procedures, judges are ill-equipped to make political decisions which determine the way in which administrative authorities fulfil their duties. The courts of law are not designed as research centres, and judges in our system are most reluctant to assume an inquisitorial role and to seek to discover all the relevant facts. They rely on the adversarial method and take judicial notice only of those matters and those arguments presented to them. This position is carried to the extreme of not enabling a party to obtain discovery of documents unless he can show their direct relevance to his case.

In *Air Canada v. Secretary of State for Trade (No. 2)*[48] Lord Fraser said:

> In an adversarial system such as exists in the United Kingdom a party is free to withhold information that would help his case if he wishes, perhaps for reasons of delicacy or personal privacy. He cannot be compelled to disclose it against his will. It follows in my opinion that a party who seeks to compel his opponent, or an independent person, to disclose information must show that the information is likely to help his own case.

Lord Wilberforce said: 'There is no independent power in the court to say that . . . it would like to inspect the documents, with a view to possible production, *for its own assistance*' (emphasis added). Lord Edmund-Davies said, 'To urge that, on principle, justice is most likely to be done if free access is had to all relevant documents is pointless, for it carries no weight in our adversarial system of law.' The contrary view was put by Lord Templeman who said, 'The judge must decide whether the public interest in maintaining the confidential nature of the document prevails over the public interest in ensuring that justice is achieved.' So also

47. See C. Harlow and R. Rawlings, *Law and Administration* (1984), pp. 327–9.
48. [1983] 1 All ER 161.

Lord Scarman said, 'Discovery is one of the few exceptions to the adversarial character of our legal process. It assists parties and the court to discover the truth.' But they agreed with the majority in the event.

If the judiciary were willing to adopt a more inquisitorial role, they could insist that evidence be called on specific matters. The evidence of those directly concerned in both policy-making and the administrative process would clarify the issues and enable the courts to come to a more complete understanding of the nature of the public interest involved. Counsel can put the general situation before the court but their arguments are likely to be less effective and less well-informed than those of the individuals directly involved, be they politicians or public servants. Expert evidence also can play a most important part in the instruction of the judiciary.

In *Pickwell v. Camden LBC*,[49] a strike by the council's manual workers was settled on terms which were more favourable to those workers than the terms on which a parallel national dispute was settled. And a year later the council added a further cost-of-living increase, negotiated at the national level, and did not absorb it within the extra pay margin. The district auditor asked the court for a declaration that both payments were unlawful. But the court held that the council had not acted unreasonably or considered irrelevant matters or failed to consider relevant matters. The district auditor's calculations were challenged in an affidavit from a professor, expert in the field of pay and employment. Forbes J said: 'Whether the district auditor or Professor Metcalfe be right, the existence of so fundamental a divergence of opinion on a matter so important must cast some doubt on whether it can properly be said that no reasonable authority could possibly have acted as did Camden in this instance.' In the *GCHQ* case two people knew the real reason why the Government did not consult the unions: the Prime Minister and the Foreign Secretary. Neither could be required to give evidence.[50] How far such evidence should

49. [1983] 1 All ER 602.
50. See my article 'Judicial Decision-making in Public Law' in [1985] *Public Law* 564; and above p. 155.

be on affidavit and how far by oral testimony (and so open to cross-examination) would be for the court to decide.

Two objections may be made. The first is that it would prolong the hearing of cases. This may well be so but if the judiciary are to continue to review decisions of the kind in *Bromley v. GLC*, the *Laker* and the *CRE* cases, they must have relevant evidence before them.

The other objection is more serious. If the judiciary were to adopt a more investigatory role, the danger is that they would be encouraged to encroach even more on policy matters than they do at present. So it would be necessary to curtail the scope of their enquiries.[51] Lord Scarman has said:

> When one turns away from the field of legislation to that of executive discretion and decision, co-operation calls for a high degree of judicial restraint. The ambit of executive decision and executive discretion must be defined by statute: and judges must respect it. They will, of course, become the watch-dogs empowered to compel compliance with the conditions to which executive power is subject. But within these limits executive power is not to be curtailed by judicial action unless there be infringements of basic human rights such as liberty or natural justice or unless it can be demonstrated that the power was exercised in such a way as no reasonable person invested with the power could have exercised it. In other words, within the ambit of the power there can be no judicial challenge save to protect human rights or to curb abuse of power.[52]

It has been said that the House of Lords as the upper chamber of the Legislature does nothing in particular and does it very well. It could be said of that House in its judicial capacity that, in the field of public law, it does too much in particular and does it rather badly.

51. See my chapter in P. Archer and A. Martin (eds.), *More Law Reform Now* (1983), pp. 54–9.

52. In a lecture at the Royal Institute of Public Administration on 4 November 1982.

Conclusion

In suggesting that the senior judiciary look to a view of the
public interest to inform their attitude to the controversial
matters of law and order, of political and economic conflict,
of sexual and social *mores*, of personal liberty and property
rights, of protest, of governmental confidentiality, of race
relations, of immigration and the rest, I mean to absolve
them of a conscious and deliberate intention to pursue their
own interests or the interests of their class. I believe that in
these matters and within the considerable area of decision-
making open to them they look to what they regard as the
interest of the whole society. However, we are left to consider why it is that their view of that public interest is what
it is.

It is common to speak of the judiciary as part of the system
of checks and balances which contains and constrains the
power of the government; or as one of the three principal
institutions of the State, each of which acts to limit the
powers of the other two. The image has a pleasing and
mechanistic appearance suggesting some objective hidden
hand which holds the constitution in perpetual equilibrium.
The extent to which the image reflects reality is less obvious.

If we limit our examination to the working of the three
institutions – Parliament, the government, and the judiciary
– in their relationships with each other, then it is clear that
each of these groups influences the way in which the others
act. And it is clear, in particular, that the judiciary may
oppose the government to the extent of declaring its actions
invalid or requiring it to pay compensation or even subject-
ing one of its members or servants to penalties.

If however we look more broadly and more widely we
see that this judicial activity of opposing governments is a
deviance from the norm, an aberration, which occurs most
infrequently and in very special circumstances. The judiciary
is not placed constitutionally in opposition to the government but, in the overwhelming mass of circumstances, alongside it.

In our society, as in others, political power, the power of
government, is exercised by a relatively small number of

people. Senior ministers are most obvious of that number, as are senior civil servants, the chairmen and chief officers of the largest public authorities. Among those who are not members of State institutions should be added a few industrialists and, under Labour governments, a few trade union leaders. And the leading members of Her Majesty's Opposition are also, from time to time, a part of the decision-making process at this highest level. The whole group numbers a few hundred people. They represent established authority.

The rest are outside. Some may be influential as advisers. Others may be very important as professional men and women. But they, along with the population at large, remain outside the governing group. Of course there are many organizations which exercise many different kinds of power within their own sphere. In this narrow sense, we live in a pluralist society. But the political power of governing the country is oligarchic, exercised by a few.

The senior judges are undeniably among those few. The importance of their task, their influence on behaviour, the extent of their powers, the status they enjoy, the extrajudicial uses to which they are put, the circles they move in, the background from which they come, their habits of mind, and the way in which they are regarded by other members of the group confirm beyond question their place within the governing group of established authority. And, like other members of the group, they show themselves alert to protect the social order from threats to its stability or to the existing distribution of political and economic power.

I have said that judges look to what they regard as the interests of the whole society. That, in itself, makes political assumptions of some magnitude. It has long been argued that the concept of the whole society suggests a homogeneity of interest among the different classes within the society which is false. And that this concept is used to persuade the governed that not the government but 'the State' is the highest organization and transcends conflicts in society. It is a short step to say that it is the State which makes the laws, thus enabling those in political power to promote their own interests in the name of the whole abstracted society. Inevitably the judiciary reflects the interests of its own class. Lord Wedderburn has written that 'the eras of judicial "creativity", of new doctrines hostile to trade union interests, have been largely, though not entirely, coterminous with the periods of British social history in which the trade unions have been perceived by middle-class opinion as a threat to the established social order'.[53]

My thesis is that judges in the United Kingdom cannot be politically neutral because they are placed in positions where they are required to make political choices which are sometimes presented to them, and often presented by them, as determinations of where the public interest lies; that their interpretation of what is in the public interest and therefore politically desirable is determined by the kind of people they are and the position they hold in our society; that this position is a part of established authority and so is necessarily conservative and illiberal. From all this flows that view of the public interest which is shown in judicial attitudes such as tenderness towards private property and dislike of trade unions, strong adherence to the maintenance of order, distaste for minority opinions, demonstrations and protests, the avoidance of conflict with Government policy even where it is manifestly oppressive of the most vulnerable, support of governmental secrecy, concern for the preservation of the moral and social behaviour to which it is accustomed, and the rest.

Professor Mancini of the University of Bologna has singled out 'the susceptibility of English judges to be analysed as a politically cohesive group' – what I have called their homogeneity – as the factor distinguishing them from judges in Italy, France and Spain. 'What I mean', he says, 'is (a) that English judges seldom make decisions of a nature to challenge a universally received notion of public interest; and (b) that when they happen to do it, their decisions are a result of strictly individual options.' He draws a very sharp contrast: 'the trend towards a more politicized and politically polarized judiciary . . . in Italy, France and Spain . . . has

53. See *Industrial Law Journal* (June 1980) at p. 78.

acquired, or is in the process of acquiring, traits so neat and forcible as to rise to the dignity of a major national issue.'[54]

One reason for this continental phenomenon is historical and political: the greater divergence between the right and the left in Italy and France as compared with Britain. But it is made possible by the fact that in those countries judges are appointed in their early or mid-twenties after open competitive examinations. It is therefore possible for men and women with widely different, and, at the time of their examination, unknown political opinions to reach the bench and to remain there, effectively, until retirement. If they display political attitudes of which their superiors disapprove, their promotion may not be speedy. And these superiors continue to be 'politically cohesive'. But to remove the dissidents from office is much more difficult. This split between right and left among the judiciary in those countries is highly significant and wholly without parallel in Britain.

Any analysis which places the judiciary in the United Kingdom in a wholly subservient position to the government misreads history and mistakes the source and nature of the common law. Those who criticize existing institutions in the United Kingdom need always to remember that, in comparison with most other countries, this country enables its citizens to live in comparative freedom. To what extent is this a consequence of our judicial system and of our judges?

That they play some part is undeniable. They will even, on occasion, enforce the law which forbids arrest without reasonable cause or imprisonment without trial, and support the right of free association or, within its limits, of free speech. The idea of the rule of law is not wholly illusory.

In Britain, laws are rules made by governments, with the authority of Parliament, or by judges. Without these rules governments would not be able to perform their traditional functions. But these laws, which empower governments, by so doing define their powers. And if governments exceed these powers, they may be controlled by the courts and their actions declared unlawful.

54. G. F. Mancini, 'Politics and the Judges – the European Perspective' in 43 *Modern Law Review* (1980) 1.

What then is meant by 'the rule of law'? The law rules in this sense: that government and all who exercise power as part of established authority are themselves bound by the existing body of laws unless and until they repeal or reform any of those laws. When a government makes a law under Parliamentary authority it makes a rod for its own back as well as for the backs of others. The Declaration of Rights of 1689 declared illegal the suspending or execution of laws by royal authority without the consent of Parliament; and the power to dispense with laws. The exercise of arbitrary power by governments is contrary to the rule of law and the true mark of the despot is that he can, at his own wish and without restraint, set aside the existing laws in any case. Judges are similarly constrained in their law-making function by the doctrine of precedent.

So, because the powers of governments in Britain are limited by law (even though governments may make new laws and change existing laws), there is always the possibility that the exercise of power by governments may be challenged; and because judges, however much they share the values and aims of governments, are not governmental servants, the challenge may be successful.

There is a sense, however far it falls short of what is claimed for it, in which those who exercise legalized force in our society must have regard to the existence of a judiciary which may be prepared to condemn them in some circumstances and will be supported in so doing. Nevertheless, in the event of an attempt by a government to exercise arbitrary and extensive powers, curtailing individual liberty, it cannot be forecast how the judges would react. The political circumstances would be crucial and the judiciary would be divided, as Lords Parker and Gardiner were divided over official torture in Northern Ireland (see above, p. 52). A left-wing attempt would meet with judicial opposition more immediately than a right-wing attempt. And there is little evidence to suggest that the judiciary would be quick to spring to the defence of individual liberty wherever the threat came from.

To whatever extent we seek to define more precisely the function of the judiciary in our society so as to take account of the power of judges to act independently of others, their place as part of the governing group remains unaffected. Nor must we lose sight of two major determinants of the whole. The first is that we in the United Kingdom do live in an increasingly authoritarian society and that this is the outstanding phenomenon of all modern states. I do not mean to belittle the authoritarianism of the great systems of government in the past. But modern authoritarianism deals with millions where the tyrants of the past dealt with thousands. And the means of control today are obviously more scientific and much more thorough. It is within such systems that the judges operate; and they operate to help to run these systems. And authoritarianism is always, by its essential nature, conservative and reactionary. It must preserve itself.

Secondly, judges are the product of a class and have the characteristics of that class. Typically coming from middle-class professional families, independent schools, Oxford or Cambridge, they spend twenty to twenty-five years in successful practice at the bar, mostly in London, earning very considerable incomes by the time they reach their forties. This is not the stuff of which reformers are made, still less radicals. There are those who believe that if more grammar or comprehensive schoolboys or schoolgirls, graduating at redbrick or new glass universities, became barristers and then judges, the judiciary would be that much less conservative. This is extremely doubtful for two reasons. The years in practice and the middle-aged affluence would remove any aberration in political outlook, if this were necessary. Also, if those changes did not take place, there would be no possibility of their being appointed by the Lord Chancellor, on the advice of the senior judiciary, to the bench. Ability by itself is not enough. Unorthodoxy in political opinion is a certain disqualification for appointment.

Her Majesty's judges are unlikely to be under great illusions about the functioning of political power in the United Kingdom today. And I think we come close to their definition of the public interest and of the interests of the State if we identify their views with those who insist that in any society, but especially societies in the second half of the twentieth century, stability above all is necessary for the health of the people and is the supreme law.

It follows that governments are normally to be supported but not in every case. Governments represent stability and have a very considerable interest in preserving it. The maintenance of authoritarian structures in all public institutions is wholly in the interest of governments. This is true of all governments of all political complexions, democratic and authoritarian. Whenever governments or their agencies are acting to preserve that stability – call it the Queen's peace, or law and order, or the rule of law, or whatever – the judges will lend their support and will not be over-concerned if to do so requires the invasion of individual liberty. But individual property rights have a strong claim on judicial protection as is shown in the *Laker*, *Padfield* and *Anisminic* cases (but not, in Major's competitive Britain, so as to weaken the operations of the Monopolies and Mergers Commission). And a few judges are occasionally moved to protest against, and even (however rarely) to strike down, Ministerial action which seems to them to be unjust, particularly in social security cases. Ministers are not amused by this and, as we have seen, seek to circumvent the decisions. It is interesting to speculate what would happen if the judges seriously tried to restrain Governments from acting against the public interest. Lord Devlin, writing about the *Padfield* decision, wondered, 'whether the courts have moved too far from their base' which, he said, was 'the correction of abuse'. He continued, and here he was also speaking of the *Tameside* decision:

> One may also share to some extent the apprehensions of the Civil Service. All legal history shows that, once the judges get a foothold in the domain of fact, they move to expand. Questions of fact become in a mysterious way questions of law. The fence between error and misconception crumbles with the passage of time. The civil servant may fear the day when he dare not reach a conclusion without asking himself whether a judge will think all the deciding factors as relevant as he does. I do not think that the judiciary should be thrust out of the domain of fact.

Lord Devlin wanted above all to see judicial review 'preserved as a weapon against arbitrary government and I am conscious that its efficacy depends upon the good will of Whitehall'. Because of the power of government to exclude judicial review by statutory provision 'judicial interference with the executive cannot for long very greatly exceed what Whitehall will accept'.[55] Or, as the Prime Minister said in 1977 in the House of Commons: 'We should beware of trying to embroil the judiciary in our affairs, with the corresponding caveat that the judiciary should be very careful about embroiling itself in the legislature.'[56] And in *Duport Steels Ltd v. Sirs* Lord Scarman said: 'If people and Parliament come to think that the judicial power is to be confined by nothing other than the judge's sense of what is right . . . confidence in the judicial system will be replaced by fear of it becoming uncertain and arbitrary in its application. Society will then be ready for Parliament to cut the power of the judges.'

Sometimes, no doubt, the 'judge's sense of what is right' cannot be applied even by so devoted and self-confident a judge as Lord Denning as he reluctantly concluded in *Smith v. Inner London Education Authority* (1978) when some parents sought to prevent the Authority from closing St Marylebone Grammar School as part of the change to comprehensive schooling. 'Search as I may,' said Lord Denning, 'and it is not for want of trying, I cannot find any abuse or misuse of power by the education authority . . . It is sad to have to say so, after so much effort has been expended by so many in so good a cause.'[57]

Lord Scarman's plea for the introduction of a Bill of Rights is relevant here.[58] The purposes he has in mind may be wholly admirable being based largely on the Universal Declaration of Human Rights. But others who have also spoken in favour of such a Bill, whose provisions would be

55. *The Times*, 27 October 1976.
56. 941 HC Deb. col. 909 (15 December 1977) (Mr Callaghan).
57. [1978] 1 All Er 411; see also *North Yorkshire County Council v. Secretary of State for Education and Science*, *The Times*, 20 October 1978.
58. Sir Leslie Scarman, *English Law, the New Dimension* (1975).

entrenched and only repealable or declared inapplicable with the approval of a special (perhaps two-thirds) majority in Parliament, have amongst other things hoped it would prevent the curtailment of freedom of speech in the Race Relations Acts, the educational policies of the Labour Government which denied parental choice, the right of entry of factory and health inspectors, and a tax policy, the effect of which would be (it was claimed) to destroy a substantial proportion of independent businesses.[59]

The European Convention on Human Rights, also a candidate for entrenchment in our law, after listing a number of desirable purposes, adds provisos to each in terms like:

> No restrictions shall be placed on the exercise of these rights other than such as are prescribed by law and are necessary in a democratic society in the interests of national security or public safety, for the prevention of disorder or crime, for the protection of health or morals or for the protection of the rights and freedom of others. This Article shall not prevent the imposition of lawful restrictions on the exercise of these rights by members of the armed forces, of the police or of the administration of the state.

It is difficult to see how the welfare of the individual would be promoted by the enactment of such provisions if they were to be interpreted by the judiciary of today.

To some, the judicial view of the public interest appears merely as reactionary conservatism. It is not the politics of the extreme right. Its insensitivity is clearly rooted more in unconscious assumptions than in a wish to oppress. But it is demonstrable that on every major social issue which has come before the courts during the last thirty years – concerning industrial relations, political protest, race relations, governmental secrecy, police powers, moral behaviour – the judges have supported the conventional, established and settled interests. And they have reacted strongly against challenges to those interests. This conservatism does not necessarily follow the day-to-day political policies currently

59. See the examples collected by M. Zander, *A Bill of Rights?* (1981).

associated with the party of that name. But it is a political philosophy nonetheless.

The two outstanding groups of cases in the second half of the 1980s were those concerned with miscarriages of justice – the Guildford Four, the Maguire Seven, and the Birmingham Six – and those concerned with freedom of speech. Of the first, the best that can be said of the judicial performance is that the courts were shown to be worse than useless as protectors of innocent persons charged with highly unpopular offences. The second – comprising *Spycatcher*, the other curtailments of press freedom, and the protection of Government information – demonstrates, as I have said, the deep reluctance of the courts to stand on principle when opposed by special interests.

During the same period the courts failed to develop a coherent doctrine of judicial review. In *Oladehinde* (see above, p. 190, note 85), where the Court of Appeal overruled Lord Justice Woolf by the use of semantic trickery, Lord Donaldson MR said:

> It would be a mistake to approach the judicial review jurisdiction as if it consisted of a series of entirely separate boxes into which judges dipped as occasion demanded. It is rather a rich tapestry of many strands which cross, re-cross and blend to produce justice.

This is rhetorical nonsense. Each of the three possible bases of judicial review – illegality, irrationality, procedural impropriety – is sufficiently imprecise to enable judges to jump with the cat in any direction they choose. Illegality contains all the possible variations of statutory interpretation based on what the courts decide Parliament may or may not have intended. Unreasonableness sometimes seems to be limited to a rule or decision which, in Lord Diplock's words, is 'outrageous in its defiance of logic or accepted moral standards',[60] but may also include one which is merely 'so unreasonable that no reasonable authority could ever have

60. *In re the Council of Civil Service Unions* 1984 3 All ER 935.

come' to it,[61] or even one which is partial and unequal, or manifestly unjust.[62] Procedural impropriety includes or excludes a great variety of action or inaction. If this is tapestry it is very loosely woven.

Many regard the values of the bench and bar in Britain as wholly admirable and the spirit of the common law (as presently expressed) to be a national adornment. The incorruptibility of the English bench and its independence of the government are great virtues. All this is not in issue. When I argue that they regard the interests of the State or the public interest as pre-eminent and that they interpret those interests as meaning that, with very few exceptions, established authority must be upheld and that those exceptions are made only when a more conservative position can be adopted, this does not mean that the judges are acting with impropriety. It means that we live in a highly authoritarian society, fortunate only that we do not live in other societies which are even more authoritarian. We must expect judges, as part of that authority, to act in the interests, as they see them, of the social order.

The judges define the public interest, inevitably, from the viewpoint of their own class. And the public interest, so defined, is by a natural, not an artificial, coincidence, the interest of others in authority, whether in government, in the City or in the church. It includes the maintenance of order, the protection of private property, the promotion of certain general economic aims, the containment of the trade union movement, and the continuance of governments which conduct their business largely in private and on the advice of other members of what I have called the governing group.

Far more than on the judiciary, our freedoms depend on the willingness of the press, politicians and others to publicize the breach of these freedoms and on the continuing vulnerability of ministers, civil servants, the police, other public officials and powerful private interests to accusations that these freedoms are being infringed. In other words, we

61. Lord Greene MR in *Associated Provincial Picture Houses Ltd v. Wednesbury Corporation* [1948] 1 KB 223.
62. Lord Russell CJ in *Kruse v. Johnson* [1898] 2 QB 91.

depend far more on the political climate and on the vigilance of those members of society who for a variety of reasons, some political and some humanitarian, make it their business to seek to hold public authorities within their proper limits. That those limits are also prescribed by law and that judges may be asked to maintain them is not without significance. But the judges are not, as in a different dispensation and under a different social order they might be, the strong, natural defenders of liberty.

Judges are concerned to preserve and to protect the existing order. This does not mean that no judges are capable of moving with the times, of adjusting to changed circumstances. But their function in our society is to do so belatedly. Law and order, the established distribution of power both public and private, the conventional and agreed view amongst those who exercise political and economic power, the fears and prejudices of the middle and upper classes, these are the forces which the judges are expected to uphold and do uphold.

In the societies of our world today judges do not stand out as protectors of liberty, of the rights of man, of the unprivileged, nor have they insisted that holders of great economic power, private or public, should use it with moderation. Their view of the public interest, when it has gone beyond the interest of governments, has not been wide enough to embrace the interests of political, ethnic, social or other minorities. Only occasionally has the power of the supreme judiciary been exercised in the positive assertion of fundamental values. In both democratic and totalitarian societies, the judiciary has naturally served the prevailing political and economic forces. Politically, judges are parasitic.

That this is so is not a matter for recrimination. It is idle to criticize institutions for performing the task they were created to perform and have performed for centuries. The principal function of the judiciary is to support the institutions of government as established by law. To expect a judge to advocate radical change is absurd. The confusion arises when it is pretended that judges are somehow neutral in the conflicts between those who challenge existing institutions and those who control those institutions. And cynicism replaces confusion whenever it becomes apparent that the latter are using the judges as open allies in those conflicts.

Thus it is usual for judges in political cases to be able to rely on the rules of law for the legitimacy of their decisions. As we have seen, there are innumerable ways – through the development of the common law, the interpretation of statutes, the refusal to use discretionary powers, the claims to residual jurisdiction and the rest – in which the judges can fulfil their political function and do so in the name of the law.

General Index

Aberfan disaster, 47
Abortion Act, 43
Abse, Leo, MP, 56
Ackner, Lord, 212, 253, 277
  on reform of legal profession,
    68–9, 70, 71–2
Act of Settlement (1701), 23
Acts of Parliament *see* statute law
ACTSS, 100–1
Administration of Justice Bill, 59
Advisory, Conciliation and
    Arbitration Service (ACAS),
    97–9
air transport *see* civil air transport
    cases
Air Transport Licensing Board, 311
Amalgamated Society of Railway
    Servants, 81
Amalgamated Union of
    Engineering Workers
    (AUEW), 90–1
APEX *see* Association of
    Professional, Executive,
    Clerical and Computer Staff
Appeal Court *see* Court of Appeal
appeals, 39, 40–1, 190–7
  see also Court of Appeal; Lords,
    House of
Argyle, Judge, 37–8
arrest, causes for, 158–9, 163, 287
Arrowsmith, Pat, 158
ASLEF, 119–20, 122–3, 127
Asquith, Lord, quoted, 81
Associated British Ports, 109
Association of Professional,
    Executive, Clerical and
    Computer Staff (APEX),
    100–1, 102
asylum *see* political asylum cases
Atkin, Lord, 101, 151–2, 299
Atkinson, Lord, quoted, viii
Attlee, Clement, Prime Minister,
    15, 22
Attorney-General, 22, 44
  appointment of, 25–6, 27
  and the Crossman diaries, 204

GLC case, 134
  judicial office, 25–6
  Official Secrets Acts, 236
  refusal to consent to relator
    proceedings (Gouriet case),
    123–5
  Spycatcher case, 207–14 *passim*
  thalidomide case, 199–200
  Zircon programme, 224–5

Baldwin, G. R., quoted, 311,
    312–13
Baldwin, Stanley, 81
ballots *see under* trade unions
banks
  account information, 287
  employees dispute, 50
  leakage of bank rate, 47
  TSB, 66
barristers
  judges appointed from, 21, 22,
    25, 27, 28, 34–5, 275, 300, 322
  and judicial bias, 36–7
  as Lord Chancellor, 22n
  monopoly under law reform, 68,
    70
  Recorders appointed from, 19,
    22, 40
  as Treasury Counsel, 29
Benson, Lord, 71, 72
Bill of Rights (1688), 258
Birkenhead, Lord Chancellor, 56
Birmingham six (pub bombings),
    195–6, 289–90, 292, 326
'blacking', 87, 94, 95, 99, 103
block grants, 126
Blom-Cooper, Louis, QC, 34n,
    55–6, 127–8
Boyd-Carpenter, J. A., 52
Bracewell, Circuit Judge, 62
Brandon, Lord, 129, 178, 181, 212
breach of confidence *see*
    confidentiality
breach of contract, 85–7, 99, 100,
    103, 113
breach of the peace, 82, 83, 84, 158

Index of cases